IMMIGRANTS AT TH

M000034476

Law, Race, and Exclusion in Southern Europe

Spain and Italy have recently become countries of large-scale immigration. This provocative book explores immigration law and the immigrant experience in these southern European nations, and exposes the tension between the temporary and contingent legal status of most immigrants, and the government emphasis on integration. The book reveals that while law and the rhetoric of policymakers stress the urgency of integration, not only are they failing in that effort, but law itself plays a role in that failure. In addressing this paradox, the author combines theoretical insights and extensive data from myriad sources collected over more than a decade to demonstrate the connections among immigrants' role as cheap labor – carefully inscribed in law – and their social exclusion, criminalization, and racialization. Extrapolating from this economics of alterité, this book engages more general questions of citizenship, belonging, race and community in this global era.

KITTY CALAVITA is Professor of Criminology, Law and Society at the University of California, Irvine. She has published widely in the area of law and society, and her research has been funded by the National Science Foundation, the National Institute of Justice, and the Fulbright Program. She was President of the Law and Society Association from 2000 to 2001. She has lived and traveled extensively in southern Europe.

CAMBRIDGE STUDIES IN LAW AND SOCIETY

Cambridge Studies in Law and Society aims to publish the best scholarly work on legal discourse and practice in its social and institutional contexts, combining theoretical insights and empirical research.

The fields that it covers are studies of law in action; the sociology of law; the anthropology of law; cultural studies of law, including the role of legal discourses in social formations; law and economics; law and politics; and studies of governance. The books consider all forms of legal discourse across societies, rather than being limited to lawyers' discourses alone.

The series editors come from a range of disciplines: academic law; socio-legal studies; sociology; and anthropology. All have been actively involved in teaching and writing about law in context.

Series Editors

Chris Arup
Victoria University, Melbourne
Martin Chanock
La Trobe University, Melbourne
Pat O'Malley
Carleton University, Ottawa
Sally Engle Merry
Wellesley College, Massachusetts
Susan Silbey
Massachusetts Institute of Technology

Books in the Series

Constituting Democracy
Law, Globalism and South Africa's Political Reconstruction
Heinz Klug
0 521 78113 2 hardback
0 521 78643 6 paperback

The New World Trade Organization Agreements
Globalizing Law through Services and Intellectual Property
Christopher Arup
0 521 77355 5 hardback

The Ritual of Rights in Japan
Law, Society, and Health Policy
Eric A. Feldman
0 521 77040 8 hardback
0 521 77964 2 paperback

The Invention of the Passport
Surveillance, Citizenship and the State
John Torpey
0 521 63249 8 hardback
0 521 63493 8 paperback

Governing Morals
A Social History of Moral Regulation
Alan Hunt
0 521 64071 7 hardback
0 521 64689 8 paperback

The Colonies of Law
Colonialism, Zionism and Law in Early Mandate Palestine
Ronen Shamir
0 521 63183 1 hardback

Law and Nature
David Delaney
0 521 83126 1 hardback

Social Citizenship and Workfare in the United States and
Western Europe
The Paradox of Inclusion
Joel F. Handler
0 521 83370 1 hardback
0 521 54153 0 paperback

Law, Anthropology and the Constitution of the Social
Making Persons and Things
Edited by Alain Pottage and Martha Mundy
0 521 83178 4 hardback
0 521 53945 5 paperback

Judicial Review and Bureaucratic Impact
International and Interdisciplinary Perspectives
Edited by Marc Hertogh and Simon Halliday
0 521 83178 1 hardback
0 521 54786 5 paperback

Immigrants at the Margins
Law, Race, and Exclusion in Southern Europe
Kitty Calavita
0 521 84663 3 hardback
0 521 60912 7 paperback

Lawyers and Regulation
The Politics of the Administration Process
Patrick Schmidt
0 521 84465 7 hardback

IMMIGRANTS AT THE MARGINS

Law, Race, and Exclusion in
Southern Europe

Kitty Calavita

University of California, Irvine

CAMBRIDGE
UNIVERSITY PRESS

CAMBRIDGE UNIVERSITY PRESS
Cambridge, New York, Melbourne, Madrid, Cape Town, Singapore, São Paulo

CAMBRIDGE UNIVERSITY PRESS
The Edinburgh Building, Cambridge, CB2 2RU, UK

Published in the United States of America by Cambridge University Press, New York

www.cambridge.org
Information on this title: www.cambridge.org/9780521846639

First published 2005

Printed in the United Kingdom at the University Press, Cambridge

A catalogue record for this book is available from the British Library

Library of Congress Cataloguing in Publication data
Calavita, Kitty.
Immigrants at the margins : law, race, and exclusion in Southern Europe / Kitty Calavita.
    p.   cm.
Includes bibliographical references and index.
ISBN 0 521 84663 3 (alk. paper) – ISBN 0 521 60912 7 (pbk. : alk. paper)
1. Emigration and immigration law – Europe, Southern.   2. Europe, Southern – Ethnic relations.
3. Marginality, Social – Europe, Southern.   4. Immigrants – Government policy – Italy.
5. Immigrants – Government policy – Spain.   I. Title.
KJC6048.C35   2005
342.408′2 – dc22   2004056817

ISBN-13   978-0-521-84663-9 hardback
ISBN-10   0-521-84663-3 hardback

ISBN-13   978-0-521-60912-8 paperback
ISBN-10   0-521-60912-7 paperback

In loving memory of my mother, May Shannahan Cecil, who treated friends and strangers alike with dignity and respect, and my father, Arthur Bond Cecil, whose actions always spoke louder than words.

CONTENTS

TABLES

PREFACE

I began research for this book over a decade ago, and started the writing in the summer of 2001. During this time, numerous changes have taken place. New federal and regional laws and policies are drafted and passed almost weekly. The political landscapes in Italy and Spain are shifting once again as this goes to press. The bankruptcy of, and corruption charges against, the Italian dairy empire, Parmalat, have shaken popular support for Italian Prime Minister Silvio Berlusconi even more than his own past and present scandals have, with skyrocketing inflation since conversion to the euro adding to growing discontent with "Il Cavaliere." Spanish Prime Minister José María Aznar, having lost favor due to his alliance with US President Bush in the unpopular invasion of Iraq, amplified by the tragic train bombings in Madrid, is poised to step down and his Popular Party is to be replaced by the Socialists who won election in March, 2004. The dizzying frequency of new immigration laws and this transitional political climate virtually ensure that by the time this book is read, new political administrations will be in place and immigration policies will have undergone several rounds of changes.

While I have tried to incorporate updates throughout the writing process, it is ultimately a losing battle, and I have finally surrendered to the indomitable force of the passing of time and the daily remaking of history. But, if my analysis is correct, the kinds of legal and political changes we can expect are not likely to affect significantly the argument I make here. To the extent that the tension between immigrant incorporation and exclusion that I document inheres in the use of immigrant labor as a workforce that is both shunned for its otherness and extolled for the contribution that otherness makes to these late capitalist economies, it will not be resolved by the busy tinkering that has come to characterize these immigration regimes.

By the same logic, while the topical focus of this book is on Italy and Spain as new countries of immigration, this tension permeates to one degree or another most other post-Fordist capitalist societies including those with long immigration histories. On January 7, 2004, President George W. Bush proposed a new guestworker program for the United States, whereby immigrant workers would be given three-year work permits, renewable a limited number of times, and with no special track toward permanent legal residence or citizenship. The program would apply both to undocumented workers already in the United States and immigrant workers of the future. It would not replace the green card system for permanent residence, but its scope – applying to an estimated eight to ten million undocumented workers currently in the United States as well as untold millions of future entrants – would dwarf the older system and supplant it with the kind of codified contingency characteristic of the Italian and Spanish systems. Whether the proposal can overcome intense political opposition is still an open question. But, such convergence between this proposal from one of the world's most notorious and longstanding countries of immigration and the policies of these newcomers across the Atlantic, offers striking affirmation of the power of the structural tensions outlined here and little solace to those who dream of societies of inclusion.

ACKNOWLEDGMENTS

Many colleagues, friends and informants were critical to the writing of this book. First, I would like to thank the many people in Italy and Spain who agreed to be interviewed for this study and who graciously gave me more of their time and expertise than anyone could reasonably expect. They are government officials, administrative functionaries, immigrants and representatives of immigrant associations, union officials, NGO workers, and employers. In most cases, they remain anonymous, sometimes by their preference and sometimes by my own perhaps overly cautious decision on their behalf, both reflections of the volatile and hotly political quality of the immigration debate in these countries. Without their generosity and patience I could never have made sense of the maze of laws and policies and the day-to-day realities recounted here. No doubt, they will still find that I have something wrong. My apologies in advance for any misinterpretations or mistakes, and my heartfelt appreciation for their invaluable input.

Among the many academic experts on immigration in Spain and Italy who provided me with their collegial support and shared their extensive knowledge, I would like to extend special thanks to Maurizio Ambrosini, Rosa Aparicio, Marzio Barbagli, Ricard Zapata Barrero, Roberto Bergalli, John Casey, Francesca Decimo, Mario Giovanni Garofalo, Katia Lurbe, Monica McBritton, Dario Melossi, Salvatore Palidda, Lidia Santos, Carlota Solé, Liliana Suárez-Navaz, and Alessandra Venturini. Special thanks also to Miguel Pajares, indefatigable advocate for workers and dedicated public intellectual. My understanding has been considerably advanced by the research of all of these colleagues, by my conversations with them, and – in the case of Liliana – by our co-authorship. Finally, Roberto Bergalli and Serena Barkham helped make my sabbatical in Barcelona so enjoyable that the joke around my house was that when it was time to come home I would turn up missing.

I also thank my colleagues in the Department of Criminology, Law and Society and the School of Social Ecology at the University of California, Irvine, for contributing to an ideal environment for getting the book written. I am especially grateful to my good friend and department Chair, Valerie Jenness, for keeping my spirits up, for our many thought-provoking and challenging discussions, and for helping to provide the intellectual, professional, and interpersonal climate that makes long-term projects such as this one possible. I don't think I could have persevered without her.

Susan Bibler Coutin joined our department as I began writing the book. I could not have wished for a more energizing and insightful colleague. Her work on the *Legalizing Moves* of Salvadoran immigrants in the United States has influenced my own thinking and is in some ways the counterpart of, and runs concurrent with, the journey to the margins story told here. Her tireless work in organizing the Citizenship and Immigration Collaborative Research Network within the Law and Society Association has done much to bring visibility to international scholarship on immigration and belonging.

My mentor and friend, Bill Chambliss, continues to be an inspiration to me. I cannot thank him enough for his many insights, provocations, and encouragement over almost three decades. Other colleagues who have contributed to the development of the ideas expressed here are too numerous to name. I would, however, like to extend thanks to Wayne Cornelius for prompting me to begin an investigation of immigration to Italy in the early 1990s, thus launching this comparative project. I have benefitted substantially from his scholarship and from the many conferences and workshops that his Center for Comparative Immigration Studies at the University of California, San Diego, has sponsored and of which I have been a part.

I have enjoyed the unrivaled efficiency and day-to-day support of our departmental Office Manager Judy Omiya, the good cheer and patient help of our Administrative Assistant Marilyn Wahlert, and the unfailing expertise of Dianne Christianson in helping format the manuscript. Undergraduate students Jennifer Cheung, Oliver Chang, and Hung Ngo helped prepare the bibliography, and in the process became my teachers.

The research was funded by a grant from the Law and Social Sciences Division of the National Science Foundation. I am especially indebted to Marie Provine, then Division Director, for her support of the project and to the anonymous proposal reviewers who believed it worthwhile.

Finally, I thank John Hagan and the anonymous manuscript reviewers for such thoughtful feedback, Susan Silbey for promoting the book for the *Cambridge Studies in Law and Society* series, and Finola O'Sullivan, Jane O'Regan, and the rest of the team at Cambridge for such a smooth and collegial publication process.

MAPS

Map 1   Italy

Map 2   Spain

CHAPTER ONE

INTRODUCTION

> We are discovering the richness that diversity brings ... We are
> dedicated to the effort of integrating immigrants into Spanish society.
>> Director-General of the Spanish Institute of Migration
>> and Social Services[1]

> Legal immigration that is integrated into the economic and social
> fabric ... is a precious resource.
>> Italian Minister of the Interior[2]

> We don't work with immigrants of color.
>> Sign posted in apartment rental agency, Parma, Italy

On February 5, 2000, a group of local men in the Spanish province of
Almería set up barricades across the roads leading to the remote agricultural town of El Ejido. Then they stormed the neighborhoods of North
African farmworkers, burned tires, turned over cars, and ransacked a
Muslim butchershop. The rampage continued for days, as locals armed
with knives, rocks, crowbars, and baseball bats set fire to immigrants'
homes, stores, and cars, and went on a "caza del moro."[3] By the time it
was over, more than seventy people had been injured and hundreds of
immigrant farmworkers left homeless.[4]

A year later, in the small, southern Italian town of Salandra, angry
nationals attacked an orphanage where thirty-one Albanian children
were staying. Crying "Lynch the Albanians!" and carrying rocks and
clubs, the mob of five hundred people was outraged that some Albanian
boys "had looked at" local girls during a neighborhood get-together.[5]

with these two episodes not because they are particularly
ادly such anti-immigrant violence is quite common – nor
 ̣̣...er hand because they are representative of the attitudes of
most Spaniards and Italians. But, they serve here as emblems of something both more subtle and more consequential – the real and perceived
status of such immigrants as marginalized Others.

Ghassan Hage introduces his book, *White Nation*, with the insight–
gleaned from an analysis of graffiti in western Sydney, Australia – that
there is a "structural affinity ... between what is characterized as 'racist'
and the discourse of the dominant culture," even when that discourse
calls for tolerance and extols the benefits of multiculturalism.[6] Just
so, these outbursts of anti-immigrant racism in Spain and Italy may
be the violent cousins of more civilized folk like "suspicion," "economic marginalization," and even "tolerance." The affinity is structural
because underlying all of them is not just the common perception of
immigrants as different but, at least as important, the structural location of immigrants as third-world laborers in first-world economies that
in fact *makes* them different.

Immigration from third-world countries[7] to Spain and Italy has
increased dramatically in the last two decades. In the face of this influx,
immigration policies – even those of the right-wing governments currently in power – place a priority on immigrant integration. In fact,
"integration" has become a mantra on the lips of government officials, opposition party members, and immigrant advocates alike. But,
despite all the rhetoric and policies aimed at facilitating integration,
immigrants remain a class of pariahs, vulnerable to the kinds of attacks
described here, and vulnerable too to the everyday experiences of exclusion that derive from and signify their marginality.

I explore here what that marginality and exclusion consist of, and
how they are constructed and reconstructed in the web of daily practices, the operating procedures of local institutions, the economy,
racialization, and law. Secondly, and related to this, I want to make
sense of the paradox that while the law and the rhetoric of policymakers stress the urgency of immigrant integration, not only are they
apparently failing in this endeavor, but law itself seems to play a role in
that failure. Finally, the empirical focus on the dialectics of immigrants'
inclusion/exclusion in these southern European countries will allow me
to problematize more broadly the nature of citizenship, belonging, and
community in this global era.

The El Ejido and Salandra incidents serve a literary purpose as an emblem of law's failure, but my use of them may have been misleading. This is not a "look-at-the-racists-freak-show."[8] On the contrary, it is a look at something far freakier by virtue of its ordinariness: the largely routine and systematic practices that comprise exclusion, and that produce its entrenchment despite apparent government efforts to reverse it. In a moment, I will describe the circuitous route by which I came to this project and introduce the concepts and theoretical frameworks that are central to my argument. But, first, the context must be filled in.

SPAIN AND ITALY AS NEW COUNTRIES OF IMMIGRATION

Spain and Italy have long been countries of labor emigration, sending millions of working men, women, and children to virtually every corner of the globe beginning in the late 1800s. In the decades after World WarII, Spaniards and Italians found labor opportunities closer to home, shuttling back and forth to north and central Europe where they supplied the backbone of the industrial labor force for the post-war economic boom.[9]

By the late 1970s and early 1980s, this migrant stream began to reverse itself, as many former emigrants returned home, and these southern European countries themselves attracted large numbers of immigrants from beyond their borders. The initial influx occurred at precisely the moment that northern European countries were closing their doors to third-world workers. To some extent, Spain and Italy became the "back door" for immigrants' intent on reaching the rest of Europe, but they also became alternative destinations.[10]

Italy experienced its own "economic miracle" in the post-World War II decades, and by the mid-1970s the gap between Italy and its northern European neighbors had narrowed. The increased employment opportunities and higher wage levels associated with this transformation attracted immigrants from Africa, Asia, and Latin America, much as in earlier years Italians had migrated north to better jobs. By 2003, an estimated 2.4 million foreigners lived, legally or illegally, in Italy, with the vast majority coming from outside the European Union.[11] Most non-EU immigrants work in low-wage sectors of the economy such as domestic service, tourism, construction, and agriculture, but they are increasingly found in manufacturing too, especially in the small and medium-sized factories of the northeast.[12]

Spain's economy has traversed quite a different course from that of Italy, and has been shaped by a unique set of historical circumstances, most notably the Francoist regime. Since Franco's death in 1975, the Spanish economy has grown by spurts and starts, undergoing unprecedented levels of expansion between 1986 and 1990, when over two million new jobs were created, more than in any other European country.[13] And, the economy has continued to expand, with the number of jobs growing by 24.2 percent from 1996 to 2001.[14] While still lagging behind Italy in terms of real wages and standard of living, Spain too has gone far in narrowing the gap with the rest of the European Union. As in Italy, Spain's social protections have expanded rapidly and its welfare state is now almost comparable to that of other Western European democracies.

By 2004, over 1.6 million foreigners had legal residence in Spain, with almost two-thirds coming from outside the EU, and the vast majority of these coming from the third world.[15] Even more concentrated in certain niches than in Italy and less likely to be found in manufacturing, most immigrants in Spain work in agriculture, domestic service, tourism, construction, or other low-paying and underground sectors of the economy.[16] And, as in Italy, immigrant labor is lauded for the flexibility it provides the economy. The former Director-General of Migration once pointed out that a high unemployment rate and the need for immigrant workers are not mutually contradictory, noting that the Spanish labor market "contains certain rigidities" that third-world labor helps counteract.[17]

Despite much talk of coordinating policies at the EU level, most European immigration laws remain localized within the nation-state. It is true that borders have come down between the countries of the EU, and summits held and pacts signed on how to manage external migration. The Treaty of Maastricht in 1992 and the Schengen Agreement in 1995 provided for the free movement of EU citizens within the European Community and developed new technologies of collective security against migration-related crimes like drug-dealing, terrorism, and smuggling. The Treaty of Amsterdam three years later reiterated the commitment to solving collectively what was increasingly being seen as the immigration "problem," and the European Council of Tampere in 1999 floated a common refugee and asylum policy. But, by the time of the European Council summit in Seville, Spain, in June,

2002, virtually none of the many proposals for common immigration and refugee laws had been ratified. And, despite considerable posturing by the then President of the European Council, Spanish Prime Minister José María Aznar, the Seville summit produced mostly squabbling and dissension, with the right-wing Spanish and Italian governments locking horns with more progressive states like France and Sweden.[18]

Spain and Italy passed their first comprehensive immigration laws in 1985 and 1986, respectively, and have subsequently enacted amendments, revisions, and regulatory changes with dizzying frequency. Academics and even government officials I spoke to complained of the difficulties of keeping up with the changes. (One can only imagine the frustrations of those whose lives and livelihoods depend directly on the ever-shifting black letter and red tape.)[19] But, despite what seems like constant tinkering, some consistent themes characterize these laws. Above all, they are oriented toward immigration as a contingent or emergency labor supply; as such, they contain few provisions for permanent legal residency or naturalization, although as we will see later, that is beginning to change. "Regularization," or legalization, programs are implemented every few years, with applications reaching several hundred thousand.[20] Those who are legalized, however, generally are given only temporary legal status and have to demonstrate continued formal employment and navigate a maze of government bureaucracies to renew their permits.

Side-by-side with this emphasis on immigrants as contingent workers, government policies stress the importance of immigrant "integration." I use this admittedly vague term deliberately, as it is the term used by policymakers and in the law itself. As I explain in more detail in Chapter 4, judging from the rhetoric and from the programs devised in its name, "integration" refers generally to social and cultural inclusion and tolerance for diversity, and is contrasted to segregation, exclusion, and rejection. The vagueness of the term is compounded by the varied strategies devised to enhance it, ranging from language courses and socialization classes designed ostensibly to *assimilate*, to tolerance campaigns that pitch the benefits of cultural *difference*, and multiculturalism.[21]

The first Spanish immigration law in 1985 was introduced with a Preamble proclaiming that its purpose was to guarantee foreign residents' rights and to integrate immigrants into Spanish society. A subsequent law in January, 2000, was titled "Law on the Rights and Liberties of Foreigners in Spain and their Social Integration." The Italian law of

1998 perhaps went furthest in this direction, calling for proactive efforts like the construction of ambitious reception centers that would provide arriving immigrants with food and shelter, and a wide range of cultural and social services designed to ease their transition into Italian society. Much of the emphasis on integration in both Spain and Italy is located at the local level, with a plethora of regional and municipal programs, including language courses, programs publicizing immigrant rights and how to access them, job training, multicultural aides in public schools, and what one might loosely call "diversity work" – the government rendition of the Colors of Benetton.[22]

In previous work, I have focused on the myriad ways Spanish and Italian laws marginalize immigrants, and the economic uses of that marginalization.[23] While recognizing the integrationist language in these laws and policies, in that work I interpreted the rhetoric as just that – political language designed for symbolic purposes – while the substantive provisions of these policies marginalized and dis-integrated. In the present study, I revisit this emphasis on integration and find I am forced to take it seriously (for reasons I will elaborate in a moment). Instead of focusing solely on the economic uses to which immigrant marginality contributes, and consigning integration policies to the analytical sidelines, I ask here how and why apparently genuine integration policies fail, and how this failure is (or is not) linked to economic marginality and the laws that reproduce it.

My empirical focus on Spain and Italy is partly pragmatic: I can get along in both languages and have contacts in both countries. But, this focus also has substantial theoretical advantages. As countries that have undergone rapid economic (and, for Spain, political) transformations over the last several decades – almost overnight joining the roster of advanced capitalist democracies – they arguably experience the contradictions of capitalist development in intensified fashion, providing the observer with access to insights that might otherwise be missed. And, these brand-new countries of mass immigration give us a chance to watch the formulation of immigration policy and the incorporation of immigrant workers "from scratch" as it were, without the encumbrances of historical commitments or precedent, but replete with all the stubborn dilemmas and contradictions that are nonetheless structurally embedded in them. Finally, the dual-country focus both confirms the generalizability of the patterns exposed here, and allows us to interrogate the minor differences that emerge. Ultimately, I will argue that the dynamics of racialization and exclusion, and their links to the economic role that immigrants play in these late capitalist economies, roughly parallel those in the United States and other Western European nations despite considerable differences in political structures and historical contingencies.

The information on which the book is based was gathered over the course of more than a decade beginning in 1992, but mostly during a sabbatical in Barcelona in 1996 and – between 2000 and 2003 – during stints lasting from several weeks to two months in Spain and Italy. The data are eclectic, and include interviews with government officials, leaders of immigrant associations, union officials, academics, and employers; news media coverage; published and unpublished government documents; press conferences; and scholarly and other secondary sources. Many of these sources are in Italian or Spanish (and, in a few cases, Catalan), and the quotations I use here are my own translations. I have tried to remain as close to the original phraseology as possible, using literary license only to get around the untranslatable, or grossly infelicitous constructions.

As I explain in the following section, data sometimes make themselves heard even when we are busy focusing elsewhere. I do not subscribe to the extreme positivist position that data speak for themselves with no need for translation (metaphorically speaking), or emerge full-bodied from an unambiguous objective reality. But, sometimes they do scream at us over the din of other distracting noise and force us to pay attention. This is what happened to me as this project evolved.

I agree with Ben Agger that there is far too much "secret writing" in social science, in which both authorial agency and the deliberative process are obscured.[24] In part to offset this tendency and in part to underscore the fluidity and complexity of the reality on the ground, I intersperse the academic voice in which this book is primarily written with a more personal narrative in which I expose the vagaries and serendipities of field work and the inevitable periods of confusion that are visited on all honest researchers.

TAKING FAILURE SERIOUSLY

The project began as an investigation of the relative importance of economic versus political factors in accounting for the outcome of immigration policies "on the ground." As summarized in my grant application to the National Science Foundation, I intended to study the effects of the 1998 and 2000 laws in Spain and Italy, respectively, expecting

t the integrationist dimensions of these laws failed, regard-
different political stripes of the country or region. I antici-
:xample, that these laws with their emphasis on social inclu-
have little impact on the number of illegal immigrants or
on immigrant access to social services. And, because of the benefits
of immigrant workers' marginality for these economies and especially
for employers, I expected a convergence of outcomes (e.g. integration
policy failures), despite the presence of more powerful, pro-immigrant
labor unions in Italy and a governing coalition (at the time) of center-
left forces that advocated on behalf of immigrants.[25] Finally, I predicted
that there would be more political emphasis on inclusion and integration in Italy's traditionally communist region of Emilia-Romagna
than in the conservative region of Veneto where the anti-immigrant
Northern League is strong, but that the economic utility of marginalized
immigrants in both regions would result in similar levels of exclusion.
So, armed with notions of symbolic law that had been useful in other
contexts, I was prepared to find more talk of integration in politically
progressive regions than in conservative ones (but similar outcomes of
exclusion), and I was prepared to chalk it up to politics – or as Edelman so elegantly called it, "Political Language: Words that Succeed and
Policies that Fail."[26]

My field research proved me wrong on both counts. I found that there
is at least as much attention given to the issue of integration in Veneto
as in Emilia-Romagna, and that in both cases the efforts go far beyond
rhetoric or symbolism. Huge budgets are expended and substantial programs launched. As we will see in Chapter 4, the Director of Immigration in Veneto – himself a member of the right-wing National Alliance
Party – has taken the lead in coordinating the effort to facilitate immigrant integration. It would be hard to dismiss these activities, which
sometimes seem almost frenzied in their intensity, as empty symbolic
gestures. In any case, there is no apparent political reason for policymakers in a conservative region like Veneto, where *anti-immigrant*
rhetoric is more likely to win votes, to tout immigrant integration.

After an initial period of confusion in which I tried unsuccessfully
to make sense of these realities within my symbolic law framework, I
relinquished my preconceived notions – or, more accurately, they were
forcibly taken from me. In the process, my empirical focus shifted to
the far more difficult, and maybe ultimately more interesting, question of how immigrant marginality and exclusion get constructed and
reconstructed despite apparently strenuous efforts to reverse them. In

this focus on the constitution of immigrant otherness and exclusion, I draw from and hope to speak to several sets of literature and theoretical perspectives, most important of which are the law and society literature on law in action and the contradictions within law that get played out locally in daily administrative practices; the literature on anti-immigrant backlashes and fear of the "other" or "stranger"; Critical Race Theory and discussions of racial formation more generally; and the rapidly increasing scholarship on the concepts of citizenship, membership, and community within the context of globalization.

THE LIMITS OF LAW

At one level, this is a study of law's failure. A long tradition in the law and society field examines the discrepancy between law's apparent intent and its practice and outcome, now iconically referred to as the gap between the "law in the books" and the "law in action." While more recent work on the constitutive quality of law and society reveals this representation of two distinct stages of law to be overly simplistic,[27] it may still be heuristically useful, as we will see.

Much early work in the area of legal impact focused on law's indeterminacy, concentrating on the courts and judicial decisions.[28] More relevant here are studies that address the limitations of statutory change. Horny and Spohn's work on the limited effects of statutory reforms in the processing of rape cases is exemplary of this tradition.[29] Their study reveals that despite lawmakers' assumptions that improvements in the treatment of rape victims would increase their willingness to participate in criminal prosecutions, the reforms had little effect on the number of reported rapes, rape arrests, or convictions. The authors conclude: "[R]eformers...overestimate the role of legal rules in controlling the behavior of decisionmakers...Statutory changes...must be interpreted and applied by decisionmakers who may not share the goals of those who championed their enactment." Citing "the large body of literature detailing the failure of legal reforms," they warn that to understand the potential for legal impact, "[I]t is important to understand not only the characteristics of the reform itself but also the structure of the system on which it is imposed."[30]

Another law and society tradition takes as its point of departure the administrative discretion on which law in action ultimately hinges. Lipsky's case study of enforcement discretion among social service workers concludes, for example, that public policies are effectively made in the field by low-level personnel who constitute a kind of "street-level bureaucracy."[31] Other important work in this area, most notably Sudnow's study of the categorization of "normal crimes" and Emerson and Paley's research linking such classifications to institutional needs, focus on the impact of the perceived "downstream consequences" for the agency.[32]

Janet Gilboy, in her excellent study of the US immigration inspection process at a busy international airport (pre-9/11) has drawn attention to the external pressures that complicate inspectors' work (as, for example, when powerful Congressional constituents complain that their nanny was denied entry or hassled).[33] Some of my own work on immigration law enforcement places such constraints in a structural context. For example, I have explored the ways the stubborn dilemmas of contemporary immigration law enforcement (and the external pressures those dilemmas are most tangibly constituted of) may ultimately derive from the structural contradictions surrounding immigration. In my study of the Bracero Program and my work on employer sanctions, the tension between recurring political demands to control the border versus the economic benefits of a cheap immigrant workforce, take center-stage.[34]

In more recent work on the Chinese Exclusion Laws of the late nineteenth century, I found a different kind of contradiction compounding the mix, as the conflicting cultural assumptions about race, class, and identity embedded in the law (and the ability of aspiring immigrants to capitalize on those conflicts) stymied inspectors as they struggled to sort Chinese entrants into a host of ambiguous, overlapping, and ultimately arbitrary conceptual categories.[35] In contrast to Gilboy's work on typifications and Sudnow's portrait of routinization through the perceptual construction of normal cases, these inspectors faced dilemmas that were not only not resolved by attempts at routinization and typification, but were frequently compounded by them.

In a later study that focused on the importance of the lucrative trade with China during this period and the perceived dangers of alienating Chinese merchants, I located these dilemmas in their broader context. Drawing from Chambliss's dialectical-structural theory of lawmaking, I argued that the contradictions among extant material and political interests (for example, the tension between the political pressure to exclude the Chinese and the vast material interests relating to trade with China) produced a law and an accompanying set of ideological justifications (including assumptions about Chinese racial inferiority

and the class superiority of Chinese merchants that apparentl
their race) fraught with logical inconsistencies and internal ‹
tions. These inconsistencies, and the contradictions in the
economy they represented, confronted inspectors with the awesome
task of reconciling the irreconcilable.[36]

The present study is located within this broad tradition of research on
the law in action, and draws from and extends my previous work on the
contradictions of immigration law. Briefly, Italian and Spanish immigration laws emphasize integration, but at the same time treat immigrants
exclusively as workers, their legal status contingent on continued work
permits. They thus pull in two directions at once, cautiously welcoming
immigrants as workers and restricting their ability to put down roots by
denying them permanent residence, while at the same time underwrit-
ing ambitious programs designed to integrate them into the social and
cultural life of the community.

It has often been remarked that immigrants in some contexts are confined to "economic citizenship" and excluded from "social or political
citizenship."[37] It is not particularly novel to point out that immigrants
are often welcomed as workers but rejected as community members.
Aristide Zolberg captures the irony well, calling this the "'wanted but
not welcome' syndrome."[38] There is an extensive literature that speaks
to the function that *illegal* immigrants perform in this context, as a
uniquely marginal workforce that provides a critical element of flexibility in post-Fordist economies. Some observers, myself included, even
suggest that the precarious and fleeting quality of legal status is a way
to preserve the advantages derived from a marginalized and vulnerable
workforce.[39]

I am interested here not just in this marginalization, but in the tension in Spanish and Italian immigration laws that on the one hand
effectively construct immigrant illegality and thus difference, and on
the other strive to undo perceptions of immigrant difference, integrate
immigrants into mainstream social and cultural life, and contain anti-
immigrant backlash. I argue here that this tension is the manifesta-
tion in the legal and policy arena of the broader dialectic in political-
economic relations. That is, immigrants are useful as "Others" who are
willing to work, or are compelled to work, under conditions and for
wages that locals now largely shun. The advantage of immigrants for
these economies resides precisely in their Otherness. At the same time,
that Otherness is the pivot on which backlashes against immigrants
turn. For, if marginalized immigrant workers are useful in part *because*

they are marked by illegality, poverty, and exclusion, this very marking, this highlighting of their difference, contributes to their distinction as a suspect population.

The tension is similar to the "catch-22" that Zolberg notes in reference to Chinese, Mexican, Irish, and southern European immigration to the United States in the past: "[T]he very qualities that make a group suitable for recruitment as 'labour' demonstrate its lack of qualifications for 'membership.'"[40] Immigration law then must simultaneously preserve immigrant Otherness, and combat the political, social, and fiscal fallout of that Otherness. In concrete terms, it both constructs and reconstructs illegality and difference, and spends millions on doomed projects of integration.

If this explanation of the contradictory thrusts in Italian and Spanish immigration policy is accurate, we should find the tension particularly apparent in the northeast of Italy where immigrants are critical to a booming economy, where there is one of the lowest unemployment rates in Europe, and where there is a recent history of anti-immigrant populism. In this context, we would expect to find integration efforts especially intense given both the importance of the immigrant workforce, and the potential for backlash in this cradle of Italian xenophobia. The point is not just that immigrants must be rendered acceptable to a citizenry predisposed to reject them, although this is certainly part of it. Rather, it is that immigrants' Otherness, *on which their utility hinges*, is both constructed through law and must ultimately be dealt with. As we will see in Chapter 4, this dynamic is so powerful in the Veneto region that immigrant integration is being spearheaded by the very populist governor who rode into office on the back of anti-immigrant sentiment.

Considerable attention has recently been paid to the irony of the increasing importance of space, place, and territorialization in this global era.[41] Clearly, immigration is at one level about space, about the movement of people across spatial and territorial boundaries. But, it is about more than physical or even political space; it is about social and cultural space as well. For immigrants' crossing of national boundaries and their particular location in the host economy results in the formation of boundaries of difference that marginalize from within. Law is a pivotal factor in shoring up this marginality and the economic flexibility that is its welcome byproduct. Not only does immigration law sort people according to their suitability for inclusion in the national territory, but for third-world peoples who cross geo-political borders into developed countries, it creates and perpetuates from within their outsider status.

We can also talk about the spatialization of law itself in this context. Many case studies have addressed the workings of law within a particular institution or bureaucracy, or as it permeates individual lives, in the "common place of law."[42] Just as the ideological and material contradictions of law are most apparent in its daily practice, it is at the regional, municipal and neighborhood levels that the contradictory thrusts of these immigration laws that at once marginalize and call for inclusion, are most conspicuous. National politicians may reap benefits from playing both sides of this precarious juxtaposition and may never be questioned for their logical inconsistencies or their fancy footwork. Local policymakers have no such luxury. For, it is they who must implement strategies that are doomed to failure, and who must deal with the inevitable fallout of that failure.

CITIZENSHIP, EXCLUSION, AND COMMUNITY

This is in part then a study of the dialectics of law's failure. But, it is more generally about the construction of immigrant difference, the ways law itself contributes to their Otherness even as it struggles to deal with it, and the material and cultural sources of marginality and racialization that interact with law, but that exert their own independent force as well. In the end, I hope to make sense not just of immigrants' marginal status in southern Europe; my more ambitious goal is to explore the dynamics of exclusion and the meaning of citizenship and national community in this era of globalization.

In reading the literatures on immigration, citizenship, and community, a set of contradictory themes emerges. One theme that pervades the literature on immigrants in affluent countries is that of the "stranger" who is feared and marginalized by virtue of coming from outside the community. In this depiction, the immigrant-outsider is sharply contrasted to the citizen-member, a dichotomy that is affirmed in some of the theoretical literature on citizenship as well. But, much of the more recent literature on citizenship and community implies a destabilization of this dichotomy. By unpacking the concept of citizenship and problematizing the notion of national community, this scholarship not only begins to undermine the clear distinction between immigrants and citizens but also suggests the question of whether there is a community for immigrant-outsiders to be excluded *from*, and if so, what its nature is. In a moment I want to explore how we might reconcile these apparently conflicting themes, but first let us examine them more closely.

Sociologist Georg Simmel long ago discussed the notion of the immigrant as "stranger" – physically present in a community but not part of it.[43] More recently, Bourdieu has described the immigrant as "'atopos,' without place, displaced," a "bastard" between citizen and real outsider.[44] And Rogers Brubaker talks about "the modern figure of the foreigner – not only as a legal category but as a political epithet... condensing around itself pure outsiderhood."[45]

While some of this work – such as Simmel's – implies that the fear of the immigrant stranger is embedded in our collective subconscious, other authors have focused on the political and cultural functions of this identification of the immigrant as Other, and the social control work that shores up that politically useful identification. Thus, Ali Behdad argues that immigration in the United States is "both a necessary mechanism of social control in the formation of the state apparatus and an essential cultural contribution to the formation of national identity."[46] He contends that these identity functions are particularly important in the United States where "nation-state" has historically been an "ambiguous concept." In this context, "the figure of the 'alien' provides the differential signifier through which the nation defines itself as an autonomous community, [and] the juridical and administrative regulations of immigration construe the collective sovereignty of the modern state."

Along these same lines, Bonnie Honig, in *Democracy and the Foreigner*, shows how the foreignness of outsiders has been used historically to define and shape the national community. Fear of the foreigner, she says, plays an important role in shaping the self-identity of those who are, by way of contrast, "insiders." Thus, "it is often their foreignness itself that makes outsiders necessary even if also dangerous to the regimes that receive them. Indeed, sometimes foreignness operates as an agent of (re)founding."[47]

What all of this work has in common is the implicit or explicit dichotomy it draws between the immigrant-stranger and the citizen-member. Scholarship on the concept of citizenship often further solidifies this dichotomy. T. H. Marshall's now classic essay on citizenship and social class in England did not directly treat the issue of *non*-citizens, but instead traced the evolution of the meaning of social membership.[48] In Marshall's model, the three dimensions of citizenship – civil, political, and social – were developed sequentially, with civil rights belonging

14

to the eighteenth century, political rights emerging in the nineteenth, and social rights developing in the twentieth. Contemporary citizenship in Western capitalist societies was described in Marshall's 1950 essay as comprising the full panoply of civil, political, and social rights that have evolved over the last three centuries.[49]

Since Marshall's seminal work, much of the scholarship on citizenship has drawn a distinction between this kind of full membership in a political community, and the status of non-members. For example, Brubaker argues, "Although citizenship is internally inclusive, it is externally exclusive. There is a conceptually clear, legally consequential, and ideologically charged distinction between citizens and foreigners."[50] And, Michael Walzer, one of the most prolific political philosophers writing on citizenship today, articulates a sharp descriptive and normative distinction between citizens who belong to the national community and non-citizens who do not. Noting that stranger and enemy are the same word in Latin, Walzer argues, "We might think of countries as national clubs or families" made up of citizen-members who get to choose whom to admit.[51]

Joseph Carens, while taking the opposite normative stance from Walzer and making "the case for open borders," nonetheless reaffirms this dichotomy. Beginning his essay, "Borders have guards and the guards have guns," Carens continues, "Citizenship in Western liberal democracies is the modern equivalent of feudal privilege." Those who have it are privileged, while alien outsiders are presumably the equivalent of serfs.[52] Similarly, Alessandro Dal Lago argues that Italian society consists of two distinct groups – the majority who have citizenship rights and formal guarantees, and foreigners who are effectively "non-persons."[53]

Much of the empirical literature that depicts immigrants as a distinctly marginal population affirms this dichotomy as well. From Castles and Kosack's classic study of immigrant workers in Western Europe, to Piore's depiction of immigrant "birds of passage" in America's segmented economy, to Cornelius's analysis of Mexican workers in southern California, the picture of immigrants as an especially vulnerable and exploited workforce has been well established.[54] Established too is the notion that *illegal* immigrants are the prototypical marginalized worker, confined to the worst jobs not only by virtue of their status as immigrants but by their illegality.[55]

This dichotomy between the immigrant-stranger-outsider and the citizen-member-insider is so well entrenched that it is the academic equivalent of conventional wisdom. Oddly enough though – and to my knowledge it is an oddity unremarked upon – a series of competing ideas runs through some of the recent literature on citizenship (including some of the same works cited above) and community. For example, it is frequently noted that the meaning of citizenship has declined, blurring the lines between citizens and non-citizens. Some, like Jim Hollifield and Yasemin Soysal, argue that this is the case in Europe where immigrants have accrued more civil and legal rights, sometimes even voting in local elections.[56] Peter Schuck makes a similar point about immigrants in the United States, declaring that changes in immigration law over the last decades "have reduced almost to the vanishing point the marginal value of citizenship as compared to resident alien status."[57] According to Schuck, Brubaker and others, not only has the distance between citizen and non-citizen narrowed, but the dichotomy is more like a continuum, with *degrees* of membership distinguishing citizens, legal residents, and illegal immigrants, or as Robin Cohen calls them "citizens, denizens, and helots."[58]

Further blurring the lines of this dichotomy, citizenship in the global era increasingly crosses the boundaries of nation-states, not just with the formation of the European Union and other such supranational political entities, but with the rise of a wide variety of transnational political activities in which "people lay claim to a political space that may or may not conform to the spaces allowed by the existing system of government."[59]

Others have questioned the distinctive nature of citizenship from quite a different perspective. Rather than seeing the gap between citizens and non-citizens narrowing because of increased rights for non-citizens, this scholarship explores the limitations of citizenship. Formal citizenship in Western democratic societies is meant to confer a universalistic set of rights and duties on those who are thus included in the national political community, à la Marshall. "Equality, universalism, and participation" are the defining features of what has been called this "Whig" interpretation of citizenship.[60] Or, as Richard Falk has put it, under the Westphalian system, "Citizenship . . . is a means of ensuring the full rights of membership."[61]

But, citizenship-in-the-books and citizenship-in-action are not coterminous. As Brubaker says, "Formal citizenship is neither a sufficient nor a necessary condition for substantive membership . . . That it is not a sufficient condition is clear: one can possess formal state membership yet be excluded (in law or in fact) from certain civil, political, or social rights."[62] Race, class, gender, religion, sexual orientation, and even region, continue to distinguish "substantial citizenship" from merely "nominal citizenship."[63] Kenneth Karst, Ediberto Román, Leti Volpp, Kevin Johnson, Roger Wilkins, and many others have amply demonstrated that the history of Western democracies can be seen in part as an ongoing struggle for inclusion.[64] Renato Rosaldo refers to this struggle as the demand for "cultural citizenship," by which he means "the right to be different (in terms of race, ethnicity, or native language)...without compromising one's right to belong, in the sense of participating in the nation-state's democratic processes."[65] While race and ethnicity are often at the forefront of this struggle and take a central place in this literature, Ronald Beiner notes, "To these formidable challenges may be added what is probably the greatest challenge of all to contemporary citizenship, namely, persistent mass unemployment, which offers the surest prospect of excluding tens of millions of people even within the richest nations on earth from a sense of full membership in civic community."[66] In *Buddha Is Hiding*, Aihwa Ong eloquently documents the exclusion of those who find themselves on the wrong side of the intersection of race, nationality, and class, as she recounts the day-to-day struggles of Cambodian refugees in northern California.[67]

While the literature on expanding rights for immigrants and the critique of citizenship's limitations come from dramatically different ideological positions, they both destabilize the conventional dichotomy between citizen-members and immigrant-outsiders. Before exploring the repercussions of this destabilization for the current study, one more piece of the picture has to be filled in, namely, the question of the relevance of the "national community" in this era of globalization. Because, after all, the issues of membership and inclusion presuppose that there is a viable community to be included *in*.

The concept of community is notoriously difficult to define, and much of the literature is marked by definitional disagreements instead of, and/or permeating, more substantive discussions. Most commentators would agree with Walzer, however, that at a minimum a community consists of like-minded members, usually spatially bounded, "with some special commitment to one another and some special sense of their common life."[68] The national community is thus a politically and territorially defined group of members with bonds of solidarity and a sense of their shared identity and destiny as a nation. As Benedict Anderson pointed out long ago, it is largely an "imagined community," "because the members of even the smallest nation will never know most of their

17

fellow-members, meet them, or even hear of them, yet in the minds of each lives the image of their communion."[69]

Zygmunt Bauman and others argue persuasively that this kind of community is on the decline, as globalization, with its amalgam of economic integration, collapsing cultural boundaries, and the diminishing significance of the nation-state, erodes its boundaries and disintegrates its ties, leaving little (but nostalgia) to the "imagination." In other words, the complex forces we call globalization may have undermined the significance of both the nation-state's external boundaries and the internal ties of solidarity that define a community.

Bauman's elegant treatise traces the decline of community in Western capitalist societies to economic restructuring, particularly the end of the Fordist social contract between workers and their bosses, and relatedly, the "secession of the successful."[70] As super-affluent corporate executives with no permanent address are increasingly uprooted from any spatial community, these extraterritorial cosmopolitans "no longer need the services of the community" and within it stand to bear only the brunt of others' needs. Their secession means that they – in the words of one AT&T executive – "consider themselves the sort of citizens of the world who happen to carry an American passport."[71] Epitomizing cosmopolitans' secession from any national community, they can now purchase "homes" on an enormous cruise-residence ship that continuously circles the globe. Priced at $2 million to $6.84 million, the residences are for sale "by invitation only." In the unrestrained immodesty of the class that makes their home there, the ship is called *The World*.[72]

Of course, it is not just Bauman's cosmopolitans who are on the move. The dramatically increased rates of migration that have accompanied globalization, and that are the topic of this book, have also complicated the meaning of space and, in so doing, the connection of people to any national community. Focusing on the "turbulence of migration" in the contemporary world, Papastergiadis warns, "Despite the rhetorical appeal of multiculturalism and the intellectual popularity of concepts like diaspora and hybridity, the horizon of the migrant's imaginary is increasingly filled with experiences of itinerancy, ghettoization and illegality. Displacement is not only a more common but also a more complex experience."[73]

The flip-side of the secession of privileged elites is the further ghettoization not just of immigrants, but of the poor and near-poor, spatially and socially, as the ties of solidarity that once defined the advanced welfare state unravel, and the "City of Walls" rises up in its place.[74] As Richard Falk[75] puts it:

> Passivity, despair, and alienation result, with the privileged 20 percent feeling more and more detached from the misfortunes of their fellow citizens ... Bonds of solidarity among the citizenry, never too strong in the face of antagonistic interests and against the grain of individualism, have been fraying badly as of late.

David Abraham argues that the retrenchment of the welfare state in the United States, Germany, and Israel represents a replacement of the ideal of community by the ideal of the free market and individual autonomy. As the meaning of community and mutual obligation shrinks, so too does the significance of citizenship, which Abraham describes as "thin" – "so thin that even non-citizen residents may enjoy almost all of it."[76]

Side-by-side with this "fraying" of internal ties, the national community has lost significance by virtue of the declining significance of national boundaries. While the debate about the demise of nation-state sovereignty in this globalizing era may still be open, there is little question that the territorialized national community has decreased in significance. Thus, the new "citizens of Europe" join Bauman's cosmopolitans, as the national-territorial basis of community is stretched and strained.[77] With its internal ties shattered and the significance of its external boundaries in flux, much of the meaning of the national community on which the concept of citizen-members ultimately hinges has been gutted.[78]

In sum, these literatures alternately tell us that immigrants in affluent societies are marginalized, feared as strangers, and excluded from membership in the national community of citizen-insiders; that this conventional dichotomy is problematic in the globalizing era of transnational citizenship, extraterritorial elites, a burgeoning underclass of second-class citizens, and multiple gradations of "citizens, strangers, and in-betweens";[79] and that, in any case, the concept of community may be obsolete. How can we make sense of this kaleidoscope of ideas that are at once so eminently persuasive and so apparently contradictory? This book, at one level focused on the dialectics of immigrant inclusion/exclusion and the reciprocal roles of law and economics in that process, more generally may begin to reconcile some of these tensions in the literature surrounding concepts of citizenship, belonging, and community, a theme I will return to in the conclusion.

OVERVIEW OF THE BOOK

The book begins by providing a description of the political and economic systems that are both the backdrop for, and the major forces shaping, immigration law and the immigrant experience in Italy and Spain. Chapter 2 opens with a brief overview of political developments since the influx of immigrants in the early 1980s, and then describes the various immigration laws that have been crafted, from the first ones passed in 1985 and 1986 to the recent "toughening up." The chapter concludes with a discussion of the illegality built into these laws, and connects it to the logic of a system that welcomes immigrants solely for their economic function as third-world workers.

Chapter 3 gives a thumb-nail sketch of the size, make-up, and distribution of the immigrant populations; describes the Spanish and Italian economies, with their myriad regional and structural divisions, and striking juxtaposition of Fordist, post-Fordist, and pre-Fordist economic relations; and traces the economic location and working conditions of immigrants in these variegated systems. By the end of Chapter 3, what becomes clear is that what I call "the economics of alterité" not only helps explain the apparent paradox that high rates of immigrant employment are found even in areas of high local unemployment, but that immigrants' location in the economy reproduces their Otherness through the stigmata of poverty.

In Chapter 4, I explore the slippery concept of immigrant "integration," its discursive and substantive centrality to immigrant policy in Spain and Italy, and the sense of urgency that local politicians, including even some from anti-immigrant parties, attach to their integration efforts. Chapter 5 then looks at the everyday dynamics of exclusion despite these sometimes frenzied integration efforts. With an empirical focus on the difficulties immigrants have in accessing housing and healthcare – fundamental indicators of, and prerequisites for, social belonging – I revisit points made in earlier chapters about the marginalization implicit in policies that construct immigrants as contingent workers, the economic reproduction of their marginality through precarious work, and the interdependence and compounding effects of these legal and economic forces. The chapter concludes with a nod to human agency, describing the resistance of immigrants who are increasingly organizing, going out on strike, staging sit-ins, demanding that the social and economic rights spelled out in law be realized, and otherwise surprising those who had counted on their complacency.

Chapter 6, "Fuel on the Fire," examines the criminalization of immigrants, the political and media exploitation of immigrant difference, and, most importantly and relatedly, racialization – a theme that has lurked just beneath the surface throughout. I call this racialization, following Tahar Ben Jelloun, the "aesthetics" of immigration, and suggest that it is part and parcel of the economics of alterité, not just in these southern European countries but in other late capitalist societies that simultaneously construct, exploit, and denounce immigrant marginality.[80]

In the Conclusion, I extrapolate from my analysis of immigrant difference to reconcile the tensions in the literature discussed above. Proposing that the mirror of immigration reveals more generally the deep lines of fragmentation and structural inequality across the face of late modern society, I draw out the theoretical implications of this discussion of immigrant inclusion/exclusion through law and economics for our understanding of citizenship, race, belonging, and national community.

CHAPTER TWO

LEGAL FRAMEWORK AND THE WAYWARD "LEGS OF LAW"

Spain and Italy are often referred to as new countries of immigration. In this portrayal, they are culturally homogeneous national communities experiencing an influx of culturally and ethnically diverse populations for the first time. But of course the reverse is more historically accurate. For one thing, the territories of Spain and Italy have long been the stage for invasions, migration, and ethnic mixing; furthermore, in the case of Italy, the status of nation is a relatively recent achievement.

By the time Italy was established as a republic in the 1860s, it had witnessed more, and more diverse, population influxes than perhaps any other place in Europe. People from Asia Minor – later to become Etruscans – landed on the Tuscan coast in the tenth century BC; the Greeks colonized Sicily and eventually much of the rest of southern Italy two centuries later; Phoenician traders migrated into Sardinia during the same period; Carthaginians landed on the southern coast of Sicily in the sixth century BC; Gauls crossed the Alps in the fifth century BC; nine hundred years later, as the Roman Empire was being dismantled, the Visigoths made the same journey across the Alps; in the ninth century, Arabs took over Sicily, a perennial target; Normans conquered southern Italy and Sicily in the eleventh century; and the fifteenth and sixteenth centuries brought invasions from both the French and the Spanish. When Italy was finally unified in the late nineteenth century, it was both one of the oldest recipients of immigration in Europe (and enjoyed a long history of "multiculturalism") and the newest nation.

Spain was host to many of these same peoples over the centuries, with the Phoenicians, Greeks, Carthaginians, and Visigoths setting up colonies and populating the Iberian peninsula. The Roman Empire secured virtually all of Spain by the first century AD and transformed much of its language and culture. Arabs from North Africa took over from the Visigoths in the eighth century, bringing with them strong religious, linguistic, and cultural influences, and were not expelled for seven hundred years. The Moorish occupation of Spain ended in the fifteenth century, but the multiple influences of this earlier Arab migration into Spain are still evident.[1] While Spain's identity as a nation – most notably under the iron fist of Ferdinand and Isabella – preceded that of Italy by hundreds of years, only after the death of Franco in 1975 did it join the roster of democratic republics. And, it still struggles with issues of national versus regional identity, with the Basques and Catalan people fiercely clinging to their distinctive local identities and exercising substantial political autonomy.

Clearly, population influxes and cultural pluralism are not new to either Spain or Italy, which for centuries have served as among Europe's hottest melting pots. But, unlike their neighbors to the north, for most of the *twentieth* century they exported far more migrants than they received, first to the new world and later to northern Europe. Labor migrations into the northern industrial regions of Italy and Spain accompanied their economic booms in the 1950s and 1960s, but this immigration was almost entirely internal as impoverished peasants from the south flocked to jobs in northern cities.

So, while Spain and Italy have a long history of population movement, the external labor immigration they began to experience in the 1980s was new. Before turning to an overview of the laws and policies that deal with this new migration, it will help to have at least a thumbnail sketch of the political systems within which they were hammered out.

THE POLITICAL CONTEXTS

Italian politics have gone through major changes in recent years, in part triggered by a series of corruption scandals in the 1990s.[2] After several decades of post-World War II governments led by Christian Democrats (DC) and nominal socialists (PSI), with one of Western Europe's most powerful communist parties (PCI) exerting pressure mostly from the outside, the party system was radically reshaped in the early 1990s. The PCI collapsed in 1990 and was reformulated in the Democratic Party of the Left (PDS) that represents social democratic values and the Refounded Communist Party (RC) that still pays at least lip-service to communist ideals. The Christian Democrat Party dissolved entirely in 1992, beleaguered by both scandal and stagnation.

It was during this period that billionaire media tycoon Silvio Berlusconi launched his new party, Forza Italia (literally "Go Italy!" – a not so veiled reference to his ownership of Italy's most successful soccer team), located to the right of the former Christian Democrats. Neo-fascists formed the National Alliance party (AN), and a new region-alist, right-wing party, La Lega Nord (the Northern League), appeared in the north led by populist demagogue Umberto Bossi. Espousing an anti-immigrant platform and lambasting the centralization of political power in Rome (which it associates with what it claims is an inefficient and corrupt south), the Northern League won over 9 percent of the vote in the 1994 elections (20 percent in the north, and almost 30 percent in some areas of Lombardy).[3] Berlusconi and his Forza Italia party, in a coalition with the Northern League, pushed Italian politics to the right with their electoral victory in 1994.

Attempts to impose unpopular austerity programs and a massive national strike by organized labor contributed to Berlusconi's rapid ouster, and he was replaced by a grouping of center and left forces known as the "Olive Tree" coalition, headed up by the Democratic Party of the Left (PDS). While the old Communist Party was by now splintered, the left's influence was not substantially diminished, with the PDS in power and the more radical RC (the "unreconstructed" communists) exerting opposition from the outside. As we will see in a moment, it was this leftist coalition – and their labor union allies – that spearheaded the liberal Turco-Napolitano immigration law in 1998.

By the time of the national elections in the spring of 2001, Berlus-coni was able to capitalize on the dismal failure of the Olive Tree to deliver on its promises of economic growth and solidarity with labor, and on his own media empire that saturated television and the print media with campaign rhetoric constructing him as a national icon.[4] Berlusconi's Forza Italia party handily won the right to form a new coalition government, bringing together the National Alliance and the Northern League in the most right-wing government since World War II.

Comparable shifts and upheavals have permeated the trade union movement. The three confederated unions – CGIL, CISL, and UIL – have traditionally been connected to the Communist Party, the Socialists, and the Christian Democrats, respectively, and until the mid-1980s together comprised one of the most powerful forces of organized labor in Western Europe.[5] After a period of internal conflict and relative demise in the 1980s, by 1995 labor unions had made a stunning comeback. Indicative of their renewed political potential, a general strike in October, 1994, played an important role in undoing the first Berlusconi government.

Much of Italy's political life transpires at the local level.[6] Its twenty geo-political regions have pronounced cultural, economic, and political differences. Politics in the southern regions are permeated with clientelism and patronage and have traditionally been heavily influenced by the Catholic church and, before its demise in 1992, the Christian Democratic party. The industrial central regions (the "Red Zone") have a long tradition of communist political culture and are more responsive to the labor movement than to the Catholic church. The "industrial triangle" in the northwest is social democratic in political stripe, while the "White Zone" in the northeast has historically been staunchly center-right and identified with the Catholic Christian Democrats, and now with the Northern League.[7] It is at this regional level – with its patchwork of sometimes dramatically diverse political ideologies and cultures – that much of Italian immigration law and policy is implemented.

The political development of Spain over the last thirty years has taken quite a different course, driven in part by its isolation from the rest of Western Europe imposed by the Franco dictatorship.[8] The "redemocratization" of Spain, launched after Franco's death in 1975, has been characterized by an almost universal desire for consensus-building and stability – an impulse that was further strengthened after a nearly successful military coup in 1981.[9]

A decisive victory in 1982 by the Socialist Workers' Party (PSOE) initiated a twelve-year government by social democrats. Despite their rhetorical commitment to workers' welfare and labor unions, the PSOE platform was largely centrist, with economic development, privatization, and deregulation the key planks. When government austerity programs, combined with high unemployment and rampant corruption scandals, eroded PSOE support, voters made a tentative turn to the right, ushering in the conservative Popular Party (PP) and Prime Minister José María Aznar. Since winning the right to head up the coalition government in 1996, the PP under Aznar has steadily increased its share of the vote, and in 2000 won an absolute majority for the first time, freeing them from their sometimes fickle coalition partners.[10]

Just as Spanish party politics in the last twenty-five years have been less dramatically oppositional, more inclined to consensus, and more oriented to centrist positions than in Italy, so has the labor movement. Some have argued that the relative weakness and disinclination to militancy of Spanish labor unions results from the emphasis on "sociopolitical consensus" in the aftermath of the Franco repression.[11] Others contend that it is due to the "political marginalization of labour" and its exclusion from the "elite pacts" formed to facilitate the transition after Franco.[12] Whatever the reasons, the Spanish labor movement is widely recognized as the least powerful in Western Europe, in terms of its economic clout and political weight.

Even more than in Italy, political power in Spain is decentralized in semi-autonomous regions (called "autonomous communities"). Indeed, the struggle between the national government and the regions has characterized Spanish politics since the nineteenth century. Following the repression of regional culture, politics, and even local language during Franco's reign, regional nationalism returned with renewed vigor after his death. The Constitution of 1978 gives Spain's seventeen regions broad autonomy and grants them their own executive powers, parliaments, and courts. Spearheaded by the demands of nationalist Catalonia and the Basque Country, Spain's autonomous communities have acquired increasing independence and ever-larger shares of the federal budget in recent years.[13]

While Spain's regions differ economically and culturally, there are no clear "red" regions of overwhelming support for left-wing political parties or powerful labor union influence, as there are in Italy. Perhaps the nationalist parties that dominate Catalonia and the Basque Country have preempted the working-class identity dominant in much of Italy's industrial heartland. Whatever the reasons, with the exception of strong nationalist politics in some regions, the political composition of Spain's regions is less dramatically diverse than in Italy.

It was in these political contexts that the main thrusts of Italian and Spanish immigration laws were developed. As we will see, despite their divergent political landscapes for much of this period, their immigration laws and policies have followed remarkably similar paths.

EMERGENCE OF THE CONTEMPORARY IMMIGRATION REGIMES

Spain began to experience substantial influxes of immigrant workers for the first time in the mid-1980s, and increasingly large proportions of these foreigners come from the third world. While in 1980, about 66 percent of foreign residents in Spain were from Western Europe and North America, and tended to be retirees and others seeking the pleasures of the Mediterranean climate and lifestyle, by the 1990s this percentage had shrunk to just over 50 percent, with the other half being workers from less developed nations.[14] One observer has wryly characterized this shift as the "tercermundalización" ("third worldization") of immigration.[15]

A terminological curiosity reveals the disproportionate weight of third-world immigration in the public discourse. The official term for all foreign residents in Spain is "extranjero" ("foreigner"). But, in popular parlance a distinction is made between "extranjeros" and "inmigrantes," with the latter reserved for people who come from less developed countries seeking work. When immigration is discussed in government circles, in the media, among academics, or in public opinion surveys, it invariably refers to third-world immigration, leading one scholar to refer to first-world immigrants as "authentic desaparecidos."[16]

Spain passed its first immigration law just as this "tercermundalización" was gaining momentum. Prior to 1985, it had no explicit immigration policy, nor any specific legislation regarding the treatment of foreign residents. This legislative void created a benign legal limbo for immigrants "who carried out their work and social lives without any great anxiety and without a consciousness of being illegal."[17] One study of pre-1985 Moroccan immigrants found that they were better integrated into the social fabric of Spanish society than later cohorts, were more likely to be self-employed, and often had their families with them.[18]

In June, 1985, Spain joined the European Community, and that same month five EC member countries (Belgium, France, Germany, Luxembourg, and the Netherlands) signed the Schengen Agreement, designed to dismantle their internal borders.[19] The primary purpose of Schengen was to facilitate EC unification, but security and external border controls were central themes. Just days after Spain entered the EC, Parliament passed the Organic Law on the Rights and Liberties of Foreigners in Spain (referred to by its Spanish acronym, LOE).[20]

According to its Preamble, the LOE had the dual purpose of guaranteeing foreigners' rights and controlling illegal immigration.[21] Together with its regulations, which were finally published in May, 1986, it made sharp distinctions between different types of foreigners, with a clear line being drawn between the *Regimen Comunitario* (which applied to EC members) and the *Regimen General* (applying to those outside the EC). EC members were granted all the rights of free circulation, residence, and work in Spain associated with membership in the "Community." In contrast, it required for the first time that those who came from outside the European Community have visas. In addition to entrance visas, those who intended to stay and work in Spain longer than ninety days had to obtain residence and work permits. Legal residents were to have certain rights of assembly, public education, and unionization, with the proviso that these rights were operative only as long as they did not conflict with the "national interest, security, public order, health, morality, or the rights and liberties of Spaniards."[22] And, those in the country without permits (which now comprised the bulk of non-EC foreigners) were explicitly excluded from any of these rights. In recognition of the vast numbers thereby denied the most basic rights, immigrants could apply for legalization within a brief window of opportunity.[23] Finally, the LOE spelled out the grounds for deportation, including lack of proper residence and work permits, being involved in activities that were "contrary to the public order or internal security," being convicted of a felony, and being without sufficient funds.[24]

The LOE comprised barely five pages in the Federal Bulletin, leaving not just the details, but vast terrains of uncharted policy to be worked out through administrative channels. This administrative shunting has become a hallmark of Spanish immigration law, leading one constitutional expert to call it the "à la carte" approach to immigration policy.[25] Among the items on this administrative menu was another legalization plan agreed to by Cabinet Ministers in 1991. One of many such plans over the years, it applied to illegal immigrants who either had ongoing work contracts, were self-employed in a legitimate enterprise, or had previously had residence and work permits. Legal status was valid for only one year, with renewal contingent on the above conditions persisting.[26]

Another administrative action that same year imposed visa requirements on entrants from the Maghreb countries (Morocco, Tunisia, and Algeria) and from Peru and the Dominican Republic, which had been exempt from the requirement under the 1986 law. The new controls followed reports that these countries were the source of large numbers of illegal residents, together with stepped-up pressure from the EC as Spain signed the Schengen Agreement in June, 1991.

In 1993, with restrictions on new immigration tightening and employers complaining of labor shortages, another Cabinet agreement launched an annual foreign worker program, establishing annual quotas for foreign workers in three sectors where there were said to be shortages: agriculture (10,000 workers), unskilled construction work (1,100 workers), and various services (5,000 for domestic service and 3,500 for other services).[27] While the numbers vary slightly from year to year, the program remains an integral part of Spain's immigration policy.

A government decree in 1996 announced the third legalization program in a decade, applying this time only to those who had once had residence and work permits but who for a variety of reasons had been unable to renew them. The same decree, with a low profile and no fanfare, made one of the most significant steps toward recognizing the permanence of its new immigrant population. This relatively inconspicuous document created for the first time a permanent residence status and work permits for those who could show they had been legal for at least six years, successfully renewing their temporary permits with no lapses.[28]

While the constitutional authority for immigration ultimately rests with the federal government,[29] the actual operation of the system is decentralized in the regions, provinces, and municipalities. The seventeen regions in Spain in effect have their own immigration micropolicies and procedures. These are in theory just administrative blueprints for the execution of federal policy, but in part because the latter is so ambiguous, the regions enjoy substantial discretion.[30] As we will see later, this radical decentralization plays an important part in the uncertainty and ambiguity that plagues immigrants who are attempting to secure legal residence, work permits, and access to social services.

Throughout this early period of immigration policymaking, political rhetoric focused on the need to control illegal immigration on the one hand, and integrate legal immigrants on the other. Every law, government decree, and regional program reaffirmed this dual focus, drawing a sharp (although, as we will see, largely fictitious) line between legal and illegal immigrants. A 1991 Congressional resolution called for the fight against illegal immigration and for "the social integration of (legal) immigrants."[31] In 1992, the Minister of the Interior told the House of Representatives, "[T]he objective of all our immigration policies is the successful and harmonious integration between the local population and the immigrants who come to live and work among us." He continued, "There are two key concepts: control [of illegal immigration] and openness [to legal immigrants' integration]."[32] In 1994, the Council of Ministers formulated the "Plan for the Social Integration of Immigrants," with ambitious goals to "eliminate all types of unjustified discrimination"; "promote peaceful coexistence and tolerant attitudes"; "combat barriers to integration"; "eradicate all signs of exploitation"; and "mobilize the whole society to fight racism and xenophobia."[33]

A controversial law passed in early 2000 (known as LO 4/2000), over the opposition of Prime Minister Aznar's center-right government, expanded the emphasis on integrating immigrants. The "Organic Law on the Rights and Liberties of Foreigners in Spain, and Their Social Integration" contained several key provisions that enhanced immigrants' rights and broadened their access to social services.[34] It included yet another legalization program, this time for immigrants who had been in Spain continuously since 1999, and had held a work or residence permit at some time in the preceding three years. It granted five-year legal status to undocumented immigrants who had been in Spain for at least two years, were registered as residents in their local municipality,[35] and had a demonstrable means of support. After this five-year period of legal status (during which one still had to secure annual *work* permits), the immigrant could apply for permanent legal residence.[36] LO 4/2000 extended the right to public education to all immigrant children, regardless of legal status, and all immigrants were given the right to access the national health care system, public housing services, and social security protections. As with the legalization provisions, the key to accessing these rights was not legal status, but registration in the local municipality as a *de facto* resident.

The law was broad in scope and, for its brief life, was "considered the most liberal law on the rights of foreigners in Europe."[37] The Popular Party of Prime Minister Aznar called it "the NGO Law," with barely disguised disdain for the immigrant advocates they claimed were behind its framing and passage.[38] As we will see in a minute, many of its most generous provisions were repealed within a few months, when Prime Minister Aznar won an absolute majority in the 2000 election.

Italian immigration policies evolved in tandem with their Spanish counterparts, with Italy passing its first comprehensive law in 1986, less than a year after Spain. This law, "Foreign Workers and the Control of Illegal Immigration," was the product of pressure from unions and opposition parties who contested the exploitation of the growing number of illegal immigrants, combined with pressure from the European Community which was keeping a nervous eye on these southern doors of the European fortress.[39]

One provision stated that all legal foreign workers in Italy must receive equal treatment to that of Italian workers. Others provided for family unification, access to housing, and nondiscrimination in services such as health care. And, employer sanctions were included, specifying that smuggling immigrants or hiring illegal immigrant workers "for the purpose of exploitation," could elicit a fine the equivalent of $1,000–$5,000 a piece, and one to five years in prison. But, the undisputed centerpiece of this law was an expansive legalization program.

Fast on the heels of this law, another one was passed in 1990. The Martelli Law, named after then Deputy Prime Minister Claudio Martelli, provided the first blueprint for a quota worker system, and included another legalization program.[40] Residence permits issued in this legalization were valid for two years, renewable for four years if the immigrant could demonstrate that he or she was continuing to work. For those employed in the underground economy, it was possible to make an "auto-certification" of income, but this required divulging the name of one's employer.

With immigration increasing rapidly throughout the 1990s and with Italy's economy more and more dependent on immigrant labor, the liberal-left coalition government in 1998 passed one of the most liberal immigration laws in Europe – the Turco-Napolitano Law, on which much of Spain's LO 4/2000 law had been modeled.[41] Turco-Napolitano set up a more precise mechanism for determining the annual quota for foreign workers and mandated that the consultation process include consideration of the number of foreign workers already on government hiring lists, employers' labor needs, and unemployment rates. Employers were to request workers, either by name or by the number of workers needed. If the annual quota was not already filled, the employer would receive the workers requested, who – even if specified by name and even if already in Italy – had to return to their country of origin and re-enter with the requisite paperwork.

Foreign workers who came as part of the quota could have their residence permits renewed indefinitely without returning to their home country if they continued to work. In most cases, residence permits were issued for two years, and were renewed if the original conditions (usually work in the formal economy) continued to be met. For the first time, immigrant workers who lost their jobs did not lose their residence permits, but instead were given a year to find new employment.

The law also provided for a quota of seasonal workers. Within this quota, contracted workers could enter for periods of up to six months, extendable to nine months. If they secured permanent work during this period, they had to leave Italy and come back in through the permanent quota. Employers requesting seasonal workers had to specify, in addition to the conditions of work and housing assistance, how they intended to get the workers to leave once the work was completed.

Among its more liberal provisions, a sponsor system was established, whereby any public entity could sponsor immigrants to come to Italy to look for work, as long as the sponsor could guarantee a source of livelihood and the immigrants came within the annual quota. Employers' associations, labor unions, immigrant advocacy groups, and NGOs were all eligible to sponsor aspiring immigrants. The Turco-Napolitano Law also provided for family unification, again within the quota, and extended family members could automatically get work permits.

It also expanded the rights of foreigners within Italy. Among its major provisions were the right to equal treatment in the workplace; access to the universal health care system; and, for the undocumented, the right to urgent care, and the right to attend public school. In addition, it set out an ambitious plan for a network of reception centers throughout Italy to provide legal and illegal immigrants with emergency food and shelter, as well as language instruction and a wide range of other cultural and social services.

Finally, it provided for a "carta di soggiorno" or residence card, that for the first time created a category of permanent legal residents. After five years of continuous legal status, if immigrants had a legitimate job and sufficient income to support themselves and their family, they and their spouses and minor children were eligible for this residence permit which, unlike all previous residence permits, was open-ended in duration.

More than with any previous Italian policy, the focus in this 1998 law was squarely on the importance of immigrant integration, as exemplified by the new permanent resident status and the delineation of extensive immigrant rights and access to social services. Consistent with this focus, executive regulations for the Turco-Napolitano Law called for an annual report to be issued by a commission of experts to evaluate the progress of immigrant integration.[42]

In the spring of 2001, Silvio Berlusconi and his coalition of rightist, anti-immigrant parties came to power, replacing the center-left coalition government that had shepherded Turco-Napolitano through the Italian legislature. The year before, Spanish Prime Minister Aznar's Popular Party had won a majority in Spain's elections. Premiers Berlusconi and Aznar, spurred on by political allies to their right and by the opportunity to score political points by sounding the immigration alarm, quickly set about reversing what they claimed were overly generous provisions in their countries' immigration laws.

TOUGHENING UP

In the same Parliamentary session in which LO 4/2000 was passed, the Popular Party announced its intention to repeal it. Capitalizing on the violent events of El Ejido in February, 2000 (Aznar argued that you "had to be there" before judging the anti-immigrant mob),[43] Aznar won a decisive victory in the national elections the following month. True to their word, Aznar and his Popular Party "boycotted" Law 4/2000 – which they claimed had been responsible for the El Ejido violence by implicitly encouraging immigration – effectively calling a halt to its implementation.[44] They submitted a Bill to reform it by September, and by the end of the year the reform was enacted into law. One expert observed that the reform was enacted "in haste," before the government's newly created immigration commission had made its recommendations. "In the end," he said, "the process seemed characterized by pure improvization."[45]

Improvizational or not, Law 8/2000 – referred to by some as the "Counter-Reformation" – was in line with the administration's tough anti-immigrant stance, even smacking of payback for the humiliation of the previous year's enactment of a liberal law in the face of Aznar's opposition.[46] According to its Preamble, Law 8/2000 was designed to bring Spain into compliance with the EU agreement at Tampere (Finland) in 1999 and the Schengen Agreement, which the Popular Party claimed had been violated by the permissiveness of Law 4/2000.[47]

The new law denies illegal immigrants the rights of assembly, collective bargaining, striking, and even joining labor unions.[48] It allows police to hold undocumented immigrants for up to forty days in detention centers, and to deport them within seventy-two hours. It eliminates most rights to social services for illegal immigrants except health care, compulsory public education, and legal assistance for asylum proceedings or for any proceeding that might result in denial of future entry or deportation. Indicative of its policing orientation, the law moved more responsibility for immigration issues into the Department of the Interior where criminal justice functions are located.[49]

Legal immigrants are also affected, as family unification rights are now restricted to immediate family members. Access to most legal aid and to public aid for housing is cut off even to legal immigrants. Technically, permanent residency is still possible after five years of legal residence (that is, after one temporary permit of one year and then two, two-year permits), but these documents must be renewed every five years. Finally, the quota system was revised to eliminate it as an avenue of legalization. While in the past illegal immigrants already in Spain could apply for the annual quota worker system (effectively constituting a legalization program), quota workers now must be imported from abroad and enter with work contracts in hand.

Although the emphasis in the law was on cutting back on rights for immigrants, it also launched another legalization program, presumably to offset the dramatic consequences of Law 8/2000 for the undocumented. And, after several mass protests over the plight of illegal immigrants under this new regime, soon after the law was passed two more legalization programs were announced, one for those who had put down roots in Spain but who for whatever reason had not qualified in earlier programs, and another specifically for Ecuadorians.[50] While these legalizations signal some recognition of the need to integrate immigrants already present, the overall effect of this law has been to curtail the rights of both illegal and legal immigrants and increasingly to spell immigration as a police function. As one Spanish immigration scholar put it, the law and its related executive policies represent "a progressive hardening of Spanish policy."[51] A former immigration official interviewed for this study quipped that under the current government, the "Ministry for Immigration" is really the "Ministry *Against* Immigration."[52]

In Italy, Silvio Berlusconi soon moved in the same direction as his Spanish counterpart, if anything going further and faster to accommodate his coalition partners, the notoriously anti-immigrant Northern League and the National Alliance Party. While not quite as vitriolic as his unruly and sometimes politically toxic partners,[53] Berlusconi lost little time pushing the "immigration problem" to the top of his political agenda. When a boatload of 928 Iraqi Kurds landed in Sicily in March, 2002, a national emergency was declared, giving police the power to expedite deportation procedures and to destroy smugglers' boats (see Chapter 6).[54]

Four months later, the Berlusconi government passed a new immigration law.[55] Named for its principal sponsors, Reform Minister Umberto Bossi of the Northern League and Deputy Prime Minister Gianfranco Fini from the National Alliance Party, the Bossi-Fini Law modified many of the liberal provisions of Turco-Napolitano, more closely linked legal residence with work contracts, and added symbolically potent security and police measures. Bossi's words to one of his Northern League colleagues summed up the mentality behind the law: "On immigration, we must hit hard, as hard as possible." Or, as the Northern League vice president of the Senate put it, after the new law went into effect, there was to be "below-zero tolerance" ("toleranza sottozero") for illegal immigration – an interesting choice of words, presumably placing even legal immigrants on notice.[56] A reporter called the administration's approach "a turning of the screw on all fronts."[57]

Bossi-Fini did away with the sponsor system that had allowed immigrants to enter Italy to look for work; instead, it stipulated that only immigrants who have a work contract in hand can enter legally, and then only within the annual quotas. If immigrants lose their job, they lose their residence permit and automatically fall into illegality if they do not get another work contract within six months (instead of one year under Turco-Napolitano). Bossi made its purpose clear: "The concept," he said, "is that immigrants are to come to our country for one purpose only: work. Otherwise, they will be sent back."[58]

Residence permits are for a maximum of two years, and renewals must be requested three months before expiration (instead of thirty days in Turco-Napolitano). The "carta di soggiorno" that provides for the possibility of permanent residence survived the retrenchments, but the duration of temporary legal residence required to secure it was extended from five years to six. Finally, the right of legal immigrant workers to bring family members with them is limited in this law, applying only to spouses and minor children – as in Spain – not the extended family as in the past.

Besides this tightening of the connection between work and legal status, Bossi-Fini heightened the police function of immigration policy.

Although Bossi's proposal that illegal residence itself should be considered a felony and carry a prison sentence was over-ruled as impractical, the law does criminalize re-entry after deportation. The aspect of Bossi-Fini that received the most publicity and provoked the most debate was the mandate that all non-EU immigrants be fingerprinted when they apply for or renew their residence permits.

With great fanfare and after months of rancorous debate, a special legalization program was established for maids and caregivers. Employers were given sixty days from the law's effective date in September, 2002, to request legal status for their domestic helpers, at a cost of approximately $300 a piece (limited to one per family for maids, with no limit on caregivers of the elderly and/or disabled). Application kits were available at Italy's 14,000 post offices, which were also designated to receive the anticipated 100,000 completed applications. Another legalization plan – which the Under-Secretary of the Interior insisted was a "regularization," not an "amnesty" – was for immigrant workers in the underground economy, and was ostensibly meant to "emerge" the submerged economy.[59] These applications cost $800 each, and employers had a thirty-day window of opportunity to apply on behalf of their workers.

Summarizing the impulse behind Bossi-Fini, a former Cabinet member rued, "The philosophy behind Fini-Bossi [sic] is clear: We do not want immigrants, except for the minimal number necessary for the requirements of our economy, for the minimum amount of time possible, and in conditions of absolute precariousness, so that it will be easy to free ourselves of them when we are ready."[60] The *Corriere della Sera*, in announcing the passage of the law, captured the simultaneous focus on immigrants as workers and as potential criminals with its headline, "Fingerprints and Work Contracts: Here Are the New Rules."[61]

The new laws in Italy and Spain have been roundly criticized by opposition parties, by the Catholic church, by a wide coalition of NGOs, and even by the business sector that is normally allied with these governments. In Italy, hundreds of priests mobilized against Bossi-Fini, which they said "violates the principles of solidarity and human rights." An archbishop declared that the law "creates problems of conscience," and urged the Church to engage in civil disobedience.[62] Another bishop called it "racist."[63] Former Cabinet member and Social Democrat, Livia Turco, said the law was "bad and unenforceable" and added, perhaps somewhat self-interestedly (given her key role in sponsoring

No rights / animosity

the Turco-Napolitano Law), "Before, immigrants had rights; now, they will be exploited."[64] Another member of the leftist Olive Tree coalition said Bossi-Fini was "inequitable, racist, intolerant."[65] An association of Italian Jews offered sarcastically, "We will be the first to give our fingerprints!"[66] Even the president of a major industrial association in the conservative Veneto region criticized the law: "Veneto needs to be able to count on immigrants."[67] In Spain, NGOs called Law 8/2000 "inhumane and ineffective," and hundreds of thousands of immigrants and their advocates marched against it, protesting its suppression of civil rights.[68]

Even in these laws that elicit such criticism for their siege mentality, however, integration remains an underlying theme. Immediately after the enactment of the "Counter-Reformation" in Spain at the end of 2000, the Ministry of the Interior published its comprehensive plan to address immigration issues. Its authors introduced this "Global Program for the Regulation and Coordination of Foreign Residents and Immigration in Spain" (known by its Spanish acronym, the Plan GRECO), with the declaration, "Integration of new immigrants must be a fundamental element of any immigration policy."[69] As we will see in Chapter 4, the Plan Greco launched a host of new integration programs and refurbished existing ones.

In Italy, where anti-immigrant rhetoric among government officials is now legion, the Bossi-Fini law also includes a nod to integration. While engaging in tough talk on immigrant fingerprinting and deporting immigrants who lose their jobs, the Berlusconi government supported legalization plans for domestic helpers and caregivers and others in the underground economy. And, as in Spain, the central government continues to contract with the local regions to implement extensive integration programs. Some of this activity is no doubt designed to mute criticism of their harsh policies, but the scope of these programs, and – as we will see in Chapter 4 – their vast expense, suggests that the government's concern over immigrant incorporation is more than just political talk.

THE "LEGS OF LAW"

Several themes are apparent in this evolution of Spanish and Italian immigration policy. First, there are continuous starts, shifts, impasses, and changes of course. In less than two decades, there were four major pieces of legislation in Italy (1986, 1990, 1998, and 2002) and three in

Spain (1985, 2000, and 2001), with dozens of additional policies established by administrative decrees and government circulars. In the same period, there were six legalization programs in each country, always accompanied by statements underscoring the extraordinary circumstances justifying this by-now ordinary component of their immigration policies.

Another recurring theme is the glaring gap between the stated purpose of these laws and their actual effects. An essay on immigration law in Italy sums it up eloquently: "Laws, like ideas, walk with men's legs. The latter can go where the law seemed to want to go, they can stand still, or they can go elsewhere altogether."[70] Employer sanctions, for example, have rarely been enforced, and indeed there is some confusion as to how they are intended to work.[71] In the early 1990s, an Italian Ministry of Labor official told me that employer sanctions were entirely a civil matter (despite the possibility of a prison term).[72] The labor inspectors I spoke to had divergent opinions about who was responsible for enforcement. One inspector explained that it was the jurisdiction of the Ministry of Labor, which had wide discretion over the imposition of fines; another insisted with equal certainty that upon finding employers in violation, labor inspectors were to notify the police. While there is some evidence that this latter interpretation was accurate, those responsible for immigration matters at the central police agency in Rome seemed far less interested in the early 1990s in enforcing employer sanctions than in arresting and repatriating Brazilian prostitutes.[73] So obscure was the employer sanctions provision that I had to show Labor Department officials the pertinent section of the law before it was clear to them what I was asking about. When asked how many fines had been levied for employer sanctions, a senior official from the Ministry of Labor smiled and said, "What shall I say?"[74]

Legalization programs, which have enjoyed a far higher profile than employer sanctions, have also been fraught with difficulties. In the first Italian legalization in 1986, only about 107,000, out of up to 1.2 million undocumented immigrants present in Italy at the time, applied. Both employers and workers had their reasons for refraining, among them "the bosses' interest in not regularizing underground labor ... in order to save on health and social security contributions and the minimum wage, and ... the general vulnerability of immigrants to their employers that led them not to seek regularization for fear of losing their jobs."[75]

Early predictions of a low turnout for the Bossi-Fini legalization in 2002, based on this logic, proved wrong. Over 700,000 applications were received from domestic helpers and underground workers, with the applicants about equally divided between the two categories, and the largest number concentrated in and around Milan and Rome.[76] At the time of this writing, it was unclear how many would actually qualify, but the filing itself provided a six-month window of legality. The Northern League was clearly taken aback by the numbers: "We are not absolutely happy with this regularization, and above all the numbers that are emerging. We are sure there are a lot of illegals who applied [sic]: now there will be a verification and they [presumably, the fraudulent applicants] will be thrown out of the country."[77]

More than six months after the application deadline, regulations had still not been issued to deal with the monitoring of the new work contracts, staff had not been brought on to process applications, and only a tiny fraction of applicants – about 2,500 – had been legalized. In Rome, where over 107,000 immigrants applied, only 300 had received the coveted notification of legalization by late January, 2003. One reporter characterized the slow pace of this "ghost law" thus: "Delays will be of biblical proportions."[78]

Besides these problems of low turn-out and administrative delays, immigrants to Italy who manage to legalize are often returned to illegality after one or two years. Only about half of those who were legalized under the Martelli Law of 1990 retained their legal status a decade later.[79] Those who are legalized under Bossi-Fini are likely to experience even higher drop-out rates, given the program's focus on the underground economy.

In Spain, of the original 128,000 applicants for legalization in 1991, only 64 percent were legal after two years.[80] Antonio Izquierdo explains: "[It is] difficult for the regularized to maintain legal status, because they tend to work in precarious and unstable jobs in sectors (such as construction, textiles, agriculture and personal services) where irregular contracts and the underground economy are the norm."[81] In other words, laboring in the underground economy nullifies – not just de facto but literally – immigrants' hard-won "denizen" status, and thrusts them back into the netherworld occupied by "helots," belying the categorical nature of the distinction.[82]

The quota worker systems are plagued by controversy and paralysis too. The annual quota for 1998 in Italy was not announced until October, by which time it was too late to import workers, and undocumented workers already in Italy were allowed to take the unfilled slots. The quota for the following year was not issued until August, was not preceded by any analysis of labor needs, and simply reused the 1998 numbers. Since 2000, the annual quotas have been augmented *ad hoc* throughout the year as employers complain of shortages. In addition to the unwieldy and reactive way the quota is determined, the requirement that temporary workers who secure a permanent job must return to their home countries to be called back in under the quota has produced its own share of criticism. McBritton and Garofalo explain: "The regulations reproduce . . . the same bureaucratic *iter*, so Kafkaesque, that the law was meant to avoid and results in a powerful incentive [for immigrant workers] to stay and become illegal."[83] The same "Kafkaesque *iter*" paralyzes the quota program in Spain. With employers unwilling to hire workers sight-unseen, they are shunning the quota system that now requires them to contract with workers in their countries of origin. In one dramatic example of employer reaction to this requirement, the government allocation of 30,000 special quota slots for Ecuadorians in 2002 resulted in only *four* contracts.[84]

The Turco-Napolitano plan to provide immigrant reception centers throughout Italy also fell short of its goals. Most of what were euphemistically called "reception" centers were in fact detention centers for illegal immigrants. Under the heading, "Is This Any Way to Welcome Them?," a journalist visiting one of the largest of these centers called it "a maximum security prison" for illegal immigrant "guests."[85] Caritas, the Catholic charity, provides food and shelter for immigrants in most major cities, but space is limited, and these shelters bear little resemblance to the cultural and social service oases envisioned in the Turco-Napolitano law. I visited one of these centers on the outskirts of Venice that was more like a halfway house, with residents let out during the day to work but otherwise kept under close scrutiny (see Chapter 5).

Finally, relatively few permanent residence cards have been issued, and, as we will see in Chapter 5, the holy grail of "integration" has remained just that – a legendary treasure to be talked about but never found. Indeed, throughout this short history of Italian and Spanish immigration policies, whether the issue is restrictions and controls (such as employer sanctions, or control over the borders) or the rights accorded immigrants by law (such as access to permanent residence cards), the "legs" of law rarely "go where the law seemed to want to go."

One explanation for the wayward ways of the law resides in the realm of public administration and the difficulties of obtaining (and retaining) legal status in the face of often obdurate, slow, and sometimes fickle bureaucracies. One Spanish scholar estimates that applicants for residence or work permits wait on average ten months to one year to receive their permits or be denied.[86] An official for the immigrant services division of one of the largest unions in Spain, whose job is mainly to help immigrants apply for permits, said the process can take up to three years, and that nationally about 365,000 immigrants were waiting for their "papers."[87]

Ewick and Silbey have eloquently described the power of documents to validate one's "social existence." As they put it, "Often to receive one's papers, whether a green card or a handicapped parking permit, is to become someone different, to be officially recognized, and thus to enter the social script."[88] There is a catch-22 built into the permit systems that dispense such critical validation of one's existence in Italy and Spain. In order to secure or renew legal status in Spain or Italy, foreigners must generally (1) get a preliminary work contract with which to secure a provisional work permit; (2) take this work permit and other documents to the police for a residence permit; and (3) finally, secure work and residence permits (which usually expire after one or two years). The labor contract, the work permit, and the residence permit are in effect mutually dependent on each other, a fact that one observer of Spanish law has called "the vicious circle in which clandestine immigrants are trapped."[89] One indignant member of Spain's House of Representatives told his colleagues: "It is the famous fish that ate its tail: you can't get residence if you don't have a work permit and you can't get a work permit if you don't have residence."[90]

A Mexican worker living in Catalonia for three years described his experience in this way: "The work permit was very difficult to get because [first] you need to present a work contract ... but to get a work contract you need a permit, no? So, which comes first, the chicken or the egg?"[91] On some occasions, one permit expires while waiting for the other to be issued.[92] A Gambian worker tells this story:

> My boss signed a year's pre-contract with me, but my work permit kept being delayed ... I went every two months to Barcelona to get the official stamp ... Well, after a year, still no work permit. One day, my boss says to me, "Well, the year is up already!" I say, "Yes, I know, but tomorrow I'm going to Barcelona again to see if I can get my papers." So, I go to the provincial authorities in the Interior, and they say, "Your papers are at the Labor Department," and I go to the Labor Department and they say, "Your papers are with Interior." When I go back to Interior, I tell them my name, they finally give me my papers, but then they say, "Oh, but your residence permit has expired ... ".[93]

41

Another explanation for the wandering legs of these laws lies in the extensive discretion accorded regional officials, the effect of which can be seen in the vastly discrepant distribution of permanent residency cards – one of the few routes out of the "fish-and-its-tail" predicament. As with much immigration policy in Italy and Spain, implementation of the residence card system is left to local authorities, usually the municipal or provincial police. A study of its implementation across three provinces in the Italian region of Lombardy found dramatic differences in what is required to obtain this coveted document. In all three cases, the documents requested by local police in the application process exceeded what was required by law. In one province, it was the local policy *not to release any permanent residence cards at all*, in clear violation of both the letter and the spirit of the law.[94] The Director of Immigrant Affairs at the CGIL office in one large Italian city told me that the local authorities there were "fussy" about giving out these residence cards, and that the only ones he had seen issued were given to foreigners married to Italian citizens.[95] In Spain, unions have denounced officials in the region of Valencia for "boycotting" the issuance of even temporary permits.[96]

Underlying these bureaucratic quagmires and the "fussiness" of local authorities, and with an impact that can scarcely be exaggerated, is the fact that the two central features of these immigration systems – integration and control – are on a collision course, as we see in the following section.

LAW'S "PERVERSE CONSEQUENCES"[97]

Since their beginnings in the mid-1980s, immigration law in Spain and Italy has been predicated on the principle that the increasing influx of immigrants from the third world must be controlled, or at least managed. For one thing, as these Mediterranean countries became the southern gate of a European fortress that was steadily dismantling its internal walls, pressure mounted to control the numbers who slipped across their borders. At least as important, it was from the beginning a labor migration. Not only do immigrants come to Italy and Spain seeking work, but their welcome there has been, and remains, contingent on their willingness to work in jobs and under conditions that locals increasingly shun (see Chapter 3).

While the term "guestworker" is long outdated, the concept remains entrenched. Since the post-World War II experience in Germany with

"Gastarbeiter" who stayed around to become permanent members of German society, few are naive enough today to believe that immigrant workers can be brought in and expelled at will. But, immigrants in Italy and Spain are first and foremost *workers*, and they are begrudgingly tolerated because there is work to be done. Like uninvited (and unpopular) dinner guests who are the only ones willing to do the dishes, they are allowed to stay, but only under certain conditions and only until the dishes are done.

Mercedes Jabardo, an anthropologist studying African farm labor in Catalonia, observed of the first Spanish immigration law: "The legislation...generate[d] irregularity among the vast majority of the immigrant community...In other words, the law create[d] the legal category of immigrant and thereby generate[d] the category of the 'illegal.'"[98] This is true in the obvious sense that before the LOE there was no comprehensive immigration policy in Spain, and thus no illegal immigrants.[99] But, the law produced "irregularity" in a more subtle way as well, for lapses into illegality are *built into* both Spanish and Italian immigration law. This construction of illegality through law is the product of a variety of overlapping factors, the most important of which is the temporary and contingent nature of legal status.

Prior to 1996, it took ten years of continuous legal status before one could apply for permanent residence in Spain (reduced to five in the latest laws). Italy first introduced the concept in 1998 with the possibility of applying for a "carta di soggiorno" after five years of uninterrupted legal status (extended to six under Bossi-Fini). But, there are still relatively few permanent legal residents in either Spain or Italy, largely because of the near impossibility of piecing together five or six years of uninterrupted work and residence permits.

The contingent nature of legal status is underscored by the instability inherent in the very programs designed to legalize immigrants. Virtually all of these legalization programs are specifically and exclusively for foreign *workers* (and under some limited conditions, their families), and are usually dependent on having a legitimate work contract or having had one in the recent past. The difficulties of illegal immigrants meeting this standard, given their concentration in the underground economy, are legion. Not only are underground employers often unwilling to formalize work contracts, but some clearly *prefer* the undocumented status of their workers, and the vulnerability that status ensures. A union official told me of an asparagus grower in the poor agricultural region of Extremadura who fired all his legal workers and replaced them with

200 undocumented Ecuadorians, a move that brought him a 60-million pesetas fine in a rare implementation of the employer sanctions law.[100]

According to ethnographic studies with Latin American and African immigrants in and around Barcelona and Madrid, many have been fired for broaching the possibility of legalization.[101] An Equatorial Guinean in Spain who lost his job when he asked his boss to help him legalize, put it this way, "Here when they hire an immigrant they prefer that he work in conditions that are not legitimate, and preferably illegal; that way they can pay what they want and under conditions convenient to them." A Gambian immigrant explained: "If you work in the fields, and you go to your boss and ask for a contract, that's the day you lose your job."[102] In one extreme and highly publicized case in Italy, an underground employer in the construction industry was convicted of murder after pouring gasoline over and setting fire to a Romanian worker who had asked to be legalized.[103]

The legalization provision for underground workers in Italy's Bossi-Fini law, purportedly designed to "emerge" the submerged economy, is interesting in this context. While early reports suggesting that few employers would volunteer for legalization proved wrong, the program has apparently been used by some to "extort" money from their workers to cover estimated losses from any such "emersion."[104] In Rome, nine out of every ten construction workers whose employers applied for legalization were required to pay the administrative costs, and many had to pay their employers an additional "incentive" fee.[105] A Peruvian maid in Rome told reporters that her employers had discouraged her from trying to legalize, making it clear that if she insisted she would have to pay not only for the cost of the legalization, but for all subsequent social security payments and taxes, in effect reducing her wages from 15,000 lira an hour to 8,000 lira (then the equivalent of $4.50). Other domestic helpers reported being fired.[106]

As an aside, an official for the Berlusconi government, in a remark that reveals the distance between the administration and working people's lived experience, in response to reports that people had been fired, claimed that no one could lose their jobs as a result of this law: "To the complaint that some people will lose their jobs...I say that this is impossible, because the workers who lose their jobs in reality don't *have* a job. They are exploited by people who do not give them a regular contract, and so they cannot be laid off."[107] Susan Bibler Coutin discusses the "spaces of non-existence" of undocumented Salvadoran immigrants in the United States, eloquently relating such spaces to the "disjuncture between physical and legal presence" and describing the unauthorized immigrant's legal "absence" or "nonexistence." Extending the logic of nonexistence to immigrants' employment, this Italian official announced with characteristic aplomb: if it is illegal, it does not exist.[108]

Underscoring the contradictions inherent in a legalization plan for underground employers (who by definition attempt to evade government regula(riza)tion), a dispute erupted in Italy between the Northern League and the National Alliance over whether immigrant workers could take their employers to court to force them to legalize them under the Bossi-Fini law. When the Under-Secretary of the National Alliance party circulated a proposal to allow for such lawsuits, the Northern League and even some members of his own National Alliance party criticized him. The Cabinet member responsible for immigration issues chided his party colleague: "The regularization plan *allows for*, but does not *require*" employers to legalize their workers; furthermore, he argued, allowing immigrant workers to take their employers to court "would have a negative impact on the politics of integration, which is based on mutual respect between the parties."[109]

Historically, as we have seen, those who have managed to get legalized do not find it easy to retain their legal status. In fact, all these legalization programs *build in* a loss of legal status unless one can demonstrate on an annual or bi-annual basis that the original conditions persist (most importantly and most dauntingly, a formal work contract). Some immigrants do not qualify for renewal because the work contracts on which their legalization had been based have ended; in other cases, the original contract commitments were never fulfilled by employers.[110]

The point is that Spanish and Italian immigration laws, anchored by temporary and contingent permit systems, build in illegality. And, this "institutionalized irregularity"[111] is part and parcel of the labor function of immigrants in these countries. I am not referring here simply to the (important) fact that illegal immigrants "work scared and hard," a point that has been made many times before.[112] Rather, I mean that the precariousness of legal status that is doled out in small increments – and hence immigrants' inevitable stints of illegality – are the mirror image of their contingent and begrudging welcome as the uninvited guests whose job it is to clean up. The Bossi-Fini law moves this contingency front and center, with its insistence on the link between legal status and work contracts, but this logic permeates all Italian and Spanish immigration policy. "Institutionalized irregularity" is the by-product of a legal system that tolerates third-world immigrants *conditionally*, as flexible workers. And, of course, irregularity, and the contingent legality from which it derives, enhance that flexibility. As an Eritrean immigrant who has been in Italy for fifteen years told a reporter: "We risk being deported if we do not accept our employers' blackmail."[113]

Meillassoux likened the work permit system for immigrants in France and the subsequent contingency of legal status several decades ago to the South African "pass" system, an analogy that fits equally well the case of immigrant workers in contemporary Italy and Spain:

> Work permits are granted only for limited periods and renewed only on specific conditions. The "pass" system once operating in South Africa, by which African workers are moved about as it suits their racist employers, is matched in France by the various permits (residence-permit, work-permit) which leave the immigrant worker vulnerable to the hazards of police, administrative and employer control and make it easier to fix their length of stay in accordance with the needs of the economy.[114]

But, if immigration law helps construct and preserve the immigrants' Otherness on which their economic contribution rests, it must also cope with the resulting poverty and exclusion – in part because this exclusion marks immigrants as a suspect population and invites a political backlash against this useful labor force, in part because such marginal populations present fiscal and social problems, and in part because of the ideological dissonance associated with the construction of an excluded underclass in these liberal democracies. Regarding the latter, Yasemin Soysal has argued that with the expansion of universal human rights in democratic societies, immigrants have come to enjoy virtually all of the rights associated with citizenship. As part of this evolution, she contends: "The theme of 'the need to incorporate' guestworkers has supplanted that of their 'temporariness' as the dominant discourse."[115]

There is little question but that human rights discourse has had an impact in Spain and Italy as they struggle with immigration policy. But, developments in these new countries of immigration are not consistent with Soysal's argument, and the nature of the inconsistencies suggests that there are more complex dynamics at work than a linear progression of human rights and incorporation. Not only have immigrants here clearly *not* secured equal rights with citizens (and the most recent laws further accentuate the differences), but Italian and Spanish immigration policies tap *both* the "need to incorporate" *and* the "temporariness" discourses, simultaneously marginalizing and attempting to integrate.

Leti Volpp, in her discussion of the historical exclusion of Asian Americans from full citizenship in the United States, notes the contradiction of such exclusion in liberal theory. "Liberal theory," she says, "cannot explain why Asian Americans can be cast 'both as persons and populations to be integrated into the national political sphere,' deserving of the protection of rights, and 'as the contradictory, confusing, unintelligible elements to be marginalized and returned to their alien origins.' "[116] A similar contradiction lies at the heart of Spanish and Italian immigration laws, with their dual focus on the integration of immigrants and the right to return them "to their alien origins."

A central question throughout this book is, how is immigrant marginality constituted and reconstituted despite the emphasis in Italian and Spanish policies on integration? One answer lies in this tension between the integration emphasis and the countervailing effects of these same laws that confine immigrants to contingent (and thus usually temporary) legal status. As one critic of the Plan Greco in Spain put it: "No program can integrate those whom the laws 'disintegrate.' "[117] The following chapters examine in more detail this contradiction between the legally constituted function of immigrants as Others, and the push to incorporate them. As this tension is played out at the local level where concrete integration policies are constructed and implemented, we can watch close up both the urgency and the long odds of integration efforts in the face of immigrants' legal and economic Otherness.

CHAPTER THREE

"USEFUL INVADERS":[1] THE ECONOMICS OF ALTERITÉ

The president of the Banca d'Italia issued a blunt warning: "Italy needs immigrants."[2] His counterparts in Spain have raised similar alarms, with even the Spanish government conceding, "Immigration is a desirable phenomenon."[3] This sometimes reluctant acknowledgment of the importance of immigrants hinges in part on the dangerously low birthrates in these Catholic countries, and related fears that their social security systems cannot survive the shrinking revenues and expanding expenses associated with their rapidly aging populations.

Italy and Spain have birthrates of less than 1.2 per couple (compared to 1.5 for the rest of the EU), far below replacement level. By the middle of this century, they will be the two oldest countries in the world, with a median age of over 54.[4] Population declines threaten the very survival of many small towns and villages – even the legendary Italian hilltowns of Tuscany and Umbria. Writing of the demise of these towns, one journalist wrote: "Defiant through the centuries, they survived the Roman Empire, plagues, barbarians, two World Wars, famines, earthquakes, depressions and huge migrations to New York, Boston, and Philadelphia. But [this] new peril is more threatening than any of the previous ones."[5]

Immigrants are counted on to offset these trends. Under the headline, "It Will Be Immigrants Who Save Italians' Pensions," the Banca d'Italia president pointed out that only a hefty infusion of young immigrants can ward off the impending crisis in Italy, where pensioners already outnumber active workers and the pension system is $44 billion in debt.[6] A study commissioned by the construction industry in Milan concluded that the Milanese population had remained stable over the last decade "thanks to immigration."[7] In Spain, immigrants – whose contributions to the social security system have doubled in less than three years – are credited for the system's surplus. And, the birthrate is beginning to creep back up from its low in the mid-1990s, thanks in part to higher fertility rates among recent immigrants.[8]

The number of foreign residents in these southern European countries is still relatively small, with just over 2 percent of the Spanish population and 4 percent of the Italian population foreign-born (compared to an EU average of 5 percent, and 10.4 percent in the United States).[9] Precise estimates vary according to the government agency producing the data, their sources, and their administrative purpose.[10] In Italy, the primary government source for the number of legal foreign residents is the Ministry of the Interior. According to their data, there were about 1.4 million legally resident foreigners in Italy at the beginning of 2001. The Catholic service organization, Caritas, put the number closer to 1.7 million.[11] In 2003, Caritas estimated that the combined number of legal immigrants in Italy and those who had applied for legalization under the Bossi-Fini law, reached 2,395,000, nearly triple the number present just over a decade ago.[12]

Almost half of Italy's immigrants live in just two regions – Lombardy (the northern region anchored by Milan) and Lazio (the central region around Rome). Even as the number of immigrants continues to climb, their distribution remains uneven, with over 80 percent residing in Italy's northern and central regions (see Table 3.1). Most gravitate to major cities, but some of the highest per capita concentrations are found in the small towns and villages of northeastern Italy. The town of Altivole in the Veneto region, with a total population of 6,000, is home to about 900 immigrants, giving it the highest ratio of immigrants to natives in all of Italy. Of the 329 foreign residents registered in City Hall, twenty-five different nationalities are represented. As Altivole struggles with labor shortages and a declining and aging population, one out of every two new hires is an immigrant. One local resident of this remote town in the northern Italian countryside told a reporter with a glint in her eye: "I came to expect just about anything out of life, except that I would grow old in a Chinese industrial district."[13]

The size and distribution of the undocumented population – the "irregolari" – is difficult to gauge. Estimates have ranged from 250,000 (suggested by the Minister of the Interior), to 300,000 (Caritas), and 340,000 (the Organization for Economic Cooperation

Table 3.1. *Legal foreign residents in Italy, by region (January 1, 2003)*

North	887,820
Valle d'Aosta	2,913
Piedmont	107,563
Lombardy	348,298
Liguria	36,835
Trentino-Alto Aldige	38,647
Veneto	154,632
Friuli	48,304
Emilia-Romagna	150,628
Center	428,510
Tuscany	111,458
Umbria	30,965
Marche	47,169
Lazio	238,918
South	134,678
Abruzzo	21,263
Campania	58,641
Molise	2,377
Basilicata	3,505
Puglia	31,294
Calabria	17,598
Islands	61,316
Sicily	49,579
Sardinia	11,737
Total	1,512,324

Source: Ministro dell'Interno, cited in ISMU-Cariplo, *Nono Rapporto sulle Migrazioni 2003* (Milan: FrancoAngeli), 2004: 355.

and Development).[14] With the Bossi-Fini legalization programs eliciting more than 700,000 applications from undocumented caregivers and underground workers alone, even considering that some of these applications were duplicates it seems certain that the total undocumented population far exceeded original estimates. In any case, as explained in the previous chapter, legal and illegal statuses are more accurately moments in time than characteristics of distinct populations, and their numbers can shift dramatically with changes in government policy.

The majority of immigrants to Italy come from outside the European Union, with Africa the largest source region for non-EU immigrants, followed by Eastern and Central Europe. Morocco is the single largest source country, providing approximately 10 percent of the total number of legal foreign residents and a disproportionate number of unauthorized immigrants as well. The share of non-EU residents has steadily increased since 1994, including a dramatic increase in immigration from Eastern and Central Europe, and smaller but significant increases in the proportion of immigrants from African and Asian countries.

Women make up about 45 percent of foreign residents in Italy, with the gender gap decreasing over time, giving rise to the concept of the "feminization of migration flows."[15] Their distribution across Italy's regions approximates that of their male counterparts, but the gender make-up of different nationalities varies widely. While 72 percent of foreign residents from Morocco are male, women account for over 66 percent of immigrants from the Philippines, 70 percent of Polish immigrants, and 68 percent of Peruvians; the large population of immigrants from the Cape Verde Islands is almost entirely women.[16] Some of these women pre-date their male counterparts in Italy. For example, Filipinas were among the first immigrants to arrive in large numbers in the early 1970s, and with family unification and the passage of time, they are now among the most established of immigrant groups.[17]

As in Italy, Spain also experienced massive internal migrations in the mid-twentieth century, when the industrial areas in and around Barcelona and Madrid, and in the Basque region, attracted the landless populations of the rural south. But, high levels of *external* immigration beginning in the mid-1980s were new. The number of legal foreign residents in Spain rose from fewer than 250,000 in 1985 to over 1.2 million in 2002 to more than 1.6 million by 2004.[18] With just 11 percent of the EU population, Spain now receives an estimated 22 percent of its immigrants.[19] As in Italy, the primary source region is Africa, and the single most important country of origin is Morocco. Spain is also host to a substantial Latin American population, not surprisingly given its linguistic and colonial-cultural ties to the region.[20] A slightly larger share of Spain's immigrant population is unauthorized at any given point in time than in Italy, with most estimates currently hovering around 300,000.[21] Just under 40 percent of these are thought to be Moroccan, 25 percent South American, 12 percent Sub-Saharan African, 8 percent Chinese, and 8 percent Eastern European.[22]

Also as in Italy, women make up almost half of the immigrant population, with the proportions varying by nationality.[23] The "most feminized flows" of immigrants to Spain come from the Dominican Republic (about 80 percent), Colombia (about 72 percent), Ecuador and Brazil (almost 70 percent), Equatorial Guinea (66 percent), and the

L.A. = mostly female

Table 3.2. *Legal foreign residents in Spain, by region (December 31, 2003)*

Andalusia	208,523
Aragón	39,015
Asturias	12,730
Balearic Islands	75,867
Basque Country	28,600
Canary Islands	113,339
Cantabria	11,778
Castilla-La Mancha	36,540
Castilla y León	45,233
Catalonia	383,938
Extremadura	17,123
Galicia	37,522
Madrid	355,035
Murcia	58,150
Navarra	22,681
Rioja	13,621
Valencia	180,011
Ceuta	2,184
Melilla	3,225
Total	1,645,115

Source: Ministerio del Interior, Delegación del Gobierno para la Extranjería y la Inmigración, Observatorio Permanente de la Inmigración, *Boletín Estadístico de Extranjería e Inmigración*: 4.

Philippines and Peru (65 percent each).[24] Filipina and Peruvian women are more likely to arrive alone in search of domestic employment, while women from the Mahgreb countries and Pakistan usually accompany male migrants and, at least initially, tend not to work outside the home.

Most immigrants are concentrated in the wealthy regions of Catalonia (in and around Barcelona) and Madrid, with the third largest immigrant population found in the agricultural region of Andalusia, Spain's southernmost point (see Table 3.2). With the Strait of Gibraltar separating Spain from Morocco by just eight miles, many who make this treacherous journey by sea remain in Andalusia and form the backbone of the region's agricultural workforce.[25]

In a moment, I will turn to the various economic niches these immigrants occupy, and suggest that the wages and working conditions they endure are in effect their passport, but first some background must be filled in.

THE ITALIAN ECONOMIC MIRACLE AND BEYOND

Italy experienced something of an "economic miracle" after World War II. With an annual growth rate of almost 6 percent and a doubling of its GDP between 1950 and 1962, its economic expansion was surpassed only by that of Japan in the post-war years. It was not just a matter of increased productivity and capital investments either; during this period, Italy catapulted from its relatively undeveloped agricultural economy to become an industrial powerhouse. The transformation depended in part on a large internal supply of very low-wage labor. One observer noted that "Italian industry in the 60s had much in common with that of the third world, above all because it made use of such low-wage labor."[26]

The "miracle" did not affect all geographic regions equally. A prominent feature of Italy's economy was, and continues to be, its geographic and structural duality.[27] Massimo d'Azeglio famously proclaimed, upon Italy's unification in the 1860s: "We have made Italy – now we must make Italians." Since then, Italy has continued to be divided economically into a more developed and affluent north and a quasi-feudal agrarian south, or "Mezzogiorno."[28] In part the consequence of location and in part the result of government policy and private sector strategies, this uneven development is a distinguishing feature of Italian-style capitalism. Although the Italian government sponsored emergency measures in the 1960s and 1970s in an attempt to reverse the effect of decades of neglect – and in some cases outright political and economic abuse – the results were limited to the transfer of a few large factories, many of which have long since disappeared.[29]

In the decades after World War II, this uneven development supplied northern industry with an important source of cheap labor to fuel its economic miracle. Approximately seven million people left the south between 1950 and 1975, many heading to factories in northern Italy. As one Italian sociologist put it: "[B]ehind the so-called Italian 'miracle' . . . was a harsh reality of heavy sacrifices for the working class . . . and for the south."[30]

Italy's economy began to cool in the mid-1970s, and has never returned to its heady post-war growth rates. Nonetheless, with the world's fifth largest economy and the "Made in Italy" label a fixture of upscale international trade, it is now a member of the Group of Eight (G-8) industrialized nations and a key player in the post-industrial global economy. Today, the Italian standard of living and per capita income approach those of its northern European neighbors, as do its state welfare protections.

While it shares much with the other economic powers in its orbit, Italy's economy is distinct in a number of ways. For one thing, the regional duality is cross-cut with a deep structural one. To a greater extent than in any other advanced capitalist nation, Italy's economy is bifurcated, with an important monopoly sector – dominated by giant firms like Fiat and the now-infamous Parmalat food dynasty – and a larger secondary sector of small and medium-sized businesses that today are responsible for Italy's continued (albeit slow) economic growth.[31] As a measure of this split, Fiat directly employs at least 50,000 people in Italy, but over 60 percent of Italians work in firms of fewer than twenty people.[32] So central a part of the economy are these small, often family-run, businesses that this constellation is sometimes referred to as "the Italian model" of capitalism.[33] The proportion of the economy constituted by these relatively small businesses has increased dramatically over the last twenty years. While in 1981 the average size of Italian companies' payrolls was twenty, by 1997 the typical firm had shrunk to eight workers.[34]

Dotting the Italian peninsula and scattered throughout virtually every small town and city, these misleadingly humble enterprises often occupy niches with national and international markets, specialize in just-in-time production and services, and offer wages well below that of the monopoly sector. They are integral to the survival of mega-firms that contract out much of their work to them, suggesting that while there is a structural divide between these two sectors there is also a structural interdependence. An estimated 1.5 million workers – roughly 7 percent of the nation's workforce – are linked to Fiat through the thousands of smaller businesses it contracts with or that are indirectly connected to the industry.[35]

Many small firms are located in the vast underground economy. Employing from three to five million workers and accounting for about 28 percent of Italy's gross domestic product, its underground economy is the largest of any advanced capitalist country.[36] Not even Spain, with a less developed economy and lower per capita income, has as active an underground as that of its Mediterranean neighbor. And, it continues to expand, with the proportion of Italian economic activity located in the underground increasing by 10 percent between 1993 and 2001.[37] While some firms are altogether "submerged" ("sommerso") in the underground, many others are hybrid, with parts of their workforce legitimately employed and others hired off-the-books. Of the 21,431 industrial and commercial firms that the Italian Department of Labor inspected in 2002, 55 percent employed at least some of their workers "in nero," or off-the-books.[38] Many of these workers in the shadow economy are part of the longstanding practice in Italy of "doppio lavoro" (double work), or taking a second job in an effort to make ends meet.[39]

Perhaps not surprisingly, these two divisions – the regional and the structural – intersect, as 51 percent of Italy's underground work is found in its southern regions.[40] In some sectors in the south, it accounts for the vast majority of employment. In Calabria, almost 92 percent of agricultural employment is underground in some way (compared to a still-high 60 percent in the northeast and 65 percent in the center-north). In manufacturing, the figure for Calabria is 64 percent and for other southern regions it ranges from 18 percent to 60 percent (compared to only 9 percent in the northeast and 12 percent in the center-north).[41] In the province of Lecce in the southeastern region of Apulia, labor inspectors surveying 2,100 agricultural, textile/shoes, and metalworking firms found that one out of every two enterprises engaged in illegal practices or operated off-the-books in some way, with 90 percent of the province's vigorous shoe industry thus classified as "irregular."[42]

While a disproportionate amount of the shadow economy is located in Italy's southern regions, a recent Caritas report warns against overstating this concentration. Based on the large number of legalization applications coming from immigrant workers in the north and center of Italy (more than four-fifths of the total) under the Bossi-Fini law, Caritas cautions: "It is therefore not accurate to say that [irregular work] is something that only affects the south...It is in reality a national problem."[43] Similarly, a recent report from the labor confederation, CGIL, suggests that the underground economy may be larger in the north than previously suspected. According to this report, approximately 500,000 people work in the shadow economy in Lombardy alone, with heaviest concentrations in construction and domestic service.[44]

Another distinctive mark of the Italian economy is – counterintuitively, given the presence of such a vast underground and the proliferation of small enterprises – the scope and bargaining clout of labor unions. The three major confederations – the Italian General Confederation of Labor (CGIL), the Italian Confederation of Labor Unions (CISL), and the Union of Italian Labor (UIL) – collectively make up one of the most powerful union forces in Europe, and claim membership of up to 40 percent of the Italian workforce.[45] While these three confederations were originally affiliated with the Italian Communist Party, the Socialists, and the Christian Democrats, respectively, since these parties' demise and restructuring, the unions have ended their official connections to political parties. Instead, they work together as a block and as such have a significant influence not just on labor contracts but on broader social and economic issues.

Union-negotiated contracts set wages and benefits for different categories of work. These pay scales and benefit packages apply to virtually every sector of the formal economy (excluding very small firms). Employers must generally hire from government-sponsored and union-supervised "hiring lists," from which workers are employed on a first-come/first-served basis depending on their length of time unemployed. In addition, a 1970 workers' rights law – passed at the height of labor agitation and union strength – limits the conditions under which workers can be laid off. The Berlusconi government has moved to revoke this protection, setting off a fierce labor union and public reaction, including widespread demonstrations and a national strike that involved close to 13 million workers.[46]

This union strength – despite threats from Berlusconi's center-right government – together with a tradition of active state regulation, renders the formal economy relatively inflexible from the employer's point of view, and costly – with payroll taxes adding as much as 50–60 percent to wage costs.[47] An OECD study reveals gross labor costs (in the formal economy, of course) to be higher in Italy than in any other EU country besides the Netherlands, and more than 20 percent higher than in the United States.[48] Citing an "inflexible labor market," high business taxes, and organized crime, a report by the World Economic Forum in 2002 rated Italy only the thirty-ninth most competitive economy in the world in which to invest, down from twenty-sixth place in 2001, and below that of most other European nations.[49] A Banca d'Italia study concluded in 2001, in a transparently self-interested prognosis: "The Italian economy has put on the brakes but it can take off again with fewer taxes and more flexible salaries."[50]

One response to this perceived inflexibility – in addition to hiring workers off-the-books – is to employ more temporary and part-time workers. According to one report, 23 percent of all new contracts in 2000 were for part-time employment. Between 1994 and 1998, part-time and temporary work contracts increased by more than 26 percent, and today account for over 12 percent of all work contracts.[51] Suggesting that such contingent work and underground employment are alternative employer strategies designed to deal with the constraints of the formal economy, part-time and temporary contracts proliferate in the north but are rare in the south, where underground employment (which is often part-time and temporary, but without the formality of a contract) is more common.[52]

This trend toward contingent work (Italians call it "atypical" work) is of course not unique to Italy, but is integral to post-Fordist, post-industrial economies everywhere, with their emphasis on the "flexibility of the employment relationship and the deregulation of contracts."[53] It is interesting to note the tensions associated with this post-Fordist model of precarious work in Italy, tensions that reflect an underlying contradiction within the economy itself. The model fits well with the patchwork quilt of independently owned and operated small shops that increasingly dominate the economy,[54] but the demand for flexible production processes collides head-on with the tradition of state regulation and union-negotiated contracts that until recently have so defined the primary sector. Perhaps nowhere else does the Fordist model of giant factories, state regulations, and union rules on the one hand, and post-Fordist, precarious, small-scale production processes on the other, co-exist in such dramatic fashion as in Italy.

Unemployment in Italy over the last several decades has been high and remains high for much of the country, although it is declining.[55] The official unemployment rate in 2001 was 9.1 percent, but there are regional variations here as well. In the north, unemployment is at an historic low of 3.9 percent (falling to 3 percent in some areas of the northeast), while in the south it reaches close to 20 percent, affecting well over half of the region's youth.[56] An EU study reveals that in the southern regions of Calabria and Campania, unemployment is 25 percent and 22 percent respectively, putting these Italian regions in a league with some of the most impoverished areas of Eastern Europe.[57] (Of course, given the extensive underground economy in Italy, and the south in particular, it is not clear to what extent this official unemployment rate reflects the true level of joblessness.)

While the Italian standard of living, per capita income, and welfare protections all increased in the last several decades, poverty has by no means been eliminated. According to the latest national survey, about 12 percent of Italian households live beneath the official poverty level (calculated as the income it takes to secure minimally adequate housing, food, and clothing), which for a family of two is equivalent to a little more than a thousand dollars a month. Almost 5 percent of the population lives in "extreme poverty," defined as four-fifths of the poverty level. Two-thirds of all poor families live in the south (home to just 33 percent of the population), where the poverty rate climbs to 24 percent and extreme poverty reaches 11 percent.[58]

Policymakers periodically try to induce unemployed southern Italians to take jobs in northern Italy as they did in the immediate post-war period as a way to address regional imbalances, but to no avail. Despite high levels of poverty and unemployment in the Mezzogiorno, most southern Italians are no longer willing to migrate north to find employment. One factor discouraging such migration is the high cost of housing in northern industrial centers relative to the meager wages of industrial employment – at approximately $850 a month, a skilled auto worker earns little more than a supermarket clerk. With many southern Italians owning their own homes – sometimes together with extended family members – and able to count on at least one pension or disability income per household, moving north for such jobs holds little appeal.

If the economic miracle of the post-war period was performed on the backs of the southern Italians who supplied the cheap labor, that function has now migrated further south to Africa – and east to Eastern Europe and Asia, and west to Latin America. As the observers quoted above put it, "Italian industry in the 60s had much in common with that of the third world" because it benefitted from what was for all intents and purposes third-world labor.[59] Today, it imports the genuine article.

IMMIGRANTS IN THE ITALIAN ECONOMY

One out of every four new hires in Italy is an "extracomunitario," or non-EU immigrant.[60] They are street vendors, domestic workers, nurses, factory workers, gas station attendants, farmworkers, construction workers, dishwashers, foundry workers, metalworkers, sex workers, and office "errand-boys." But, they are clustered in several sectors, the primary ones being manufacturing, construction, agriculture, domestic service, and other services. Their distribution across these sectors varies considerably by region (see Table 3.3), and as we will see, by gender and nationality.

More immigrants work in manufacturing in Italy than anywhere else in the rest of Europe, where they tend to be more highly concentrated in services. Many are in metalworking, particularly in the Piedmont,

Table 3.3. *Non-EU legal foreign workers in Italy, by economic sector and geographic area, (1999) (percentages)*

	Agriculture	Manufacturing	Construction	Domestic	Services
Northwest	9.2	26.3	11.7	30.7	22.2
Northeast	22.0	39.7	7.9	8.5	21.8
Center	15.4	33.0	9.0	22.2	20.5
South	38.3	7.6	2.8	39.7	11.6
Lombardy*	5.7	31.8	5.9	31.0	25.6
Lazio*	7.3	3.1	3.0	71.6	15.0

* Lombardy and Lazio are the regions where Milan and Rome, respectively, are located.

Source: Zincone, *Secondo Rapporto:* 354.

Emilia-Romagna, and Veneto regions, but they also work in chemical-related industries, foodstuffs, textiles, foundries, tanneries, and slaughterhouses, mostly in the small and medium-sized shops so typical of northern and central Italy. A study sponsored by the CGIL union confederation found that 60 percent of the immigrants hired in 2001 and 2002 were employed in shops with fewer than fifty workers.[61] Of course there are exceptions. Several hundred immigrants are employed by the giant Electrolux factory, with its 15,000-worker payroll. In 1999, Fiat hired immigrants in large numbers for the first time, when it faced a shortage of Italian workers willing to work on short-term contracts.[62] And, the small shops in which immigrants tend to be concentrated are often subcontracted by very large firms, such as Fiat and Olivetti, that contract out their most hazardous and arduous work.

So vital is this workforce that employers in Italy's industrial northern and central regions have begun to actively lobby government for higher levels of immigration. One CEO of an auto parts company outside Milan pleaded with government officials for more immigrants. Unless he could recruit 1,500 workers over the next few months, he said, his new machinery would remain in its packing boxes, and "the train won't leave the station."[63] One solution in the Friuli-Venezia Giulia region that borders Slovenia is to hire daily border commuters – mostly Slovenes, Croats, and Serbs – an estimated 7,000–10,000 of whom cross the border daily to work in Italian factories, but also to care for the elderly, harvest crops, and do construction clean-up. Sometimes they sell their day-labor in the main piazza or in front of the Trieste train station, and sometimes they have fixed employment. Whatever the ient, the illegal hiring of these border commuters is generally od to be a "keystone" of employment practices in the region.[64]

s and working conditions for immigrants in manufacturing and industrial services, as with all sectors, vary between the north and the south, even within the same categories of work.[65] What remains constant is that they are generally worse than for local workers. Wages for immigrants in metalworking range from roughly $600 a month in the northern regions of Piedmont and Veneto, to close to $1,000 in north/central Emilia-Romagna. They make slightly more in chemical-related industries, foodstuffs, and slaughterhouses, where they perform the most grueling and precarious jobs.[66] Some low-end industrial jobs are paid by the hour or piece rate, and the proportion of illegal workers is generally higher. For example, Romanians, most of whom are without residence permits, work in the underground economy in Piedmont painting car parts for body-shops at approximately $30–35 a day. Garment workers in the south (who are predominantly Chinese and Bangladeshi) are also paid piece rate. Whole Chinese families working in the garment industry in southern Italy often earn the equivalent of $250 a month for 8–10-hour days.[67] Nor are such wages confined to the south. In Veneto, Chinese immigrants work in garment sweatshops scattered throughout the small town of Altivole, where the average wage for 18-hour days at piece rate comes to about $350 a month. An investigative reporter writes that if you work at a "phenomenal" pace in these sweatshops, you might make $500 in a month.[68]

Unlike in the manufacturing sector, the immigrant presence in construction covers the whole national territory, and is probably far more extensive than what official statistics indicate, given the predominance of the shadow economy in this sector. The construction industry overall contains the highest proportion of illegal immigrants working in the underground economy, in part because this sector is comprised of so many small firms that are relatively easy to conceal from state oversight.[69] Immigrants in construction are usually paid by the day, with overtime rarely compensated. In some northern areas, they can earn as much as $50 a day, and in parts of central Italy, where government regulations subsequent to the 1996 earthquake improved wages and working conditions, they earn up to $800 a month. But, in the south they make only $15–30 a day for 12 hours of work, making them among the most poorly paid of all immigrant workers, on a par with the undocumented farmworkers of the region.[70]

Italy (and, as we will see in a moment, Spain) differs from most of the rest of Europe in the high proportion of immigrants who are engaged in agricultural work, where they comprise 10 percent of the workforce.[71] The vast majority work on a seasonal basis, with the peak season lasting from June to September. The heaviest concentration of immigrant farmworkers is in the south, where much of Italy's richest farmland is located. It is estimated that more than 73 percent of Italian agriculture is "irregular," with the figure for the south reaching 85 percent, and immigrants play a vital role in this eminently flexible sector.[72]

Many come from Eastern Europe, particularly Poland, the Czech Republic, Slovakia, Albania, and Romania, although this varies by Italian region, as do the types of farmwork and the wages.[73] In Lombardy, Indian immigrants do most of the cattle-raising and work as stable-hands; in the southern regions of Sicily, Apulia, Calabria, and Campania, Moroccans and other North Africans work in hothouses and fish farms, harvest watermelons and tomatoes, and pick olives; in central Umbria, Moroccans work the tobacco crops; and, in the northern region of Trentino, Eastern Europeans tend honey production.[74]

As in construction, wages are usually paid by the day. In Campania, one of the poorest regions of Italy, immigrant farmworkers work 8–10-hour days for $10–15, a wage that has lost ground over the last few years. In Apulia, where labor contractors get a 5–10 percent cut of farmworkers' pay, they make piece rate, with a fast worker taking home about $500 a month. In the center and north, where agricultural work is not so often "irregular," and workers are more likely to be paid according to union contracts, they can earn up to $900 a month.[75]

While immigrant men in Italy are found in manufacturing, construction, and farm labor, women are heavily concentrated in domestic service, including cleaning services, elderly care and child care. The Italian Minister of the Interior warned not long ago that immigrants are especially critical in this area: "[T]oday we can all see that the only ones taking care of our loved ones – whether they be our elderly or our children – are immigrants."[76] The need for immigrant caregivers is particularly acute in southern Europe where the welfare state is less developed than in some areas of northern Europe where state-sponsored child care and provisions for the elderly are the norm, and the demand is further accentuated by the rapidly aging population.[77]

In 1996, almost half of the 209,726 domestic helpers registered with the Italian social security system were non-EU immigrants, of whom

71 percent were women.[78] They come primarily from the Philippines, Cape Verde and South America (particularly Peru), and in recent years more Eastern European women have entered domestic employment.[79] Filipinas so dominate this sector that "Filipina" and "domestic helper" have become synonymous in some circles.[80] As Rhacel Salazar Parreñas recounts in *Servants of Globalization*, so entrenched is this stereotype that one Filipina domestic helper in Rome has a side-job in Italian movies where she plays only domestics; in a "surreal" mimicry of life and art, Salazar Parreñas says that off-screen the actress continues to be confined to domestic work.[81] Underscoring the discrimination implicit in such occupational restriction, the educational levels, skills, and social position of these women prior to immigration often far exceed the menial work they find in Italy. Some men also work in this rapidly expanding sector, although their participation is even more patterned by nationality than it is for women. Almost entirely confined to Somalians and Filipinos, their employment in the sector is often contingent on following a wife or girlfriend into joint employment with an Italian family.[82]

Because of the in-house nature of this work, one might expect it to be disproportionately off-the-books. Many immigrants in domestic service do work outside the reach of government regulations and social security rules, and some work under conditions that constitute a flagrant violation of established labor rights.[83] An EU study concluded that there are approximately one million underground domestic workers in Italy, with half of them non-EU immigrants.[84] Interestingly, however, many immigrants in domestic service are legal, with this sector being second only to manufacturing in the numbers of immigrant workers registered with the social security system (probably because of the relatively generous quotas for domestic service in Italian immigration policy).

The large metropolitan areas of Rome and Milan account for roughly half of all immigrant domestics (three out of four domestic workers in these two cities are immigrants), with the rest dispersed throughout the northwest and south.[85] As in construction work, remuneration depends less on legal status and more on the immigrant's nationality and, especially, where they work: Live-in helpers in the north and center earn about $800 a month, while in the south they are paid no more than $500 a month. For hourly work, wages range from $3.50 an hour in the south (sometimes even for a married couple working together) to $8 an hour in the north. Wages also differ depending on the worker's nationality, with Filipinas at the top of the pay scale and Sri Lankans near the bottom.[86] Recently arrived Eastern European women in th area in the mid-1990s were said to receive less than half the sal manded by Somalian women who were more established in th An ethnographer found that this salary differential triggered a competitive race to the bottom, as the Somalians struggled to retain their jobs.[87] The most extreme version of this differential is found between immigrant domestic workers and the relatively few Italian women still found in the sector. Indeed, the sector has apparently fragmented in some areas, with hourly work done by Italian women represented by a national domestic workers' union (ACLI-COLF), and under-paid, live-in work the province of immigrants (who are largely excluded from the union).[88]

Besides working in manufacturing, construction, agriculture, and domestic service, immigrants are found in a wide range of other sectors and niches. For example, they are an important component of the tourism industry, particularly the hotels and restaurants dotting the Adriatic coast that boom during the summer season but are virtually deserted by late August.[89] In some areas, they are primarily street vendors, like the Senegalese who can be seen on the streets of large cities, selling cigarette lighters (Milan) and faux designer purses (Florence) and who ply the beaches of Tuscany and Sardinia in the summer.[90] An ethnography of Senegalese and Moroccan immigrant communities reported that the Senegalese worked as street vendors when they first arrived, moving on to factory jobs once they settled in. Recently arrived Moroccans reportedly found the market saturated by the Senegalese (who often have pre-immigration experience in commerce and networks in Italy that facilitate their entry into this niche), and so were less likely to work as street vendors.[91]

One of Italy's most respected immigration experts argues: "The process of stabilization is perhaps the most significant aspect of immigration in Italy in the 1990s."[92] By this he means that immigrants are an increasingly important part of the economy and are more and more likely to be legal residents and have "regular" jobs. Indeed, they are joining unions in record numbers. According to CGIL records, immigrant membership increased by 22 percent between 1998 and 2000.[93] Interestingly, immigrants working in factories in Italy's southern regions are more likely to be unionized (45 percent) than those working in the post-Fordist, small enterprises of the north (30 percent). In some southern areas, union membership among factory workers is higher for immigrants than for local workers.[94]

But, immigrant stabilization should not be exaggerated. For one thing, they continue to play a pivotal role in Italy's vast underground economy. While just 15 percent of Italian workers labor in the submerged economy, 30 percent of non-EU immigrants work there, and 62 percent find their first job there.[95] And, not all of them are undocumented; according to one study, the majority of immigrants working in the underground economy have residence permits.[96] Underscoring the importance of this off-the-books workforce, Italian employers save at least $13 billion annually on taxes and social security payments by using immigrant workers in irregular employment.[97]

Immigrants are often hired on a temporary or part-time basis. About 13 percent work in day labor, 15 percent are part-time, and another 10 percent are seasonal.[98] In some regions and sectors – agriculture in the south is a conspicuous example – virtually all immigrant workers are seasonal day laborers. Even in the industrial heartland of the northeast, they are more likely than locals to be employed on a contingent basis.[99] One reporter summed it up, after interviewing union officials about immigrant labor and the Bossi-Fini law: immigrants, he said, are like " 'Kleenex,' picked up by the employer as necessary, and thrown away after use."[100]

With immigrant unemployment in Italy among the lowest of any Western capitalist country (second lowest, after Spain),[101] and with the country's low birthrates and declining populations, immigrants fill critical labor gaps. Labor economists conclude that they do not usually take jobs away from Italians; rather, their employment tends to have either no effect or a complementary, positive effect on employment opportunities for locals.[102] Others note, however, that the availability of immigrant workers may allow employers to eschew strategies that would bring broad benefits to local workers. For example, the presence of immigrants in the industrial north means that firms do not have to move jobs to southern Italy where local workers might be more readily available, nor do they have to raise wages or improve working conditions to attract unemployed Italians to areas of high employment.[103]

This brings me to a critical point. Immigrants are useful to Italian employers precisely because they are *different* from locals. By this, of course I do not mean that there is some *a priori* racial or ethnic difference that constructs them as a good supply of cheap and flexible labor (although as we will see in Chapter 6, this construction is not unrelated to racial formation). Rather, their lack of integration into Italian society and culture is a critical ingredient of their flexibility. While in some regions (like the northeast) immigrants fill absolute shortages, mostly their value is that they work for wages and under conditions that locals increasingly shun, and that unemployed southern Italians will no longer move for. The foreign worker program that is now the only way to enter Italy legally to work, mandates that immigrants can be imported only after it is determined that there is a shortage of Italians who are available and willing to do certain jobs at the going rate (e.g. farmwork, domestic help and elder and child care, and unskilled construction work). Implicit in this policy is the tacit understanding that immigrants are welcome precisely because they are *not* like Italians. It is by definition their *Otherness* that is useful.

Ambrosini points out: "From a strictly economic point of view, the best immigrant is one who has just arrived, is . . . willing to work hard, [and is] undemanding in terms of health and other social services: in other words, the immigrant who is not integrated, who in other respects raises apprehensions and social tensions."[104] We will discuss the implications of this more fully later, but first let us look briefly at Spain's "useful invaders."[105]

THE SPANISH "MIRACLE," POST-FORDISM, AND IMMIGRANT WORKERS

The industrialization of modern Spain began in the 1950s and escalated in the 1960s, but it took place within the confines of a dictatorial regime and relatively scant investment in the public infrastructure.[106] After Franco's death in 1975, the Spanish economy began to catch up with the rest of Western Europe, almost paralleling the Italian miracle of a decade earlier. Its phenomenal growth is reflected in the GDP, which in 1960 stood at 56 percent of the European average and had increased to 76 percent by 1996.[107] Average wages more than doubled in real terms between 1960 and 1985, and the official minimum wage increased by a factor of 25.[108] By 2002, Spanish per capita income was about 83 percent of the EU average.[109] The structure of employment changed too, even more than in Italy, as Spain went from being a largely agricultural nation to a modern, industrial one. Between 1960 and 1985, the percentage of the Spanish population employed in agriculture fell more than twenty points, from over 38 percent to just 18 percent.[110]

Massive internal migrations helped fuel these developments – just as they did in Italy – with poorer, more rural populations from the southern regions of Andalusia and Extremadura, and Galicia in the west, pouring into Madrid and Barcelona and other prosperous industrial areas during the 1950s and 1960s. By 1970, 38 percent of the population of the Catalonia region was born elsewhere – with 16 percent coming from Andalusia – and in the regional capital of Barcelona the figure was 47 percent.[111] Much as south–north migration was central to Italy's industrialization, the massive influx of cheap labor from other regions of Spain into its industrial centers was pivotal to its economic development.[112]

Again like its Italian counterpart, large regional differences continue to characterize the Spanish economy. Its seventeen political regions, each with its own president, local parliament and courts, and a high degree of autonomy, are also divided culturally and economically, sometimes rather dramatically. The agricultural regions of Andalusia and Extremadura have per capita incomes that are less than 80 percent of the national average, while the industrial areas of Navarre, the Balearic Islands, Madrid, and Catalonia boast per capita incomes that are 20–40 percent above the average, with the GDP showing comparable gaps.[113]

The economy is cross-cut by sharp structural divisions as well. Like its Italian neighbor, it is bifurcated into a technologically advanced primary sector that is unionized and state-regulated, and an extensive underground. This underground – traditionally made up of domestic work, agriculture, and various kinds of self-employment – expanded dramatically in the economic restructuring of the 1970s and 1980s, and now includes sectors that are integral parts of Spain's increasingly post-Fordist economy. One author notes of this expansion: "The news...is that 'irregular' work has become 'organized,'" that is, it has moved beyond the confines of a relatively chaotic and small-scale, secondary economy to become a central component of Spain's industrial strategy.[114] Today, about 23 percent of Spain's GDP is provided by the underground economy, making it second only to Italy in terms of the share of GDP derived from undergound work.[115]

Long-term contracts are regulated in Spain both by the federal government and by unions, but contracts for less than three months are subject to far fewer restrictions. Not surprisingly, these short-term contracts comprise an ever greater share of the job market.[116] More than 80 percent of the young adults who work have such temporary contracts, far exceeding the EU average.[117] As a result, the labor force is increasingly split between older, long-term workers whose job security is ensured by government regulations and union contracts, working side-by-side with contingent employees on fixed-term contracts living out the precarious reality of post-Fordism.[118]

Official unemployment in Spain is the highest in Western Europe, hitting a peak of over 20 percent in 1994 before settling at about 13 percent in 2001.[119] The figures are worse for certain regions and segments of the population, with unemployment in Extremadura and Andalusia as high as 22 percent.[120] It has become popular among economists and policymakers to attribute the high unemployment rate to the rigidities of the Spanish labor market.[121] For example, some bemoan the fact that unemployed Spaniards are no longer willing to move for work, as they did in the 1950s and 1960s.[122] Indeed, internal migrations away from the poorer regions of Spain have come to an abrupt halt; in recent years, Andalusia, Extremadura, and Galicia have even registered net increases in migration into their regions, as former emigrants return home for retirement.[123]

Others blame Spain's stubborn unemployment rate on the inflexibility of government regulations and collective bargaining – which now covers 75 percent of the country's private workforce – overseen by the two major union confederations (the socialist UGT and the (nominally) communist CC.OO).[124] Counter-intuitive as it may seem, these pundits argue that the high unemployment rate is due to the laws and union contracts that make it expensive and legally complex to lay off workers (and hence, the argument goes, discourage hiring).[125] So widespread is the notion that the rigidity of the labor market is to blame for high unemployment that one public intellectual refers to it derisively as the "new dogma in Spain."[126] Whatever the reasons, high unemployment in Spain seems now to be endemic, and – unlike Italy where there are regions with virtually no unemployment – no region is immune.

State subsidies cushion the worst impacts of joblessness. Between 1980 and 1993, Spain registered one of the highest rates of growth on social spending in the EC, together with Italy and Greece.[127] While the bulk of this goes to old-age pensions and the national health care system, Spain now ranks first in the European Union in the proportion of social spending on unemployment compensation (perhaps not surprisingly, given its high unemployment rate). Benefits, which apply only to those who have been previously employed and last a maximum of two years, are less generous than those of some of its European neighbors, but are indicative of Spain's commitment to at least minimum income-maintenance policies. In part as a result of the country's economic growth and in part because of these social welfare policies, the poverty rate in Spain has fallen substantially since 1980. Still, poverty persists, with an estimated 10–17 percent of the population living beneath the poverty line – somewhat higher than in Italy, but lower than in Portugal, Greece, and the UK.[128] And, as in Italy, the center-right government in Spain has recently embarked on policies of social welfare reforms and labor rights retrenchments, the consequences of which are likely to be manifest in increasing poverty rates and rising numbers of the working poor.

The proportion of immigrants in the workforce has increased every year for the last two decades. The number registered with the social security administration doubled in just two years between 2000 and 2002, with non-EU immigrants comprising four out of every ten new workers in the social security system. And, they are even more heavily represented in the underground economy, where non-EU immigrants account for at least 15 percent of the workforce.[129]

More important than their mere numbers, they fill critical niches in the economy – usually those that have been vacated by Spanish workers. Based on Interior Ministry data from the last legalization program, immigrants are concentrated in agriculture (33 percent), construction (15 percent), domestic service (15 percent), and the tourism industry (11 percent), with a far smaller fraction in manufacturing than in Italy.[130] Mirroring this concentration and at the same time helping comprise it, of the 32,000 quota workers admitted in 2002, 53 percent went to agriculture, 20 percent to construction, and 11 percent to services of various kinds.[131] As in Italy, immigrants in Spain provide not just a supplemental workforce, but a particular *kind* of workforce, i.e. one that will do the jobs, and under conditions, that local workers no longer accept despite double-digit unemployment.

And, as in Italy, the location of immigrants in different sectors varies across regions and localities. In Almería (the rural province in Andalusia where El Ejido is located), more than 90 percent of immigrants – mostly from the Mahgreb countries – work in labor-intensive, hothouse agriculture, while in Barcelona they are distributed across construction, tourism, and a range of services, and in Madrid they are more likely to be found in domestic service.[132] Wages and (rarely) benefits vary as well. What remains constant is that immigrants are found in the most precarious sectors and are usually compensated at lower rates than comparable local workers. Perhaps most precarious of all is the sex industry, where it is estimated that up to 70 percent of the mostly female workforce are immigrants.[133]

According to data from the Spanish immigration agency (IMSERSO), 32 percent of immigrants work without a contract, with almost 50 percent of sub-Saharan Africans, 40 percent of North Africans, and 25 percent of Latin Americans falling into this category.[134] An extensive study of immigrants in Madrid found that 70 percent of them were working either without contracts or with contracts that provided little labor protection or job security. Even workers with residence and work permits often work without contracts, although wages sometimes vary considerably according to legal status. In one well-publicized case, hundreds of undocumented farmworkers hired to pick oranges in Valencia were found sleeping in caves, and receiving wages that amounted to one-fifth of what legal workers with contracts made.[135]

Immigrants in Spain's enormous hospitality and tourism industry – said to be the largest in the world – also often work without contracts. Chinese immigrants comprise one-third of the foreign workers in this sprawling sector that includes hotels, restaurants, bars and cafés, camp-grounds, and resorts. Many have no contract, and they are the lowest paid of any nationality in the sector. Despite education levels that far exceed that of Spanish workers in the tourism industry, immigrants of all nationalities often receive wages that are well below that of their local counterparts.[136]

In study after study, sector after sector, immigrants speak for them-selves: Gambian gardeners paid 20,000 pesetas (roughly $150) for a six-day workweek; Senegalese garment shop workers paid 28,000 pesetas a week working from eight at night to ten in the morning; a waiter who works for three weeks, is terminated, and not paid.[137] Sometimes they have seven or eight different jobs in a year, often overlapping, like the "doppio lavoro" so common in Italy.[138] Jamal, a Moroccan immigrant, describes one of his several jobs: "It is marginalized work...cleaning who knows what...I go in a factory and, well, I do the worst jobs: clean, gather, load, unload, do this, do that, whatever no one else can [sic] do."[139]

Turnover is high, both because people cannot survive long under these conditions, and because employment is unsteady and haphaz-ard. As the Gambian gardener cited above said: "The problem is, one week they give you work and the next week they don't. You can't live like this."[140] The razor-thin subsistence of immigrant workers and the degree to which their livelihoods are dependent on not just employer goodwill but a whole mix of factors beyond their control, is periodically underscored by highly visible, dramatic events. For example, when unseasonal hailstorms devastated fruit harvests near Lleida in northeastern Spain in the summer of 2002, over 3,000 African immigrants were left destitute and wandering the streets, sleeping in cardboard boxes, and unable to eat even the now-ruined fruit that normally makes up their meager diet while employed in the harvest.[141] The events were considered newsworthy in their drama, but they reveal an all too mundane truth about immigrants' lives and the fragility of their livelihoods.

To fully appreciate that fragility, it might help to look in more detail at the wages and working conditions of immigrants in Spanish agriculture, the sector in which immigrants are most highly concentrated. Because immigrant farmworkers are disproportionately found in the Almería province of Andalusia, and because vast amounts of data are available about that area where the most violent anti-immigrant riots in Spain took place, our discussion begins there.[142]

The arid and sparsely populated province of Almería first began developing its signature hothouse agriculture ("bajo plástico," or "under plastic") in the late 1960s. Four decades later, Almería, with a population of just 0.5 million, generated $1.5 billion from this labor-intensive industry. Much of this growth took place beginning in the early 1990s when a massive increase in the intensification of cultivation occurred, and Moroccan workers began to arrive in large numbers to work "bajo plástico." Almería now has one of the largest proportions of foreigners to local residents in Spain, with the size of the legal immigrant population more than doubling in five years, growing from 11,255 in 1995 to over 25,000 in 1999. Most of the increase in legal immigration came through the quota worker program (the Spanish government favors this region in its annual allotments of quota workers, and the small province of Almería receives 9 percent of the total). With an estimated 70 percent of immigrant workers in Almería undocumented, the size of the immigrant population approaches 100,000.

The town of El Ejido emerged only recently – a creature of the new hothouse industry – and was officially incorporated in 1987. Boasting among the highest productivity levels in hothouse agriculture anywhere, the El Ejido area contains over 6,500 "farms" – one for every six inhabitants. The vast immigrant workforce is almost entirely

Moroccan, most of whom are undocumented. According to the report released by SOS Racismo following the El Ejido riots, immigrant workers "are one of the prerequisites of the hothouse production system that requires the ability to enhance substantially the size of the available workforce at a moment's notice during periods of intense activity." Contrary to what might be assumed about agricultural production in southern Spain, their hothouse agriculture is not based on age-old techniques, but "is a paradigmatic example of the workings of late capitalism."[143]

It may not be too far-fetched to call this the agricultural equivalent of post-Fordist manufacturing in northeastern Italy. These are small-scale production units with intense levels of productivity and heavy investments in technology and equipment. And, as SOS Racismo describes it, this sector:

> is inserted in a global economy. Product prices are fixed in Perpignan, France. The speed at which crops mature can be artificially increased by modifying temperatures and ventilation in the hothouses and this requires that a supplemental labor force be permanently available – that of illegal immigrant workers. Intense [global and local] competition requires a reduction in labor costs, especially wages, with a cheap and docile workforce, and increases in the pace of production.[144]

Three harvests a year are forced from the over-worked soil, each requiring 40,000 workers for one to three weeks at a time. With only 12,000 jobs officially registered, the rest work off-the-books. Seemingly immune to labor inspections from the federal government, these hothouses depend on itinerant undocumented workers to provide the supplemental workforce, the temporariness of which is a fixture of this system of production.

The typical workday lasts ten hours, with temperatures reaching 113 degrees Fahrenheit and humidity at 90 per cent inside the hothouses. In some cases, workers sleep under the plastic structures or in nearby shacks and are expected to provide around-the-clock security, a role that effectively extends their workday to twenty-four hours. Hot, humid, and the air heavy with toxic pesticides, owners often deduct money from workers' wages for these accommodations. A 45-year-old Moroccan farmworker in El Ejido described living conditions this way: "We live eight in one room without running water or electricity. We live together, eat together, cook together. But, at the moment only two of us are working, the others either aren't working or work only one or a week."[145] What contracts exist are oral. Wages even for legal ts, at about $18–24 a day, are lower than those established for al work in this region (which already has the lowest wage-rate in Spain). Undocumented immigrants, hired for short periods of time and chasing the harvest from town to town, earn even less. In this context, "lack of protection against exploitation is absolute."[146]

These conditions are by no means unique to Almería, Andalusia, or southern Spain. A labor union recently denounced agricultural employers in affluent Catalonia for illegally employing hundreds of immigrant workers for the harvest without contracts.[147] An anthropologist studying the role of African immigrants in Catalan agriculture describes their economic contribution thus: "It is not a coincidence that the development of this intensive agriculture is linked to the phenomenon of illegal immigration." She continues: "It is precisely their urgency and dependence that make the immigrant workers more economical for employers, even more than Andalusian day laborers."[148]

ECONOMICS AND THE CONSTRUCTION OF OTHERNESS

There are a few differences in the economic location of immigrants in Spain and Italy, just as there are some differences in their respective economies. Immigrants are more likely to be found in manufacturing in Italy – particularly in the northeast and center where there are absolute labor shortages – than in Spain where they are more highly concentrated in agriculture. More substantial than these cross-national differences, however, is the variation across regions within each country. Indeed, some regions in Italy – like the south where immigrants are almost exclusively found in agriculture and construction – are more similar to regions in Spain than to other parts of Italy. Further, these new countries of immigration are more like each other with respect to their policies and the economic location of immigrants, than they are to the rest of Europe, where immigrants are only rarely found in the fields.

 More importantly here, regardless of the sector of employment or geographic region, immigrants are Others, the "new untouchables"[149] who do the work that locals largely shun. In the previous chapter, we saw the legal construction of immigrant Otherness through the reproduction of illegality and the contingent nature of legality. What we see here is that legally constructed Otherness is both compounded by and partially produced through immigrants' economic location. With their legal status dependent on legitimate work contracts, (temporarily) legal immigrants are almost as vulnerable as their illegal counterparts working in the underground economy. Furthermore, legal and economic marginality are mutually constituted – with the fragility of legal status contributing to immigrants' disempowerment *vis-à-vis* employers, and their concentration in the underground economy jeopardizing their ability to legalize. And, they both derive from the same source: the contingency of immigrants' welcome as marginalized Others. The foreign worker programs in Italy and Spain codify both the contingency and the marginality by allocating slots only to those industries and jobs that do not attract local workers, ensuring that, *by definition*, immigrant workers are distinct from the local working class. This is the basis of Ambrosini's remark that, "the best immigrant is...one who is *not* integrated."[150] Ambrosini points out that there is no real contradiction between high local unemployment rates and high rates of immigrant employment in these late capitalist economies. Indeed, they are part of the same phenomenon of a late capitalism that is made up of pre-Fordist and post-Fordist work, with little in between.[151] Remember that the three most significant areas of immigrant labor in Italy and Spain are small and medium-sized manufacturing shops (particularly in north and central Italy); domestic service (in every major metropolitan area); and agriculture (particularly in the southern regions). Despite the obvious variation in types of work, what these sectors have in common is their embeddedness in the global, post-Fordist economy, and their essentially pre-Fordist labor relations.

While domestic service and agriculture are traditional, pre-Fordist economic sectors, they have leapfrogged the period of collective bargaining rules and strict government regulations associated with industrial employment in the mid-twentieth century, and today constitute an amalgam of pre-Fordist employment relations and post-Fordist globalization. The contours of domestic service – in some areas employing almost exclusively an immigrant workforce, filling in for the now-employed wives and mothers that in earlier times provided the household labor, and picking up the slack for an inadequate and now shrinking welfare state – have changed dramatically, but quasi-feudal employment relations remain the norm. Agricultural employment too – as exemplified by the El Ejido hothouses – with its intense but temporary periods of productivity, and its global markets, price structure, and labor

73

hybrid of pre- and post-Fordist labor relations and employ-
tures, just as are the small manufacturing shops of northern
_..e effect of this accelerating combination of pre-Fordist and
post-Fordist work in late capitalism helps explain the paradox of high
local unemployment and high immigrant employment: too few good
jobs and too many bad ones.

It has long been recognized that employers welcome the vulnerability of immigrants who "work scared and hard,"[152] whose utility
is precisely their marginality, and whose exclusion is effectively their
passport. Ambrosini, Zolberg,[153] and others have already exposed the
contradictions, if not the hypocrisy, of policies that ostensibly embrace
integration for immigrants whose primary virtue is their Otherness.
What we have seen here, however, goes beyond that important insight.
Marginality is not just a characteristic that immigrants bring with them
like some third-world passport that gains them admission and ushers
them into the economy's worst jobs, nor is it solely constructed through
the legal system. Rather, their location in the economy *reproduces* that
Otherness from within, as immigrants' status as an underclass of workers with substandard wages and working conditions impedes their full
membership in the national community. So, it is not just that historical global inequalities have produced post-colonial subjects who today
provide cheap labor to first-world powers; those inequalities, and those
post-colonial subjects, are reproduced from within.

CHAPTER FOUR

INTEGRATING THE "OTHER"

David Engel, in his now classic article, "The Oven Bird's Song," recalls Yamaguchi's description of an old Japanese legend in which a "calamity that attacked the community had its origin in an alien factor inside the community . . . However . . . the alien element, which could turn into calamity at any time, was absolutely necessary for the growth of the crops. Thus the need for the alien factor had two facets which appear contradictory to each other."[1]

Just as the "alien factor" in this legend – and the outsiders in Engel's Sander County – contribute to economic development but are perceived as "calamitous" for the community, so contemporary immigrants in Italy and Spain are both wanted for their labor and suspect for their Otherness and the anticipated consequences of that Otherness for the community. The consequences are not just imagined, the paranoid fantasy of racist fearmongers. Rather, the immigrant marginality that is so beneficial to the economy creates a class of outcasts that is unacceptable to liberal democracies heralding inclusiveness, and is politically explosive as it invites nativist backlash against this element that is "absolutely necessary for the growth of the crops." As we have seen, immigration policies in Italy and Spain follow closely the contours of this contradiction.

In this chapter, I discuss the various meanings of immigrant integration, and trace the laws, policies, and programs designed to promote it. These efforts are extensive and cannot be dismissed as merely symbolic gestures or political performances. Nor are they patterned according to regional political ideology. Indeed, some of the most intense efforts at integration are being undertaken by the Italian region of Veneto, a politically conservative area led by right-wing politicians, some of whom now find themselves in the unlikely role of immigrant advocates.

ELUSIVE INTEGRATION: WHAT IS IT?

In the early twentieth century, immigrants to the United States were thought to be incorporated through "assimilation," a process by which they presumably took on the cultural values, attitudes, and behaviors of the host society, as exemplified in Thomas and Znaniecki's *The Polish Peasant in Europe and America*. While lip-service was sometimes paid to the cultural interaction of the immigrant and the host society, the main assumption in the academic literature and in policy circles was that the immigrant would, and should, be the one to adapt in an essentially one-sided process. At the level of policy, assimilation was embodied in Americanization programs designed to acculturate immigrants and cure the social problems allegedly associated with them.[2]

By the 1970s, the concept of assimilation had come under attack for its intellectual limitations and self-contradictions (Was the host society truly homogeneous? Did the melting-pot produce a stew of diverse parts or a monocultural purée? Was assimilation a process or a product?), as well as for the ethnocentricity of its assumptions.[3] In his book, *We Are All Multiculturalists Now*, Nathan Glazer summed up the multiple sources of disenchantment with the concept, and concluded somewhat ruefully: "Assimilation is not today a popular term . . . The idea that it would happen, that it should happen, has simply been discredited."[4] By the time Italy and Spain were attracting their own immigrants in the 1980s and 1990s, integration had replaced assimilation as the buzzword in academic treatises and policy circles, a substitution that may have responded rhetorically to the myriad "discontents"[5] associated with the former term, but not its inherent ambiguities.

Among those who attempt to define the concept of integration (most prefer to leave it vague), there is considerable disagreement, overlap, and inconsistency. In the Spanish and Italian immigration contexts, it has taken on many meanings, some implying that the onus is on the immigrant to fit in, others suggesting that it hinges on natives' open-mindedness and tolerance, and still others prioritizing the accessibility of social services and basic necessities. Sometimes, it is simply used as a synonym for settlement, or putting down physical and social roots.[6]

A Spanish social scientist and immigration expert defines it this way: "We can say that immigrants are integrated into a host society when they do not face additional obstacles due to their foreign origin in the main aspects of their social, economic, and family life, when compared to the native-born population." An Italian sociologist argues that integration is "a multidimensional and interactive process dedicated to the minimization of conflict and the maximization of well-being for all involved. Integration is above all a process . . . the result of a path of social insertion and cultural understanding." The Director of the Immigration Division of the Spanish Department of Labor suggests that immigrants are well integrated when, as individuals or groups, "[t]hey are able to manage the situations or issues most important in their daily lives." According to the Italian Commission on Immigrant Integration Policies, integration is comprised of two elements: "the integrity of the individual" (meaning access to work, housing, health care, etc.); and "positive interaction" (meaning, primarily, the absence of racism and xenophobia among the local population).[7] Despite the variation in such definitions, they generally include some reference to immigrants' cultural adaptation (such as language acquisition), their access to basic services, and the absence of racism and the tolerance for difference among the native population. These three components also surface in national integration policies and the local programs they support.

Before turning to official efforts at integration, I should point out that numerous non-governmental organizations (NGOs), unions, and charities are also active on this front. Labor unions in both countries have immigrant services in most major cities to help with securing documents, conducting job searches, and procuring social services. NGOs such as SOS Racismo, Medicos Sin Fronteras, and hundreds of immigrant associations, offer general and specialized services. Medicos Sin Fronteras in Spain and SOKOS in Italy provide health care. The Catholic service agency, Caritas, operates shelters and soup kitchens and offers language classes and a vast range of other services.[8] The Italian Conference of Bishops even produced a series of TV spots – one of which was filmed at their shelter in Lecce in southern Italy during the exodus from Kosovo – in their "educational campaign" to put a human face on the explosive issue.[9] These activities are considered a critical component of integration efforts, and are often the result of subcontracts and other forms of partnership with government agencies.

IMMIGRANT INTEGRATION IN ITALIAN LAW AND POLICY: BEYOND BENETTON?

Since passing its first immigration law in 1986, Italy has formally endorsed the notion of equal social rights for (at least legal) immigrants. Both the 1986 law and the Martelli Law in 1990 made reference to equal access to housing, public education, social assistance, and the national health care system. The Turco-Napolitano Law of 1998 is widely recognized as the most expansive in this series and remains the blueprint for immigrant integration in Italy today, despite the Bossi-Fini retrenchments in 2002. Article 42 of Turco-Napolitano outlined several activities directed toward immigrants' "social integration." Among them were courses in Italian language and culture; the dissemination of information regarding "opportunities for integration and personal growth"; enhancing Italians' "appreciation of the cultural, social, recreational, economic, and religious expressions" of immigrants and the prevention of racial discrimination and xenophobia; and the establishment of "intercultural mediators" to facilitate interaction in schools and other public institutions.[10]

Article 43 made it illegal to discriminate on the basis of race, religion, ethnicity, or nationality. Discrimination was defined as any activity or attitude that compromises a person's enjoyment of "full human rights and liberties in political, economic, social and cultural contexts."[11] Articles 34 and 35 guaranteed to legal immigrants and their families access to the full range of national health care services, and for undocumented immigrants, emergency care and certain preventive and prenatal services (undocumented immigrants carry a special health service membership card that has been described as a "light" version of the real thing ("una tessera leggera")).[12] Article 38 provided all immigrants the right to public education, and Articles 40 and 41 gave legal immigrants access to public housing and public assistance equal to that of Italian citizens.

Finally, a number of new federal agencies and government divisions were set up to oversee and coordinate integration efforts. Among them, the National Organism for the Coordination of Immigrant Integration Policies was established within the National Council for the Economy and Labor (CNEL) to oversee and promote local efforts to ensure immigrants' "full exercise of rights and duties." By 2001, their monthly meetings had produced a list of priorities, including: immigrant housing initiatives; access to health services; intercultural co-existence and exchange; the opening of information counters for immigrants; and the appointment of cultural mediators in institutions such as public schools and health clinics.[13]

National government decrees underscored the importance of integration, and reaffirmed the Turco-Napolitano trilateral focus on cultural adaptation, access to services, and freedom from discrimination. A 1999 decree mandated the establishment of Territorial Councils in every province[14] to bring together the disparate actors involved in various aspects of integration – employers' associations, government officials, union advocates, immigrant associations and NGOs – in order to deal with "the problems encountered by foreign immigrants and their families." Another decree announced that 68 billion liras (approximately $34 million) would be available in a general fund to be dispensed annually by the new Inter-Ministerial Commission on Immigration, to regions, provinces, and cities on a cost-share basis for the development of integration projects. Priority was given to projects that "privilege social service assistance to immigrants . . . facilitate the insertion of immigrants . . . emphasize the positive contribution immigrants make to the local economy . . . promote a positive image of immigration among the general population . . . and contribute to positive relationships between immigrants and Italians."[15]

Regional laws quickly followed, replicating the tone and sometimes the exact wording of Turco-Napolitano. The law had given Italy's twenty regions the task of developing broad integration policies, with provinces and towns responsible for working out the details and for their actual implementation; "Consulte Regionali" were to issue annual reports on their progress to the Minister for Social Solidarity. Lombardy, the region with the largest number of immigrants, with Milan as its capital city, passed Law No. 2526 on December 5, 2000, establishing the regional Observatory for Integration and Multi-Ethnicity.[16] Its stated purpose was to help monitor the integration problems of the immigrant population and evaluate the efficacy of integration policies.[17] At the other end of the Italian peninsula, and worlds away from the sophisticated bustle of the Milanese financial capital, a proposed law in rural Calabria was to "remove all obstacles" to immigrant incorporation with a "special focus on housing, language, and social integration." In addition to providing access to housing, health care, public education, and other services to immigrants, Calabria proposed "proactive" policies that would include offering Italian language courses; the prevention of discrimination and xenophobia; the hiring of cultural mediators; and "the dissemination of useful information for the positive insertion of immigrants, especially regarding . . . the various opportunities for integration and personal growth offered by the public sector and voluntary organizations." At the same time, it planned to launch courses for immigrants on the culture and language of their homelands, and to distribute information about "the possibility of immigrants' positive *reinsertion* into their country of origin."[18]

Several patterns characterize these and other regional laws in Italy. The first is that, like the Turco-Napolitano law and its successor Bossi-Fini, "integration" is an open-ended term used to refer simultaneously to cultural adaptation, access to services, and freedom from discrimination, with a heavy emphasis on culture – both the cultural *adaptation* of immigrants and, somewhat paradoxically, Italians' appreciation of immigrants' cultures.[19]

Secondly, these laws often pull in different directions at once, echoing the tension in national laws between the contingency and fragility of immigrants' legal status and the need to integrate these "cittadini stranieri" ("foreign 'citizens'"). The tension is nowhere more evident than in the proposed law for Calabria that called both for courses in Italian for immigrants and for classes in the culture and language of immigrants' homelands, that was to foster integration and at the same time disseminate information about repatriation. It might be argued that this binary approach merely recognizes the reality that many immigrants are in fact bi-national – global commuters between their workplace in Italy and their distant homes. But, this binary approach of integration policies that both exhorts immigrants to adapt and coaches them on how to repatriate, also reflects another reality – the reality of the deep ambivalence with which Italy receives them.

Thirdly, while many of the same themes are touched on in these laws, there are in fact vast differences among them. Some regions in the south only reluctantly reiterate the national policy, while others have long had proactive laws on the books.[20] Differences across regions – and even across provinces and towns within the same region – are particularly apparent when comparing their aggressiveness in seeking cost-share monies from the general fund established by Turco-Napolitano. Every region receives some monies from the fund to deal with problems related to immigration, with the amount determined by their susceptibility to immigration crises (such as in regions like Apulia and Sicily where there are frequent emergency sea-landings), the relative size of the immigrant population, and the nature of the relationship between immigrants and locals.[21] Additional funding is available for special projects that the regions and local governments propose, but only on a cost-share basis.

So dramatically do the regions and provinces vary in their pursuit of these funds that one team of researchers warns that it creates a "vicious circle," with resources directed "not necessarily where the need is most urgent, but where there already exists a greater sensitivity on the part of the powers that be and the local social fabric."[22] They explain too that because it is the provinces and towns that actually propose projects to the regions (who then request funding from the national purse), the number and scope of integration projects may vary substantially from town to town. In Venice, a radio call-in show ("Progetto Melting Pot Europa") broadcasts the latest integration policies and procedures, takes calls, and dispenses advice to its immigrant audience.[23] An experiment in Bologna had Italian filmmakers teaching their skills to a small cadre of North African students, at a cost of millions of liras (thousands of dollars) per student.[24] Rome set up a school in Tunisia that journalists dubbed "Immigration School," where prospective immigrants are taught Italian and introduced to Italian culture, so there will be "a constructive integration of young Tunisians into the Italian economic and social reality."[25] Many of the largest cities have websites for immigrants where they can download forms, retrieve documents, and get the latest information on available services.[26]

While these local governments launch creative experiments, others have not even set up the Territorial Councils mandated by law. The southern regions are generally less proactive than some areas in the north, but there are sharp differences even within the most aggressive northern regions. In one study of three different towns in Lombardy, researchers found that one had co-sponsored numerous projects with the general fund, another had funded only four, while in the third town not a single project had been proposed. In two of the three towns, the Territorial Councils that had been set up on paper were unknown even to the presumed participants. And, in one of the towns, despite a large immigrant presence, there was no provision at all for immigrant informational or social services.[27] One immigration expert explains the reluctance of some mayors to endorse such programs as politically driven: "Many mayors have avoided applying for integration funds and establishing programs for fear of the public backlash and loss of votes" if they appear to cater to immigrants.[28]

But, neither simple political calculations nor incumbents' own ideological preferences can predict the variety and scope of integration policies, as the following brief comparison of programs in Emilia-Romagna and Veneto makes clear. Emilia-Romagna and Veneto are two of the most proactive regions in Italy with regard to immigrant integration – the former a bastion of leftist politics and liberal social programs, and the latter a traditionally center-right enclave and the heartland of anti-immigrant politics.

The region of Emilia-Romagna, with a total population of approximately four million, is comprised of nine provinces, of which the regional capital, Bologna, is the largest, with a population of just under 900,000 (the city of Bologna proper is relatively small, with just 400,000). As described in Agnew's *Place and Politics in Modern Italy,*[29] Emilia-Romagna forms the backbone of Italy's "red zone" where the communist party (the old PCI, and now the PDS) and its affiliated labor unions and working-class solidarity have long dominated both party politics and the broader "territorial political subculture."

Historically an agricultural area based on sharecropping, Emilia-Romagna has become one of Italy's wealthiest and most industrialized regions. The GDP for the region has surpassed the national average virtually every year since the 1950s, unemployment (as low as 2.7 percent in 2002) is far lower than the national average, and per capita income is far higher, prompting even characteristically understated economists to praise its "consistent positive regional performance."[30] The region is known throughout Italy for its progressive politics, wealth, good food, and excellent educational system, including the oldest university in Europe. Italians, with their knack for caricature and dry wit, refer to Emilia-Romagna as the land of "la Rossa, la Grassa, e la Dotta," meaning roughly, "the Red, the Fat, and the Learned."

The labor force is largely engaged in services (60 percent, including those related to industry) and manufacturing (35 percent), with the rest in agriculture and other miscellaneous activities.[31] Much of the economy – an estimated 25 percent – is organized around (mostly for-profit) co-operatives. Despite the fact that a large proportion of workers in Emilia-Romagna are employed in small and medium-sized enterprises where underground work often predominates, the percentage of workers who are irregularly employed (either off-the-books, under conditions that violate labor laws, or in the informal economy) is lower in this highly unionized region than in Italy as a whole. Nonetheless, workers in Emilia-Romagna experience one of the highest occupational accident rates in the nation, due in part to the intense productivity levels and pace of work.[32]

Immigrants are spread throughout the region, with the largest number in the province of Bologna where they constitute about 5 percent of the population. Initially consisting mostly of young, single men, they increasingly include entire families, and by 2000, close to 20,000 immigrant children were enrolled in the region's public schools. Of Italy's twenty regions, Emilia-Romagna has the fourth largest number of immigrants (after Lombardy, Lazio, and Veneto), with its total immigrant population *doubling* between 1997 and 2001, and it ranks second only to Lombardy in the proportion of immigrant residence permits issued for the purpose of work.[33]

More concentrated in manufacturing – especially related to metalworking – than they are in huge metropolitan areas like Rome and Milan where they are more likely to be domestic helpers, immigrants fill important gaps in this labor-hungry, post-Fordist region.[34] The demand for immigrant workers is so intense that Emilia-Romagna fills its quota of foreign workers (allocated to the regions annually by the central government) within weeks of its allocation.[35] In the province of Bologna, 33.5 percent of all new hires were immigrant workers in 1999, and this figure increases annually. This intense demand for immigrant workers does not, however, seem to translate into their increased bargaining power or improved working conditions. In fact, in Bologna the percentage of immigrants who have full-time, permanent contracts (in contrast to part-time and/or short-term contracts) *fell* from 60 percent in the early 1990s to just 25 percent by 1999 (with the figure for immigrant women as low as 6 percent), testifying once again to their contingent labor status and to the post-Fordist trend of the economy.[36]

Emilia-Romagna has long been on the forefront of integration efforts. Well before the national government passed its first immigration law, much less launched integration programs, the city of Bologna began offering Italian classes for foreigners within its general Extension education services.[37] In the late 1980s, a series of visits for local officials was organized between Bologna and Birmingham and Coventry in England in the interest of sharing information and exchanging ideas for immigrant integration practices.[38] A 1985 regional law reorganizing social assistance programs included provisions for immigrant services, and the first comprehensive regional law relating to immigrants in 1990 included the first housing initiative for immigrants in Italy.[39] In 1991, another housing law added immigrants to the category of the "socially disadvantaged" who were eligible for regional subsidies, pre-dating by one year the national law to that effect.[40] By the mid-1990s, Emilia-Romagna's capital city of Bologna had launched "a great wealth of new initiatives."[41]

Since Turco-Napolitano was passed in 1998, Emilia-Romagna has been among the most aggressive regions in applying for national funds to subsidize its integration activities, receiving the equivalent of $0.5 million in 1999 for shelters and transitional housing, and approximately $2.7 million in 2000 and again in 2001 for general integration efforts.[42] Centrally funded integration programs have included a health services initiative and a public safety initiative, both in 1999; an immigrant right-to-education program and a housing initiative in 2000; and programs specifically addressing the needs of immigrant children and adolescents in 2001. In addition to these public sector efforts, the region subsidizes "socio-cultural integration" activities by NGOs and immigrant associations. For 2001, funding priority was given to associations that proposed Italian language classes; special initiatives for women and children; sports events; dissemination of information; and, the "valorization, promotion, and diffusion" of the cultures and languages of immigrants' countries of origin.[43]

Bologna has been particularly proactive on the housing front. The dearth of affordable housing is widely recognized in Bologna – and throughout Italy – as one of the most enduring and stubborn social problems, not just for immigrants but for Italians as well. Italy has one of the highest rates of occupant-owned housing of any advanced Western nation, and the meager availability of rental units and their high cost puts them out of reach of most low-income families. The problem is even more pronounced in Bologna, where rents exceed the already high Italian average. As early as 1990, in part to address the issue of affordable housing for immigrants, the city set aside the equivalent of $500,000 for the newly constituted Progetto Immigrazione, with the words: "This effort, which draws entirely from City resources and which requires a heavy reduction in the budgets of other municipal departments, is a clear testament to the fact that the immigration problem is now a real priority."[44]

That summer, the "immigration problem" took a turn for the worse. A larger than usual influx of North African immigrants alarmed city officials, especially as Bologna was about to host the World Cup of soccer. And, when the immigrants began to occupy abandoned buildings, both in protest over the lack of housing and because there was nowhere else to go, public opinion turned against them. An emergency shelter was set up, as city officials said, "to reduce social conflicts between immigrants and locals."[45] It did not help that these new immigrants were perceived to be quite different from what Bologna had experienced in previous eras, when foreigners were more likely to be students, political refugees, and internal migrants:[46] The Director of Health and Human Services for the city explained: "Past immigration never threatened to tear apart the social fabric." But, these immigrants were "unskilled labor," "devoid of the minimal means necessary for integration." The document he presented to city officials to deal with the emergency began: "Every effort must be made to govern this most delicate period of transition, made all the more difficult by . . . the illegal occupation of buildings, that has threatened the climate of peaceful coexistence in the city."[47] According to those close to the situation, "It was in this context of heavy polemics and accusations that steps were taken that would define immigration policies in Bologna for the foreseeable future."[48]

A project called "Al Bait" (meaning "the house" in Arabic, signaling its intended clientele), or "Bait-Bologna," was to consist of five newly constructed shelters/transitional housing with a total capacity of 500 beds and a separate service center, with 1,500 more beds to be acquired by restructuring abandoned schools and other public buildings. The Bait-Bologna plan was abandoned after months of heated public debate and recriminations over cost, but in 1992 a regional project put nine shelter complexes in Bologna with a capacity of 729 beds, designed as temporary lodging for up to six months for recent immigrants.

In 1996, a new entity was created – the Institute for Immigrant Services ("Istituzione dei Servizi per l'Immigrazione" or ISI) – designed to aggregate all immigrant services in one agency. According to an ISI newsletter: "The Institute has the task of promoting integration policies and actions for all kinds of immigrants, but also for citizens, making possible a co-existence that is positive and respectful of rights and differences."[49] The first of its kind in Italy, ISI was created as a freestanding, autonomous agency with a budget approaching $1 million. In addition to providing immigrants with information on their rights, eligibility for social services, and how to secure documents etc., ISI oversaw a service center for immigrant associations (of which there are close to fifty in Bologna, representing twenty different nationalities), collected and disseminated data, ran an after-school program, taught the Italian language to adults, ran a course on "cultural mediation," oversaw myriad anti-discrimination and anti-racism programs, and operated an interactive website.[50]

Among its many projects, housing was at the forefront. Having inherited the administration of emergency housing from the earlier period, by 1997 ISI operated five complexes of transitional housing, and 150 apartments for immigrant families.[51] (In addition to this housing, regional law stipulates that 15 percent of all public housing projects be available to immigrants.) So proactive was ISI in the 1997–1999 period that some argued the "intense activity" and "searching for large solutions" comprised an "excessive concentration on public sector activity."[52]

When the Bologna municipal elections of 1999 resulted in devastating losses for the left and the advent of a centrist city government for the first time in recent memory, ISI lost its status as an independent agency and was incorporated into the city's Department of Social Services. As a result of this shake-up, the city now operates its immigrant housing complexes through subcontracts with NGOs. The Forum of Immigrant Associations (the confederation of local immigrant associations) with which ISI had worked in close collaboration moved from the former ISI offices in the center of the city to the distant periphery, its new geographic isolation mirroring its lower political profile. While there are many harsh critics of this "dismantling" of ISI,[53] the restructured Immigration Services (Servizio Immigrati, Profughi e Nomadi) continues to operate a wide range of programs, with their internet homepage advertising help with housing, both emergency and long-term; "interethnic education"; "intercultural mediation"; an "intercultural" center; work-related courses; and "intercultural" training for health professionals.[54] At least some immigrant representatives have hopes for the new administration, or, rather, they are not overly concerned about the transition. As one member of the Forum of Immigrant Associations mused, "With the left . . . they want to seem like they are doing you a favor . . . They are good at spending money. They are very good at that. Maybe the right will be better for us."[55] In the meantime, Emilia-Romagna as a whole retains its "red" hue, and has funded one of the country's most proactive regional laws aimed at ensuring immigrants' access to health care.[56]

The northeastern region of Veneto, with Venice as its capital, has long been a center-right enclave. Its politics the antithesis of the "red zone" that Emilia-Romagna anchors, the "white zone" in Veneto and throughout the northeast was traditionally dominated by the Christian Democratic party (DC) and the Catholic church, and is now a cradle of the Northern League. In some other respects, however, the two regions are comparable. With a population of about 4.5 million, Veneto is only slightly larger than Emilia-Romagna. Its eight provinces and their major cities are similar in size to those of its red neighbor, with each of its largest provinces – Padua, Verona, Venice, Vicenza, and Treviso, respectively – only a little smaller than Bologna.[57]

Its economic climate is comparable too, so much so that the center-north region of Emilia-Romagna sometimes achieves honorary status as a member of the "northeast," a term that is now short-hand for economic vibrancy, small and medium-sized shops spread throughout the territory, and post-Fordist flexibility.[58] One reporter calls the northeast "a symbol of the economic boom beginning in the 1980s, not the old economy of massive factories, but the modern one, every bit Italian, of small enterprises dispersed around the region that live off of particular market niches and international markets."[59] Typical of the post-Fordist economic model, as in Emilia-Romagna, in Veneto the percentage of short-term contracts has increased rapidly in recent years, with half of all new hires in 2000 on such contracts.[60] With the huge factories in Mestre (the sprawling industrial city outside Venice) in crisis, industrial activity is increasingly dispersed outside the major cities and smaller towns that dot the area. Together, manufacturing (34 percent) and construction (7 percent) account for just under half of employment in the region, with the rest in agriculture (5 percent), services and other activities. Unemployment was 3.5 percent in 2001, effectively constituting full employment, something that, as the Director of the Veneto Department of Labor boasts, "few areas of the world can claim."[61] Despite the tight labor market, the business climate continues to be conducive to capital investment, with the provincial capital of Vicenza ranking *first* among small cities in Europe as a good place to locate a business, according to a study conducted by one of the world's largest entrepreneurial consulting firms.[62] Per capita income in the region, as in Emilia-Romagna, is far higher than the national average, and even outstrips that of some more affluent Western European countries by 20 percent. Contemplating this scenario, the regional Director of the Department of Labor observes: "The real issue now is not how to grow the economy, but how to cope with the problems paradoxically generated by full employment and the accompanying quickening of structural changes."[63]

One of these structural changes is the increase in immigrant workers. Veneto has the largest number of immigrants of any region in Italy after Lombardy and Lazio – regions with far larger populations – and the number is rapidly increasing. Between 1999 and 2000, new immigrant employment in the region rose by 35 percent, and by mid-2002 over 27 percent of all new hires were non-EU immigrants.[64] The industrial city of Treviso – home base of Benetton – is illustrative of this burst of immigrant employment, with 30,000 immigrants working in 300 factories in the area.[65] Although it varies by province, approximately 50 percent of immigrants in Veneto work in manufacturing, 30 percent in services (with relatively few in domestic service), and 10 percent in agriculture (mostly on a seasonal basis). And, as in Emilia-Romagna, the single largest group is Moroccans, but Veneto also has a relatively large (and increasing) number of Central and Eastern Europeans, and approximately 5 percent each from China, Ghana, Senegal, and Nigeria.[66] While the majority of immigrants come from this handful of countries, scores of others are represented; suggestive of the diversity involved, fifty-six different languages are spoken in the schools of Venice – a remarkable statistic given that this new immigration only gained momentum two decades ago.[67]

So tight is the labor market that annual quotas for foreign workers are filled within days of their allotment. Industry spokespersons and regional officials regularly petition the government for quota supplements, with the Veneto Director of Immigration – Raffaele Zanon, a member of Gianfranco Fini's right-wing and generally anti-immigrant Alleanza Nazionale (AN) party – taking a lead role in the lobbying.[68] In a twist on the trend of the last two decades – when immigrants were seen as replacements for the sudden dearth of southern Italian migrants – the president of the Veneto Industrial Association urged southern Italians to migrate for jobs in the north to fill vacancies left by the shortage of immigrant labor![69]

In 1990, Veneto passed its first triennial plan for immigrant integration, consistent with federal law, and in 1993 enacted another, affirming its general commitment to implementing national policy at the local level.[70] But, unlike in Emilia-Romagna, the politics of integration did not take off until later in the 1990s. Once the alarm had sounded, it was loud and long, even managing at times to drown out the cacophony of the anti-immigrant zealots (and sometimes even co-opting them, as we will see).

In 1997, the Osservatorio Regionale Immigrazione was established by the regional government as a research and data-collection entity whose job it was to oversee trends, keep tabs on labor market absorption, sponsor conferences and otherwise provide the intellectual heavy lifting critical to effective policymaking. In February, 2001, the Tavolo Unico Regionale sull'immigrazione (regional "round table" on immigration) was set up to encourage dialogue and coordination. The Tavolo Unico brings together regional, provincial, and city officials; all three major union confederations and some trades unions; the major industrial associations; the agricultural association; and the board of commerce and tourism (immigrant associations were conspicuously omitted). Organized by Raffaele Zanon, the Tavolo Unico set as its major goals: "the civil insertion of non-EU immigrants in workplaces and in the regional community"; "the harmonious co-existence of citizens and immigrants"; and "the promotion of the return to Italy of Italian and Venetian emigrants and their descendants" (a provision that representatives of the Northern League insisted upon as a condition of their participation).[71] To achieve these things, the group proposes projects that address vocational training, housing, social services, the control of immigration flows, and information networks for the analysis of labor needs. Zanon touts the model as "unique in Italy." And, he is not alone in his praise. The central government considered the Tavolo Unico so innovative that it signed an agreement with Veneto to explore the possibility of using it as a "paradigm of reference" for other regions, and backed it up with resources.[72] It is particularly significant that the agreement was arranged under the center-left coalition government before the election of Berlusconi, that is, before the central government shared any party identification with right-wing Veneto or its Director of Immigration.[73]

Six months after the Tavolo Unico promulgated its founding principles, Veneto passed its triennial plan for 2001–2003, borrowing heavily from the Tavolo's recommendations. The five-party coalition of right-wing and anti-immigrant parties, including Forza Italia, the National Alliance, and the Northern League, agreed to spend approximately $6.2 million on immigration in 2001, with the bulk of it earmarked directly or indirectly for integration. Consistent with his own party politics and pressure from Northern League colleagues, Zanon introduced the plan by announcing a preference for the return of Italian emigrants and integration policies that favor them. He also took pains to draw a "sharp demarcation between legal immigration and clandestine immigration," and offered the stern warning that "the question of immigration is also a question of public order and respect for the rules of civil society in which everyone, including immigrants, has to adapt."[74] Less predictable was what came next. To set the stage for the plan's recommendations

89

of immigrant integration, Zanon underscored the need for "recognition of, and appreciation for, the demands and real absorptive capacity of the labor market in Veneto." "This," he said, "is the real revolution compared to the past."

The Preamble to the plan flagged this new reality:

> The rapid evolution of immigration in Veneto makes it urgent that we reform local insertion policies . . . It is no longer enough to have general goals of integration; rather, they must now be concrete and specifically tailored . . . based on territorial exigencies . . . [We must] facilitate access to collective and individual services, to education, to cultural integration, to vocational training, and immigrants' acquisition of new occupational capabilities especially given the possibility of re-entry in their countries of origin. . . . It is in this complex and delicate context that the aim of the Veneto region for the next three years is to create a Venetian model of legal immigrant integration.[75]

Its authors recognized that "obstacles to this endeavor should not be underestimated"; specifically, "the invasion of foreigners often breeds suspicions"; and "cultural difficulties" were noted, relating to the attitudes of the Veneto population who were "used to constructing their own identity involving family, society, and territory."[76] Nonetheless, the plan moved forward, echoing the parameters of the Tavolo Unico. Among its priorities are facilitating access to housing for immigrants and their families. The plan makes reference not just to providing shelters and rental units but to subsidizing mortgages; providing loans to rehabilitate abandoned housing by working with lenders, employers, cooperatives, and other associations; and, encouraging "social housing" in the form of *pensiones* that would be open to both immigrants and natives on a sliding-scale basis. In all cases, priority is to be given to projects that maximize input from and dialogue with immigrants to encourage "social insertion."[77]

Almost $2 million was spent directly on various integration projects in 2000, about the same as in Emilia-Romagna, with 80 percent coming from the central government and 20 percent coming from regional and local coffers. In 2001, after the triennial plan was put in place, funding jumped precipitously. That year, $6.2 million was budgeted for integration – $2 million for housing; $750,000 each for vocational development, a network for disseminating information, and the Osservatorio Regionale Immigrazione and other research organizations; $500,000 to various pilot projects; and another $1.5 million for NGOs that work with immigrants, and for immigrant associations.[78]

In 2002, funding almost doubled again, approaching $12.(Housing was a principal "building block" of the effort, and was at almost $6 million. While Veneto continues to endorse the return o. Italian emigrants and their descendants as a top priority, and a number of programs are designed to facilitate it (for example, the "Progetto Rientro dall'Argentina" recruits Argentinians of Italian descent), the region has become a "positive example" of broader integration efforts, and is at least the rival of progressive Emilia-Romagna for innovative schemes. In one project, evocatively called "Migratools," immigrants can take distance learning classes that among other things teach the Italian language and local culture online – a program that one observer calls "the cutting edge of integration initiatives using new methodologies and innovative solutions."[79]

Employer associations have been central to these initiatives. Three months after the creation of the Tavolo Unico, employer representatives "raised their voices" at the meeting, stressing the urgency of the need for immigrant labor.[80] And, they have organized their own lobbying group for more liberal regional policies, as well as larger quotas of foreign workers from the central government. The head of one association urged that a higher quota was needed – as well as housing for them – since "immigrant workers are now a structural component of the labor market."[81] In preparation for the regional 2002 budget decisions, they declared a labor market emergency and made immigrant housing – which ultimately received close to half of the allocated budget – a top priority for government action.[82]

Employers are increasingly taking matters into their own hands. The president of the industrial association in Treviso contested the local mayor's widely publicized racist characterization of immigrants, declaring: "[Mayor] Gentilini was wrong to attack immigrants. These people are important to us." And, he pledged, "Our businesses are ready to guarantee housing [for immigrants]," starting with a plan to find accommodations for fifty-eight Moroccans.[83] In the search for creative solutions, the same organization sponsored a three-day, all-expenses-paid, field trip to Strasbourg for seventy-nine mayors from the northeast (out of a total of ninety-five) to study techniques of integration and the benefits of "tolerance" for cultural diversity.[84] In another initiative, the Veneto Industrialists Association and the major labor unions together launched a program that they called "Glocal," with housing and other integration plans for immigrant tanning factory workers around Vicenza and marble quarry workers in the Verona area.[85]

Of course, not everyone is on board in this cradle of the Northern League. Even some of the businessmen who depend on immigrant labor are ambivalent. The president of Confindustria – the largest national organization of industrialists in Italy – complained: "Here we have a situation where industry needs immigrants, but society doesn't want them. This is especially true in the northeast where businessmen say they need immigrant workers and then vote for the Northern League."[86] Some are not even ambivalent. The infamous Northern League mayor of Treviso – Giancarlo Gentilini, known colloquially as "The Sheriff" – told reporters that immigrants come from a "razza piave" (loosely translated, "alien race"), and proposed that "trucks sealed with lead" repatriate them.[87] In addition to the fingerprints now required of immigrants, Mayor Gentilini would take "nose prints and footprints," and "bury alive those priests who serve meals to the 'extracomunitari.'"[88] According to other participants of the Tavolo Unico, "The Sheriff's" participation is reluctant at best, considerably complicating the whole enterprise. In this context, a member of the policy roundtable noted: "One thing that has come out of the Tavolo Unico so far is that when it comes to immigration, one must choose one's words carefully."[89]

By and large though, Veneto's policymakers recognize the need for immigrant workers, and have adjusted their policy proposals – if not always their rhetoric – accordingly. As an official close to Tavolo Unico director Zanon explained: "He is open [to policies of integration] even if he is a member of the National Alliance party, because he has realized that without immigrants, the economic system isn't moving forward."[90] Even the Northern League is susceptible to this logic. As the head of a Caritas shelter told me just after the center-right victory in 2001, "Bossi and the Northern League operate at the theoretical level. When they face economic reality, they see they need immigrants."[91] In this region so dominated by Berlusconi's Forza Italia, the neo-fascist National Alliance, and the anti-immigrant Northern League, the economic reality of immigration is a powerful trump card, as anti-immigrant fervor has had to accommodate some of the most proactive integration policies in Europe. As David Montgomery has said in another context: "Even the most persuasive discourse can collide with the real world."[92]

This snapshot comparison of Emilia-Romagna and Veneto reveals several important patterns. Most importantly here, these regions that are so politically and ideologically different, have remarkably comparable integration policies, with conservative (and heretofore, anti-immigrant) officials in Veneto taking their place alongside their more progressive counterparts in Emilia-Romagna as leaders campaign to integrate immigrants. Furthermore, these efforts are ~~~~ sive and expensive – one gets the feeling they are almost frenetic in their intensity and scope – and go well beyond anything that can be chalked up to political posturing. If anything, political posturing is more likely to be found among conservative Veneto officials who, while busy constructing plans to house immigrants and insert them into the labor market, must throw an occasional rhetorical sop to their anti-immigrant constituents and Northern League colleagues.

INTEGRATION LAW AND POLICY IN SPAIN

Spain, despite sometimes strong ideological and political differences with Italy (especially before Berlusconi's election in 2000), has followed a remarkably similar path with regard to immigrant integration. The Preamble to Spain's 1985 law spoke of "facilitat[ing] the integration of aliens into Spanish society." By 1991, as both legal and illegal immigration increased, so too did the emphasis on integration. Congressional resolutions, administrative decrees, and speeches before Parliament regularly warned of the need "to ensure the social integration of legal immigrants" and to promote "the successful and harmonious integration between the local population and the immigrants who come to live and work among us."[93] The 1994 "Plan for the Social Integration of Immigrants" put the issue front and center. It established the national "Forum for the Social Integration of Immigrants" in part as a mechanism for bringing immigrants' voices into the debate, and the "Permanent Observatory for Immigration" as a research and data-collection institution with regional branches, closely paralleling the Territorial Councils and information networks set up in Italy. And, as in Italy, the Plan announced a commitment to ending discrimination and racism, and promoting "peaceful coexistence."[94]

As we saw in Chapter 2, Law 4/2000 was passed despite opposition from the Aznar Administration, giving immigrants equal rights to Spaniards in access to compulsory public education, health care, housing, and social security protections, and making these rights contingent on being registered in the local municipality as a *de facto* resident, rather than on formal immigration status. This pragmatic approach to integration was not altogether abandoned by Aznar's "counter-reformation" a few months later. While Law 8/2000 was decidedly different in tone and eliminated many of the rights for illegal immigrants that its predecessor had briefly established (at least on the books), it retained integration as a central concern. Much as Bossi-Fini stopped short of some of the harshest measures proposed by the Northern League, the Aznar Administration recognized the need for at least minimal efforts at inclusion. Immediately following the law's passage, the central government announced their programmatic blueprint in the Plan Greco. Similar to Turco-Napolitano in Italy, the Plan Greco reaffirmed the system for contracting with local regions and pledged resources to NGOs that promote integration. Its definition of integration was similar to the Italian understanding too; specifically mentioned were the right of (legal) immigrants to access all the fundamental human rights that Spaniards claim; their access to social services; and the importance of tolerance, "respect for cultural diversity," and "the fight against racism and xenophobia."[95]

IMSERSO (Instituto de Migraciones y Servicios Sociales), in the Department of Labor and Social Affairs, conducts studies relating to the integration and well-being of immigrants, does the actual contracting with regions, and occasionally intervenes directly on behalf of integration. A 2001 report described their goals as "eliminating discrimination"; "facilitating coexistence"; "securing a stable legal and social situation for immigrants"; "fighting barriers that impede integration"; "eliminating exploitation"; and "engaging the whole society in the fight against racism and xenophobia."[96]

For fiscal year 2002, the Aznar government budgeted more than $1.3 billion for immigration-related activities. Of this, more than $900 million was for health care, $252 million for implementation of the Plan Greco (representing an increase of 11 percent from 2001), $192 million for education, $16 million for reception centers and shelters, $7 million for contracts to local regions, and almost $6 million in subsidies to NGOs. Admittedly, not all of the Plan Greco budget was devoted to integration; of its $252-million allocation, about $79 million was earmarked for development projects in countries of origin, and $36 million went to border-patrol technology, surveillance, and counterfeit document detection.[97] But, when the Secretary of State for Immigration introduced this budget to Congress with the assurance that "[t]he Government is working for the full social integration of immigrants," he was putting his money where his mouth was.[98]

This is not to suggest that the Aznar government is unilaterally committed to immigrant integration, nor to downplay the punitive policies the new law imposed. Indicative of the hostility toward

immigrants within the administration, when the newly appoir
of the Forum for the Social Integration of Immigrants publi
multiculturalism a "gangrene," the Minister of Immigration was quic
to defend him. Multiculturalism, he said, was "unacceptable"; at most,
Spain might be a "multi-ethnic" society – presumably comprised of
those who have shed their foreign "cultures."[99] Despite such equivocation, policymakers in Spain have expended considerable effort and
resources to promote integration – efforts which, as we will see, often
backfire in the face of countervailing realities.

As in Italy, policy specifics are designed and implemented at the local
level, and, even more so than in Italy, Spain's seventeen regional governments exercise substantial autonomy. Not surprisingly, given this
autonomy and the diversity of Spain's regions, integration practices
vary considerably. One immigration scholar, referring to the policies of
rural Andalusia and industrial Catalonia, observed that they "are like
night and day."[100]

Catalonia – with 25 percent of Spain's total immigrant population –
is sometimes described as a "pioneer" of integration.[101] The first to create the position of Secretary of Immigration within the regional government in 2000, it was also the first region to write a long-term plan for
integration. Some have attributed its proactive approach to nationalist "nation-building," and there is some evidence that nationalism and
pride in the Catalan language and culture have contributed to their
integration politics. For example, an official in the Catalan Department of Education told me that when Latin American immigrants come
to Spain, "[t]hey think they are coming to the mother country, and
are surprised to find out that [in Catalonia] Spanish is not spoken in
the schools." Counterintuitively, she said it is easier to get Moroccans
to speak Catalan than Spanish-speaking Latin Americans, a fact that
may help explain the far greater preponderance of Latin Americans in
Madrid, and Moroccans in Barcelona.[102] Another Education Department official told me that because school teachers – fluent in Castillan
Spanish as well as their native Catalan – find it so difficult to persist in
using the required Catalan with their Spanish-speaking students (and
therefore often resort to Spanish), the Catalan schools are hiring extra
"cultural mediators" to deal with the issue.[103] A Catalonian government guide for immigrants in Catalonia offers advice on a wide range
of topics, including work, leisure, health, family life, housing, and taxes.
The need to learn Catalan features prominently: "When a person moves
to another country . . . it is indispensable to learn the language. It is the

How do govs/orgs see the aspects of culture that must be learned? What are they?

key to finding work, making friends, helping your children in school, shopping, etc. . . . The proper language in Catalonia is Catalan, a fundamental element of Catalan identity."[104]

The "Interdepartmental Plan for Immigration, 2001–2004" (hereinafter referred to simply as the "Plan") is Catalonia's outline for the integration process. The Plan focuses on how to deal with the multiculturalism accompanying immigration, particularly within a nationalist context like that of Catalonia. While recognizing that the transition will be "neither easy nor rapid," the Plan places its confidence in "the principle of integration":[105]

> We are in the midst of a process of increasing cultural diversity . . . It is necessary to develop a doctrine that permits us to maintain an equilibrium between social cohesion and diversity, and it seems that the principle of integration is the best given that it is most respectful of the rights of immigrants and the rights of the receiving society to maintain its own cohesion and identity . . . Catalonia has to develop a model of integration that achieves a maximum balance between respect for diversity on the one hand, and the recognition that we all belong to one community on the other.

There is a self-conscious effort here to reject the politically incorrect concept of unilateral adaptation on the part of the immigrant and to voice appreciation for immigrant cultural identity, but the facile faith placed in "integration" as a way to achieve the proper "balance" is striking. This faith – and one might say the slippery logic on which it relies – was evident too in the words of a Catalan official: "Our model is neither a 'melting pot', nor assimilation, but respect for differences. But, immigrants have to recognize that we are who we are and we are not going to change. We do not stress multiculturalism, but one community."[106] The tension between respect for cultural diversity and the desire for a cohesive community with one identity, is by far the most politically visible and remarked upon challenge in the integration process, but, as we will see later, it may not be the most daunting one.[107]

Specifics of the Plan testify to the versatility of the concept of integration. It comprises 133 different initiatives involving virtually every department of the Catalan government, and proposes such far-reaching activities as the provision of cultural facilitators in social service agencies and health clinics; the dissemination of information about and access to shelter for the recently arrived; help with job searches; treatment of social and cultural conflicts in schools; encouraging the study of diseases associated with immigrants; sponsoring street-fairs celebrating culinary and cultural diversity; disseminating pamphlets and other educational tools in the struggle against racism; funding publications addressing the special needs of immigrant women, including pamphlets denouncing female genital cutting; and co-development projects that facilitate return migration.[108]

In the area of health care alone, the Plan is remarkably ambitious.[109] The Catalan Department of Health and Social Security, in collaboration with the regional Health Services and the Institute for Health, is directed to ensure access to health care, identify health care problems, and address those problems with special research teams and clinics. Among the targeted areas are maternal and infant care; diseases treatable with vaccines; parasites; sexually transmitted diseases; tuberculosis; and mental health problems. Each of these areas is to have at least two dedicated centers, staffed by teams of doctors, nurses, and cultural/linguistic facilitators.[110]

Considerable grassroots effort has gone into the analysis of, and solutions for, the special medical problems of immigrants, including the recent publication in Barcelona alone of no less than eleven books on the health problems of immigrants and the language hurdles they face in accessing services, with three dictionaries specific to immigrants' medical needs published in 2003.[111] In addition, local health care professionals have set up a network that allows them to share their experiences in caring for immigrants, and ways to cope with the special medical, cultural, and administrative needs of their immigrant clientele.[112]

As in Italy, municipal governments have responsibility for creating and implementing their own integration activities, in addition to or as an integral part of the regional effort. Thus, alongside the Catalan Plan, the city of Barcelona has produced a vast array of reports and initiatives. In his summary of Barcelona's activities, political theorist Ricard Zapata-Barrero lists eighty-three initiatives since 1984, ranging from reports and study groups, to health care videos in multiple languages, to documentaries on depictions of the "Other" in cinema, to intercultural education proposals, and campaigns against racism.[113]

SUMMARY

The concept of integration does yeoman's work in both Italy and Spain. It fills the semantic space between the politically incorrect "assimilation" and the politically unpalatable "multiculturalism." It promises a cohesive community, while assuring respect for difference.

And, it is versatile enough to cover extensive and disparate territory, from language acquisition, to health care and housing, to freedom from discrimination, and – in some cases – even the ability to repatriate. Inclusion of this latter component suggests that perhaps the greatest virtue of this infinitely versatile concept is that in the same breath it can pull in two directions at once, perfectly tracking immigration policies and the ambiguity and contradictions they both reflect and help constitute.

Also apparent are the similarities in national integration policies in these two Mediterranean countries, despite different political climates during much of this period. Indeed, the policy variation among regions within Italy and Spain is more pronounced than their national differences, with relatively recalcitrant southern regions such as Andalusia and Apulia standing in stark contrast to proactive Catalonia, Emilia-Romagna, and Veneto. While it is beyond the scope of this book to establish precisely why the southern regions have not launched programs as aggressive as their northern neighbors, we can at least speculate that it has to do with the agricultural role (frequently sporadic and seasonal) of immigrants in these regions, their relative invisibility to the larger society, and a less urgent need to normalize their presence. Consistent with my argument that integration activities are designed at least in part to offset resistance to an indispensable "alien" population that is further "alienated" by its marginal legal status and economic function, the urgency is considerably reduced in areas where immigrant workers are neither a year-round presence nor a highly visible one. In other words, if economic reality is the driving force behind integration efforts, it is perhaps the related social reality of space and place that helps explain the distribution of those efforts.

Finally, the intensity of integration efforts cannot be ignored, nor dismissed as token gestures. When some of the most anti-immigrant political parties in northeastern Italy are spearheading integration reforms and their leaders go on industry-sponsored excursions to research the virtues of tolerance, it is only a slight exaggeration to say, as Director Zanon claimed, that there has been a "revolution." This is not to say that their intensity is matched by success. As we will see in the next chapters, countervailing forces – constituted by law, economics, immigrant racialization, and their powerful cross-fertilization – both enhance the urgency of integrating the "useful invaders" and fuel their marginalization.

CHAPTER FIVE

THE EVERYDAY DYNAMICS OF EXCLUSION: WORK, HEALTH, AND HOUSING

The staff at a hospital in Turin told a group of Senegalese immigrants they did not have the expertise to care for blacks, dismissing them with "What can we do for you here?"[1] In Spain, the baby of Moroccan immigrants died in the emergency waiting room where he had been left unattended in a critical condition.[2] These dramatic stories underscore a more routine reality of immigrant exclusion. The commissioner responsible for annual reports on immigrant integration in Italy says the picture is "somewhat 'patchy,' with a mixture of light and dark areas." Increasing family unification rates, more immigrant children in schools, and growing union membership are among the "light areas" she mentions. Among the "dark patches" are the high percentage of immigrants who are illegal; the many legal immigrants who work in the underground economy; disproportionate school failure rates; extensive homelessness and substandard housing; and high incarceration rates, with immigrants representing 25 percent of the Italian prison population overall – and 50 percent of detained minors.[3] Access to the national health system by immigrants is "extremely limited,"[4] and immigrants constitute up to 90 percent of those who use soup kitchens.[5]

A similar picture emerges in Spain. In a national study sponsored by IMSERSO, the 1,600 immigrants who were interviewed reported major difficulties finding housing, getting a fair wage, and having their skills appreciated.[6] In Madrid, immigrants comprise 64 percent of the homeless, and NGOs regularly denounce landlords for refusing to rent to immigrants.[7] The national health service in some areas denies care to immigrants, including pregnant women and children.[8]

Access to health care and housing are considered "fundamental vehicle[s]" of the integration efforts described in the previous chapter.[9] Not only are they core signifiers of membership in the national community, but they are prerequisites for the physical well-being upon which employment and other basic necessities – not to speak of the more up-scale social accoutrements of true inclusion – depend. In this chapter, I explore the breakdown of these vehicles and the obstacles to their repair. Briefly, we will see how the institutionalized irregularity constructed by law, economic marginality, administrative-bureaucratic hurdles, and racialization interact to preclude immigrants' full social participation and exercise of their rights in these core arenas of health care and housing.

As we began to see in Chapter 3, laws that make legal status both temporary and contingent ensure the economic vulnerability of hundreds of thousands of immigrants, both illegal and legal. In the face of this marginality imposed by law, the push to integrate them meets defeat halfway. The spokesman for an international immigrant advocacy group in Geneva put it bluntly: "A migrant who is illegal cannot integrate."[10] Or, as an employee of IMSERSO told me: "It is difficult to integrate if you don't have rights."[11]

I trace here the dynamics of this legal exclusion, and the ripple effects of institutionalized irregularity even for those who are (temporarily) legal. As always, law must be seen broadly to include not just formal but also informal processes; we will examine, for example, the roles that amorphous regulations, administrative discretion, and "street-level bureaucracies" play in exclusion. But, obstacles to immigrant integration go beyond the messiness of the administrative street or the self-contradictory nature of government policies – its own self-ambushing as it were – to include fundamental economic realities. For if economic reality imposes on even xenophobes the need for immigrant integration, economic realities also impede its full realization. An Italian government official, in an attempt to justify the dependence of legal status on work status in the Bossi-Fini law, claimed: "It is work that integrates."[12] But, it is also immigrants' work that *dis-integrates*. The following section looks in more detail at the connections between legal and economic marginality, before turning to the arenas of health care and housing where the repercussions of that marginality are so powerfully played out.

WORK AND MARGINALITY: DOWN BY LAW

We have already seen how immigrants' illegal status makes them vulnerable to employers, and the logic by which this vulnerability extends to legal immigrants as well. Despite the repeated pronouncements of Prime Ministers Aznar and Berlusconi, who draw sharp distinctions between legal immigrants whom they claim to welcome and illegals for whom there is "below-zero tolerance," these statuses do not distinguish populations so much as moments in time.[13] A Peruvian worker in Spain explains his economic disadvantage as an illegal immigrant: "They don't pay me much because, well, because I'm irregular; if I was legal maybe they would pay me more, no?" But, just as there is no clear dichotomy between the illegal and the temporarily legal populations, so there is often little change in an immigrant's economic fate when he or she achieves legal status. An anthropologist who studied Moroccan families in Madrid described their disillusionment over this discovery: "There was a period [after the 1991 legalization program] when Moroccans, hopeful over their new permits, tried to use them to get legal work, which many times turned out to be impossible."[14]

An article in the left-leaning Italian newspaper, *L'unità*, describes an encounter with an Egyptian immigrant, Adam, on the train between Rome and the northeastern city of Brescia. His friends had told him there was work there "even for the undocumented. More accurately, especially for the undocumented – those pressed by both fear and poverty." The reporter continues:

> The binomial fear–poverty works. Above all, it pays. Those who do not have rights work more, earn less, and pay vertiginous rents on the black market. Not to mention their labor is flexible: If the boss gets tired of him he's out the door. You have to admit, for Italians the factory that produces illegal immigrants [e.g. law] is the proverbial hen that lays the golden eggs ... Thanks to the tight sleeves of the bureaucracy the nightmare extends to legal immigrants too, permeating the entire immigrant community.[15]

So, both legal and illegal immigrants are vulnerable, but the vulnerability of the former derives in part from the threat of falling back into illegal status. As we saw earlier, this vulnerability translates into lower wages and the susceptibility to employer "blackmail." An Equatorial Guinean in Spain speaks of the low wages he received in one job, and says: "I kept my mouth shut, because I wasn't going to complain. If I complained, they'd show me the door."[16] A case study of forty-six ın and Latin American workers in an Italian recycling center documents their substandard and delayed pay, long hours without breaks, and working off-the-books that meant no benefits or social security. The study documents too the deaf ear of labor inspectors to workers' complaints and the attempts of employers first to fire workers who complained and later to threaten them all with deportation. The case is unusual in that the workers with the (belated) help of the union were ultimately victorious, but the working conditions and the employer strategies that play on immigrant vulnerability are all too common.[17]

The vulnerability is particularly intense in the shadow economy where about 30 percent of immigrants in Italy work (compared to 15 percent of Italians). The presumably disorganized underground economy can be quite well organized in its tapping of exploitable labor. A firm discovered by police in Veneto specialized in providing undocumented immigrants to businesses in the underground economy and families seeking live-in domestic help. After hiring out hundreds of illegal immigrants in this way, the network was exposed when some Moldavian/Romanian women complained to police that they were working eighteen hours straight in a factory for the equivalent of $6.[18]

Besides low wages, precarious legal status means that employers can transfer unexpected costs of production to the worker, as when thousands of farmworkers were left idle, starving, and homeless when hailstorms ruined the fruit harvest in Catalonia in the summer of 2002 (see Chapter 3).[19] It can also mean elevated incidents of workplace accidents.[20] Above all, it means work that others do not want to do. A newspaper report summarizing findings from a study of immigrants in Spain who were seeking work – headlined sardonically, "I Want To Be a Cleaner" – reveals that 72 percent were looking for positions as maids, construction crew clean-up, unskilled factory workers, or farmworkers.[21] Contrary to conventional wisdom, this concentration of immigrants in low-end jobs, and as this media account suggests their apparent "aspiration" to such jobs, has nothing to do with their skill levels or educational achievements. In Spain, non-EU immigrants are twice as likely to have college degrees, and are 30 percent more likely to have completed high school, than the native population.[22] Instead, it reflects their function as a labor supply on the margins, taking jobs under conditions that unemployed citizens will not move for and/or shun altogether. Tellingly, Italian sociologist Maurizio Ambrosini has found that vocational training, a central part of Italian and Spanish integration strategies, often leads to increased frustration among immigrants who find it *more* difficult to obtain employment after the acquisition of new skills.[23] According to Ambrosini, "[t]he more the training leads away from specialized ethnic niches and moves towards skilled occupations, the more immigrants...encounter difficulty in getting a job." In a context in which immigrants' marginality is their most marketable "skill," vocational training has failure built in.

The rest of this chapter traces the impacts of this institutionalized irregularity and labor market marginality in the areas of health care and housing, as immigration and integration policies get played out on the street.

ACCESS TO HEALTH CARE: "IT SOUNDS GOOD IN PRINCIPLE, BUT..."[24]

The integration programs discussed in the last chapter include access to the national health care systems as a central feature. An important part of the social rights of membership in these countries – T. H. Marshall's "social citizenship"[25] – health care access is considered fundamental to "real social integration."[26]

A report on integration in Italy by the National Council of Economy and Labor begins: "Their health is often the only capital immigrants bring with them for the realization of their dreams in the new country."[27] The authors go on to suggest that this capital is often squandered: "Immigrants generally only go to the clinic in an emergency...when they cannot avoid it...In such cases...the diagnosis is always late and the delay carries serious risks." Putting aside the question of who squanders what, the "serious risks" are reflected in elevated rates of infant mortality, premature births, tuberculosis, depression/anxiety, and other preventable conditions.[28] Most of the illnesses afflicting immigrants are contracted after they arrive in Italy; one study reports that 40 percent of them are brought on or exacerbated by difficulty in accessing health care, with the rest often the result of unhealthy living and working conditions.[29] Even the most optimistic report on health care access in Italy concludes that there are significant areas of concern,[30] with language difficulties, cultural disconnects, and a variety of bureaucratic barriers heading the list.[31]

The experience of one undocumented immigrant who needed medical assistance exposes the sense of disenfranchisement for those who are denied what has come to be seen as a fundamental right in Western Europe. One day, while working in a foundry in Italy, he had problems with his eyesight. He recounts: "I went to the hospital. The doctors were very nice but told me loud and clear, 'Look, we cannot care for you, you are a clandestino'... So, not having a residence permit means not even having a permit to get sick."[32]

Immigrants' access to health care in Spain is, if anything, even more problematic than in Italy. Before exploring the complex exclusionary dynamics at work there, it will help to have a grasp of the basic outlines of the Spanish health care system. Like other Western European countries, Spain has a national health care system that provides free medical care, hospitalization, and discounted prescription drugs to all citizens and entitled others. While the general principles are laid out in national policies, the system is largely decentralized, with the regions responsible for establishing policy specifics, and the municipalities overseeing the neighborhood clinics where outpatient health care and medical visits take place.

The General Health Law of 1986 grants all Spanish citizens the right to health care primarily through their enrollment in the social security system. Other EU nationals residing in Spain enjoy identical rights with Spanish citizens under this law, as do non-EU immigrants living and working in Spain legally.[33] The liberal immigration law of early 2000 (Law 4/2000) opened up access to the system to undocumented immigrants who were nonetheless registered in their local municipality as actual – if not necessarily legal – residents; to women for prenatal care, birth, and post-natal care, regardless of legal status or municipal registration; and to unregistered, undocumented adult immigrants for emergency care only. The Aznar counter-reform eliminated many social rights for immigrants, but left these health care provisions intact.[34]

It is a long and arduous journey, however, from these formal rights to actual access. Some unknowable number of immigrants experience overt discrimination on the part of administrators and medical staff. This racialized discrimination can take many forms and has many sources. Among them is the not uncommon notion that non-EU immigrants are natural carriers of particular diseases. Thus, Medicos sin Fronteras felt compelled to explain in a press release directed at the health care establishment that immigrants of color are not intrinsically disposed to tuberculosis and other such infectious diseases. As reported by SOS Racismo, the NGO doctors pointed out:

> The diseases of this population are associated with their living conditions, not the color of their skin or their geographic origins.

'Tuberculosis,' they said, 'has much to do with over-crowding and insufficient nutrition. If 16 immigrants live in an apartment without electricity and without adequate ventilation, it is likely that someone is going to develop the disease. The pathology does not lie in [the immigrants'] race but in their living conditions.'[35]

A Spanish immigration scholar has noted the naturalized attribution of various other contagious diseases to the immigrant population, including sexually transmitted diseases, as well as mental health problems.[36] Similarly, racist assumptions about immigrants' cultures are periodically exposed, as when the national health service produced a Guide to Immigrant Health and advised immigrants on how to bathe: "Wet your body with abundant water, soap yourself, and at the end dry yourself with a towel."[37] The Guide had to be recalled when immigrant groups, NGOs, and various political organizations protested its infantilizing advice.

Not only can such preconceptions lead to the mistreatment of symptoms, but the racialized fears underlying them can lead to the most blatant form of discrimination – refusal to extend treatment. SOS Racismo documents scores of cases at the end of every year in which clinics and/or medical personnel in Spain have refused treatment to immigrants who were clearly entitled to it, or have covered up inferior or delayed treatment with racial attributions of blame. After the well-publicized death of the Moroccan baby in a clinic waiting room (referenced above), the Spanish Minister of Health claimed that the mother had brought the problem on herself because she was from "a different health culture" and carrying her baby in a shawl had caused its temperature to spike.[38]

"Culture" in all its various renditions is by far the most commonly cited culprit in official, and even academic, explanations for immigrants' blocked access to care in Spain. There is little question but that language difficulties complicate the interaction between immigrants and health service administrators, nurses, and doctors – a fact regularly attested to by immigrants themselves, medical personnel, and NGOs. An SOS Racismo report even warned of the imminent "collapse" of some health clinics in Barcelona due to the serious language barriers between the increasingly immigrant clientele and the clinics' physicians. A doctor at the Barcelona clinic with the highest concentration of foreign-born patients in the city told me that, while cultural mediators and interpreters are helping in this regard, language problems persist and complicate patients' ability to navigate the health bureaucracy, as well as potentially limiting treatment.[39]

It is less clear how much strictly cultural differences discourage immigrants from seeking medical treatment. While many government and anecdotal reports claim that immigrants' cultures predispose them against Western medicine, it is difficult to untangle these reports from the kind of racialized biases discussed above. The reports are particularly suspect in light of periodic complaints from patients that their requests for treatment have been rebuffed by doctors hostile to their concerns. In one such incident, an Algerian woman legally resident for many years in Spain, asked her pediatrician to circumcise her baby boys. The specialist to whom she was referred told her in no uncertain terms that he was under no obligation to perform the circumcision (a procedure not usually done in Spain), asked her pointedly, "Why don't you go back where you came from and they will do it there?," and summarily dismissed her from the office.[40]

Recourse to narratives of immigrants' cultural aversions to Western medicine also tends to obscure their hesitation to interact with state authorities for much more practical reasons. An abundant literature addresses the reluctance of undocumented immigrants in the United States to interact with state employees, and the problems this creates for the police, health practitioners, and others who need their cooperation to safeguard the public safety and health.[41] There is some evidence that immigrants in Spain feel more comfortable approaching doctors and requesting information from clinics than they do other state representatives, with the degree of comfort varying by nationality and by region in Spain.[42] Nonetheless, in the mid-1990s, experts began to report that undocumented immigrants either avoided the public health care system altogether or frequented only those clinics that had a reputation for being "safe."[43] After Aznar's restrictive immigration law with its discourse of "below-zero tolerance" and stepped-up police action, warnings began to surface that not just undocumented immigrants but legal immigrants as well were avoiding all state authorities. NGOs in Madrid reported that many immigrants were going without health care for fear of being rounded up and deported.[44]

Besides focusing on cultural differences and appointing cultural mediators, policymakers have launched information campaigns, designed to educate immigrants about their eligibility for health services. While there are no precise data on how effective these campaigns are, many experts argue that immigrants who are legally entitled to health care are still unaware of their eligibility.[45] But, the greater informational lacuna may be found among the very administrative and professional personnel upon whom implementation of these rights directly depends. In the following section, I take the reader on a field trip of sorts, as a way to map out the various "street-level" detours of immigrants' rights to health care in Spain. Along the way, we will witness *finally* the interplay of complex and confusing rules, ideological and racial antipathies, economic marginality, and a large dose of administrative discretion, that together often nullify immigrants' rights to care.

Street-level detours: an excursion

I began my fieldwork in Spain with the requisite homework done. I felt well-versed and confident, in the way that only people who know too little can feel. I understood the following to be the case: legal immigrants have all the formal rights to the health system that Spaniards do; undocumented immigrants can access emergency care; if they are inscribed in the municipality as a resident, the undocumented can access the full package of care; in any case, children and pregnant women are covered. I was surprised therefore when early in my field research a Catalan official told me quite definitively: "Both legal and illegal immigrants have access to the public health care system. *There are no differences between them* on this point." I chalked up her apparent over-simplification to the fact that she was a public education official – not a health care expert – and/or to the excessive optimism she displayed throughout this interview that generally felt more like a public relations event. But, when my next interviewee – a reserved, senior official in the Catalan health department – told me just as definitively that illegal immigrants *only have a right to emergency care*, my own sense of confidence was shaken in the face of these two diametrically different stories, both of which conflicted with my prior understanding.

The confusion was cleared up a few days later when I visited a Barcelona neighborhood clinic. There I learned both the intricacies of the law, and, more importantly, its myriad opportunities for slippage. When I asked the doctor in charge of tropical diseases with whom I spent the morning, whether all immigrants have the right to health care, he answered carefully: "Yes, in the abstract, but there are gaps. The law seems straightforward in this regard, but many barriers exist." As I soon found out, immigrants' quest for health care resembles a frustrating treasure hunt, marked by false starts, misinformation, dead-ends, one-way streets, and narrow alleys.

From the bits and pieces I learned that morning from this doctor and, later in the day, from the administrator in charge of the clinic, this is the picture that gradually emerged.[46] For an undocumented immigrant, the first step to gaining access to the public health care system is to register as a resident at the local branch of the City Hall (these city offices are decentralized; in Barcelona, there are 132 district branches of the municipality where residents retrieve and submit birth certificates, death certificates, marriage licenses, residence certificates, and the myriad other certifications of daily life and death required by the modern state).

Registration with the city is the first in a series of potential administrative trapdoors through which the immigrant can fall out of the system. For one thing, particularly in the aftermath of Aznar's threatening Law 8/2000, many undocumented immigrants have well-grounded fears of turning themselves in to the local authorities. While some may feel comfortable enough to approach doctors at a clinic, getting access to those doctors is contingent on first going to the local authorities at City Hall, a potentially more threatening venue.

Those who overcome such fears face further hurdles, some comprised of the use and misuse of administrative discretion, others put in place by the regulations themselves, and all of which are conflated with and exacerbated by immigrants' illegality and economic marginality. When immigrants (or anyone, for that matter) apply for registration as residents of the city, they are asked for two sets of credentials: identity papers and validation that they actually live in the city. Identity papers – usually a passport – may or may not be available to immigrants, and in any case the request for them serves to heighten their anxiety. The residence validation is even more problematic because it requires: a fixed address; a papertrail to the fixed address (rental stubs, utility receipts, etc.); the appropriate number of people living at that address (e.g. no over-crowding); and a dwelling whose structure is up to regulation. As we will see in the following section on housing, many immigrants are homeless, live with relatives or friends and have no fixed address, live in over-crowded conditions, rent on the black market and thus have no formal lease or rent receipts, and/or live in substandard housing.

These requirements for registration are in some cases enhanced– against explicit regulations and directives – and in other cases waived altogether, with the consequence that immigrants' access to health care is largely determined by the particular "street-level bureaucrats" to whom fate (or, more precisely, the neighborhood they live in) has delivered them. In some districts, staff are sent out to verify the address of the applicant, the number of people in the household, and the conditions of the dwelling, although this practice appears to be dwindling for reasons of cost and feasibility. More to the point here, some districts require not just certification of actual residence, but *legal residence permits*, effectively nullifying the right of health care access to immigrants who are registered in the municipality independently of legal status. Despite a government directive in 1997 stipulating that municipalities must *not* require residence permits for this registration, of the 132 districts in Barcelona, 90 still require residence permits.[47]

At the other end of the bureaucratic street, some districts permit immigrants to register as "sin domicilio" (without residence) and to give the mailing address of a willing NGO or other institution. Thus, the clinic doctor explained to me that some districts in Barcelona allow people without a fixed address (or people who prefer not to give their real address) to use the address of the local branch of the National Institute of Statistics for the purposes of registration. The fact that the Institute is located in the same district as this clinic helps explain why their immigrant patient load is so heavy, since people are assigned to the clinic in their neighborhood. Some immigrants use the address of the clinic itself, and when the coveted health care membership card comes in the mail, the staff holds it for them. These practices of course depend on the good will of the local district officials and clinic staff who use their considerable discretion to override the logistical hurdles to registration – hurdles which others just as unilaterally, and presumably with just as much deliberation, pile up. In this regard, the administrator in charge of the clinic I visited volunteered that health centers' different administrative treatment of immigrants is "absolutely ideological."[48]

Assuming an immigrant manages to register, their next step is to apply for the health membership card, another opportunity for slippage. To secure this card, some districts require legal residency in addition to municipal registration – in apparent violation of the law – and some dismiss out of hand registrations that are listed as "sin domicilio." Others routinely process these "sin domicilio" forms in an administrative *legerdemain* that sidesteps the law's technicalities (for example, requiring a fixed address), thereby moving the immigrant one step closer to an actual medical visit.

Those who succeed both in registering and in securing a membership card proceed to their district clinic to get assigned to a primary care physician. This can be tricky even in clinics with the best intentions, and even for some legal immigrants and citizens. Assignment to a primary care physician – upon which most subsequent care depends – is typically based on one's social security number. While some experts are of the opinion that the social security number is no longer necessary, others point out that this requirement, located in the 1986 health law, has never been rescinded. My informant contended that since a 2001 government circular expressly made the social security number unnecessary for pregnant women and children, but conspicuously made no mention of changing it for other immigrants, the government meant to leave it intact.

Whatever the legal intent, health clinics across the country effectively devise their own policies in this regard. In some, people without a social security number are classified evocatively as "desplazados" (displaced, or out of place)[49] and provided with only emergency care, without access to follow-up visits or prescription drugs – that is, in the same category as people who are not registered at all. In others, such as the clinic I visited, the requirement for a social security number is often bypassed, but not without some deft bookkeeping.

The importance of this apparently mundane social security number requirement – affecting not only illegal immigrants but everyone who works in the extensive underground economy – can scarcely be exaggerated, as it brings together all the elements in this complex web of institutionalized irregularity, economic marginality, amorphous regulations, and informal lawmaking. At best, the mix spells a precarious and always fragile inclusion; at worst, it traps immigrants in a maze of information, misinformation and minutiae, and ultimately excludes them. As it turns out, both the public education official and the health expert I cited at the beginning of this section were probably right: immigrants have a broad legal right to health care, and at the same time have severely limited access to care.[50]

IMMIGRANT HOUSING AND THE LANDSCAPE OF MARGINALITY

As we have just seen, health care and housing intersect in both predictable and unexpected ways, with housing conditions substantially influencing health conditions, and the lack of a fixed address often precluding care. And, like health care, adequate shelter is a *sine qua non* of membership in these societies, with homelessness or grossly substandard housing a red flag of exclusion.

That flag is flying high. Immigrants in Spain report that housing is their most serious problem, even ahead of being paid a fair wage.[51] In Madrid, 64 percent of the people in homeless shelters are immigrants. SOS Racismo has documented numerous cases of landlords and rental agencies refusing to rent to immigrants.[52] Those who are able to find housing often must pay higher than market rents and get less than standard quality. In one large housing project with mostly immigrant residents in the center of Madrid, 10 percent of the apartments do not have bathrooms, 23 percent have no hot water, and 70 percent are in need of major rehabilitation.[53] In the mostly rural region of Murcia, a study in 1996 found that 34 percent of immigrant dwellings had no electricity, 36 percent had no running water, and 44 percent were without bathrooms.[54] The social exclusion attached to the inferior quality of immigrant housing is further compounded by spatial segregation. Immigrants are increasingly relegated to the less desirable urban peripheries and small towns surrounding major Spanish metropolises,[55] and within the urban centers they are concentrated in a few dense areas. In Barcelona proper, the vast majority of immigrants live in the four overcrowded urban neighborhoods that comprise the Ciutat Vella district, where the foreign-born comprise 23 percent of the population (compared to 7 percent for the city as a whole).[56]

Immigration experts in Italy concluded a study of housing there: "The foreigner who arrives in our territory finds a very different reception in the labor market than in the housing market."[57] As we saw in the last chapter, Italy has the highest rate of occupant-owned housing in Europe (and higher than in the US). The amount of public housing is correspondingly lower than in the rest of Europe, as is the total number of rental units (20 percent of the market, compared to the European average of 33.8 percent).[58] As a result, rents are exorbitant relative to pay scales, with disastrous consequences for people of low income, and with sometimes fatal consequences for immigrants.

According to the first annual report on integration in Italy, over 60 percent of immigrants said housing was their biggest problem in 2000, ahead of finding work or securing documents. Between 25 percent and 80 percent (depending on the region and city) of people in homeless shelters were immigrants, with their numbers and proportions growing.[59] The following year, the commission found that "vast areas of hardship persist" and that in some respects – most notably, the percentage of immigrant homeless– things had gotten worse.[60] An exhaustive study of immigrant housing in and around Milan, based on 2,500 views with immigrants, also found that the number of homeless those with "precarious" housing is increasing, and that the problem has spread to rural areas, small towns, and urban peripheries, where the greater affordability of housing had previously offered some protection. Half of the total population of homeless in Milan is immigrant, and immigrants constitute 80–90 percent of those who come to soup kitchens.[61]

Only about 30 percent of immigrants in Italy live in "normal" housing, defined as a fixed address with living conditions that meet safety standards and other regulations; 30 percent live in "precarious" and/or overcrowded conditions; and another 40 percent are dispersed in a variety of arrangements with no fixed address. Approximately one-quarter of this dispersed group rotate among relatives, one-fifth rent beds by the night, and the rest live in train stations, garages, farm structures, old railway cars, automobiles, and abandoned buildings.[62] In Rome, they live under the bridges of the Tiber River, each bridge hosting a different ethnic group – with one encampment of hundreds of Kurds set up "two steps away from the Domus Aurea."[63] Across the city, 400 African immigrants make their home in the old Tiburtina railroad station, now known as "Hotel Africa."[64] In Milan, shantytowns of cardboard shacks and container "trailers" – periodically cleared and relocated by city authorities – are home to thousands of immigrants and Roma people ("gypsies"). In "prosperous Parma" in Emilia-Romagna, immigrants build shantytowns under freeway overpasses and take refuge in railroad maintenance sheds.[65] Homelessness is not confined to single men without families either. When police raided an abandoned factory outside Milan where scores of immigrants were living, they were surprised to find middle-aged couples with children, and single women. Among them was a 51-year old former French teacher from the Ukraine who works in a Milan household as a domestic and returns to the factory to sleep at night, in a surreal reversal of the traditional home–factory commute.[66] Chinese children in a small town in Tuscany, when asked by their teacher to draw a picture of their house, replied that they did not have a house; when pressed to invent one for the sake of the exercise, the children could not even conjure one up.[67]

The profile is no better in Bologna or in the region of Veneto where so much integration work has been undertaken. In Bologna, with the most active immigrant housing program in Italy, almost 11 percent of immigrants say they sleep "wherever I can," 18 percent sleep in reception shelters, and overall 47 percent live in "precarious" housing.[68] Among immigrants who had been in Bologna ten years or more in the late 1990s, 30 percent still had no permanent address.[69] The affluent northeast, where Veneto is located, shares with the rural and poor areas of southern Italy the distinction of housing immigrants in the most "dilapidated" housing stock in the country.[70] One study, based on interviews with 140 heads of family in Schio (Veneto) found that these immigrants from Ghana, Senegal, Morocco, and the Balkans, 73 percent of whom had been in Italy five years or more, still had difficulty locating decent housing.[71] Immigrant factory workers in Veneto are said to use their first paycheck for a down payment on a used car to sleep in.[72]

Over-crowding is a chronic problem, as a press drawn to the sensational makes clear: 101 immigrant squatters crowded into an abandoned villa, 30 Chinese renting a two-room apartment, 59 immigrants from Bangladesh renting mattresses on the floor of three rooms, and 300 North Africans living in an abandoned factory so desolate it has been called "no-man's-land."[73] With 600,000 immigrants in Italy either without housing or living in such over-crowded spaces, there are warnings afoot of "grave repercussions for public order."[74] Not to speak of the more imminent repercussions for immigrants' life and limb, regularly reported in the press. Indeed, these conditions are usually raised to the level of newsworthy scandal only after the charred or frozen bodies are found.[75]

As in the realm of work, illegal status contributes to these housing problems. Since it is illegal to rent to the undocumented, they are forced onto the black market where rents are high and conditions deplorable. A Peruvian woman working as a domestic helper in Rome tells a common story about how she lost her live-in arrangement when she had her own baby:

> So I had to look for housing but if you don't have a pay-envelope ["busta paga" – in Italy, crucial evidence of a legitimate job] no one will give you a lease. So you have to rent on the black market: 300,000 liras [approximately $150] for a bed, usually 3 or 4 beds to a room... There were 12 of us in the house.[76]

Studies of housing in Milan and Bologna found a somewhat higher percentage of illegal immigrants than legal immigrants in such precarious conditions, but warn that the relationship should not be overstated.[77] The second annual report on immigrant integration concludes: "[T]here is a relationship between the quality of immigrants' housing situation on the one hand and their legality, stability, and insertion in the world of work on the other, but . . . the relationship is only a partial one." The authors continue: "Whenever a fire burns down a shack in which immigrants are taking shelter, it is discovered – with apparent surprise – that among the inhabitants are legal immigrants and immigrants who work."[78]

So, it is not just about legal status. The rents are unaffordable even for legal immigrants, whose meager wages must not only cover the already high Italian rents, but a premium as well. Indeed, the housing market is divided into two distinct niches – one for natives and the other "speculating on the needs of immigrants" – with 80 percent of the latter "underground."[79] The Director of the Integration Commission explains: "Many landlords are reluctant to rent property to foreigners, citing irregular income and poor maintenance of rental property." The result is "exorbitant rents being charged for dilapidated and crowded living accommodations."[80] In Florence, legal immigrants pay the equivalent of $300 a month for one bed in a crowded room, an arrangement the local director of Caritas remarks "is truly a form of extortion."[81] The fifty-nine Bangladeshis who slept on mattresses on the floor in three rooms near the Milan train station paid the "discount" rate of $150 each.[82] In Rome, a tiny apartment on the periphery costs Italians about $300 a month, while immigrants pay $450.[83] In some urban areas, rents for immigrants are as much as 60–70 percent above those for Italians.[84] A report by the City of Vicenza concludes that only 40 percent of immigrant workers in that area have sufficient income to pay rent, with even this conclusion probably overly optimistic.[85] Considering that immigrants earn an average income of 1.3 million liras ($650) a month, they would have to spend 90 percent of their paycheck to cover the average rent.[86] With penalties attached to immigrants' wages and a premium added to their rent, it is not surprising that so many are forced to set up house in the fields and under the bridges that they cultivate and clean by day.[87]

These legal and economic factors are enough to exclude most immigrants from decent housing, but they face straightforward racism and discrimination as well. Sometimes the discrimination comes in the form of higher rents, or renting by the person rather than by the apartment, to pay for anticipated "poor maintenance" – which in a self-fulfilling fashion is inevitable when people are forced to live cheek by jowl. Real estate agencies get into the act too, with an extra tax sometimes exacted on finding apartments for immigrants.[88]

It is not just that immigrants have to pay more. According to an immigrant advocacy group in Genoa, "Even immigrants who can pay a reasonable amount can't find housing."[89] In Brescia, a small city in the northeast, an NGO reports that it took them a year and a half to locate an apartment for a legal Pakistani immigrant family of three who had been in Italy for many years and who had full-time, long-term work.[90] The owner of a rental agency in Parma in the Emilia-Romagna region was arrested for having a sign in his window announcing, "We don't work with immigrants of color." He pleaded not guilty to charges of discrimination, saying, "I knew it was against the law, but the truth is I get complaints from landlords I send immigrants to. Out of 100 people we contract with who want to find tenants, 89 specify on the contract they don't want 'extracomunitari.'"[91] His claim is substantiated by findings from a study with a sample of 5,000 Italians in which only 22.2 percent of respondents disagreed with the statement, "If I had a house for rent, all else being equal, I would rent it to an Italian rather than an immigrant."[92]

Faced with obstacles of this magnitude, the national and regional housing initiatives launched under the rubric of integration fall far short. In 1998, it was estimated that there were 820 reception shelters for newly arrived immigrants in Italy with a total of 17,200 beds, but that the need approached 100,000. Rome alone received 16,000 new immigrants annually in the late 1990s, but had only 36 centers with 900 beds. Bologna, the avant-garde of immigrant housing programs, placed only 2,899 immigrants in these "centers of first shelter" ("centri di prima accoglienza," or CPAs) in the decade between 1990 and 2000. Only 1,962 of these residents ever left, and overall they stayed an average of five years in these "first" shelters.[93] With immigrants in Bologna allotted to CPAs by nationality and staying indefinitely, it is tempting to conclude paradoxically both that there are too few of them and that they themselves contribute to immigrants' social exclusion.

The spatial and symbolic segregation of these accommodations reaffirms this conclusion. As one in-depth study of a CPA described it:

> The area of the district where the CPA is located could best be described as 'first urban periphery'. However, within such an area, the CPA could be said to have a 'special' place. Such specificity consists of a quite evident isolation from the rest of the local residential area. In fact, the large car parking area for commuters, the heavily congested four-lane highway, another road edged by the high wall of an operating factory, and

115

ıltivated fields that constitute the immediate surroundings of the
e quite effective in providing a powerful sense of disconnection
ː nearest residential areas.[94]

A former staff member of ISI in Bologna described three CPAs for
Senegalese, Moroccans, and Pakistanis, respectively, as so over-crowded
"they should be immediately closed for health reasons." The field
researcher quoted above asked the operator of the CPA he was studying about its conformity with health and safety regulations, and the
administrator replied incredulously, "'In such a place?... You must be
kidding!" He explained to the researcher that CPAs have been designated "'exceptional residential structures' for which the regulations
about habitability do not apply."[95] A similar logic prevails in Veneto,
where a report by the City of Vicenza concluded that it would cost too
much to provide immigrants with housing of the "regular public housing type," and proposed instead "reducing costs by 50–60 percent and
incurring no costs of maintenance by using makeshift housing designed
to be used for 10–15 years and then thrown away."[96]

This spatial and social walling off of immigrant housing from "regular" housing is consistent with what Teresa Caldeira calls "a new pat-
tern of urban segregation." The "techniques of exclusion" she describes
in São Paulo and elsewhere are predicated on the fear of crime and on

the "discourses of fear" that fuel it, that are themselves the product of
broader political-economic changes. As Caldeira explains: "Both symbolically and materially, these strategies operate by marking differences,
imposing partitions and distances, building walls, multiplying rules of
avoidance and exclusion, and restricting movement."[97] Whether confined to over-crowded tenements and dilapidated urban shelters symbolically walled off from the rest of the city or dispersed in isolated
country fields, immigrants to Italy and Spain who have crossed one
set of borders confront another better-fortified and more daunting one
within.[98]

Spatial segregation inscribes into the territory immigrants' social
exclusion, as a kind of mapping of marginality – a marginality that
is at once exposed and enhanced by the *social* segregation of lowered
standards, "exceptional structures" and throwaway housing. Fabio Berti
uses the term "territorial marginalization" to refer to immigrants' residential relegation to the periphery of major cities and away from the
more prestigious historic centers.[99] But, the term might also be used to
describe this more general inscription of marginality into the territory

in the form of sometimes visible, sometimes less visible, third-world housing conditions, homelessness, and shelters walled-off by highways and industrial warehouses. In this context, it may be true that, as Castel has said, "The struggle against exclusion risks becoming a kind of social first aid." In the case of immigrant shelters and throwaway housing, the treatment risks compounding the injury.[100]

Inadequate housing and spatial segregation are the products of immigrants' legal and economic marginality, and one of the most tangible signs of the failures of integration. But, they also *reproduce* that marginality, as the crumbling and over-crowded Ghettos without gates that immigrants are confined to and the homelessness, crowding, and squatting they must resort to, reaffirm racialized fears about the "calamitous" effects immigrants have on the community. They not only are markers of integration's failure; they redouble the challenges.

STAKING A CLAIM: RESISTANCE, AGENCY, AND BELONGING

Marginalized work, inadequate health care, and substandard housing expose immigrants' exclusion and amplify their Otherness. Perhaps not surprisingly, work, health care, and housing are also central areas of resistance and claims-making. For, counterposed to the powerful structural, instrumental, and symbolic forces that marginalize immigrants are myriad *ad hoc* and institutionalized networks of immigrants, unions, NGOs and political opposition groups that contest that marginalization. It should not be missed that the most fundamental form of resistance to law's power is many immigrants' defiance of the laws that exclude them from the territory in the first place – a defiance that sometimes wins them legalized status and work permits, however temporary and precarious. Much like the Salvadoran immigrants to the United States in *Legalizing Moves*,[101] immigrants to Spain and Italy can sometimes turn the vagaries of the system to their own use and exploit its considerable contradictions, among them regular legalization programs and the begrudging nod to economic reality that they imply.

Also at the outset, the role of labor unions in fighting for immigrants' rights in both Spain and Italy – particularly the latter, where unions for decades have been a powerful social and political force – must be recognized. This struggle has been detailed elsewhere, as have its roots in leftist ideologies of solidarity, pragmatic calculations, and political strategy.[102] Unions' advocacy on behalf of immigrants has centered more on social issues – such as housing, health care, and legalization assistance – and less on labor issues per se; some commentators suggest that this underscores the perceived role of immigrants less as real workers than as socially and economically marginalized subjects in need of assistance.[103]

 That said, it is the hunger strikes, sit-ins, squatting, demonstrations, strikes, and organizing, by immigrants themselves that constitute the most direct, and increasingly visible, forms of resistance. Much of this activity is focused on the law, particularly in the aftermath of the Aznar and Berlusconi crackdowns. In Spain, tens of thousands of immigrants took to the streets to protest Aznar's Law 8/2000. The same day, up to 40,000 marched to the Interior Ministry in Barcelona and demanded that it revisit the cases of 34,000 undocumented workers who had been denied legalization in the previous round.[104] Weeks earlier, hundreds of people from sub-Saharan Africa, India, Bangladesh, Pakistan, South America, and Eastern Europe had gone on a hunger strike in the church of Santa Maria del Pi in Barcelona. Holding a placard declaring "Hunger Strike until Death," their demand was "work permits and legal residence for a dignified life."[105] In Almería, immigrants staged sit-ins at administrative offices and waged hunger strikes, demanding that an exception be made in the legalization process for those whose supporting documents had been burned in the El Ejido riots the year before, demands that ultimately met with success.[106] The following summer in Seville, as Aznar welcomed European leaders to an immigration summit there, 250 mostly Algerian immigrants occupied the university and went on a hunger strike for legalization, an event that was extensively covered in the media, and contrasted conspicuously with Aznar's confident rhetoric about integration and control at the summit meeting across town.[107]

In Italy, Chinese immigrants staged a large protest in Rome, charging discrimination against them in the processing of legalization applications.[108] Thousands of immigrants joined other protesters in massive demonstrations against the Bossi-Fini Bill when it was introduced in the Italian legislature; one immigrant carried a banner inscribed in bold letters, "Immigrants of the World Unite!"[109] Immigrant associations and NGOs pledged a boycott of the law, and organized a "Fingerprinting Day," flooding government offices with hundreds of fingerprints in a bitter mockery of the law.[110] In usually staid Vicenza, 8,000 immigrant workers left their jobs to join the protest against Bossi-Fini. One reporter, seemingly more taken with his own racialized depictions of the workers than with details of the event, called the protesters a "triumph of colors, a Babel of races." He continued:

> They march and sing the reggae notes of Bob Marley. But their thoughts are fixed elsewhere: the new Bossi-Fini immigration law, seen as a threat to their hopes of work and integration. It is the first strike of these new Cipputi[111] with their black, yellow, and brown faces. It has never happened before that immigrant workers in Italy . . . crossed their arms in defiance. And, now for eight hours [the factories where they work] . . . have had to do without those who someone recently baptized the 'new working class with the black face.'[112]

Another media outlet, less fixated on color tones and musical tastes, wrote of the immigrant workers blocking the factory gates, declaring "We are not slaves, we are honest workers, and we must have the same rights as you."[113]

Immigrants in Italy – especially factory workers – are increasingly likely to be members of labor unions, and there are signs that they might be an important component of the labor movement in the future.[114] Several months before the strike in Vicenza, all sixteen immigrant workers at a slaughterhouse near Lake Como went out on strike to protest violations of labor law in their plant, while the nineteen Italians in the plant kept working. For some immigrants, it was their first strike ever. As one worker from Senegal said: "It was [my first strike], and it was also for my colleagues from Morocco and from India, and we thought our Italian co-workers would join us . . . Oh well, it will be for the next time."[115]

Such strikes occasionally net at least modest success. At a recycling center in Bologna, forty-six workers from Senegal, Zaire, Angola, Peru, Tunisia, Rwanda, Bangladesh, and the Ivory Coast went out on strike in 1997 against the cooperative that paid them the equivalent of $4 an hour when it grossed almost $10 an hour per worker. The workers did seven-hour shifts without a break, were paid late, and few of them received a formal paycheck or enjoyed benefits. When they learned that all of this violated labor laws, they complained to their employers, and when threatened with a lock-out, staged a three-day strike and took to the streets. Aided by the CGIL union and supportive media accounts, new contracts were eventually negotiated, providing for salary increases, legitimate contracts for everyone, and the right to have an assembly of workers to help determine work rhythms and rest-break schedules.[116]

While labor agitation by immigrants in Spain is less frequent than in Italy – perhaps reflecting the lower profile of the labor movement there – periodic protests both by immigrant workers and by the unemployed underscore the progressive potential of this workforce. The Seville sit-ins discussed earlier, for example, began as a protest by several hundred North African farmworkers against the government/grower agreement to replace them with Eastern European women in the nearby strawberry fields. The strategy was widely seen as a racist effort to replace North Africans with Eastern Europeans, and, by hiring women who had left children at home, as a way to increase the probability of the workers' departure at the end of the season.[117]

Immigrants have been particularly active on the issue of housing. In Italy, demands for adequate housing date almost as far back as the first waves of immigrants in the late 1970s and early 1980s. As described in his ethnography of the Senegalese in Turin, Donald Carter says that they "were at the forefront of efforts to acquire proper housing for all migrants and in the end brought this matter to national attention."[118] The aggressive housing program in Bologna was initiated in response to squatters taking matters into their own hands and occupying abandoned schools and factories.[119] One episode in particular has become legendary in Bolognese accounts of immigrant squatting. In 1990, 400 Moroccans, including entire families, set up house in two large abandoned buildings in Via Stalingrado (Stalingrad Street), in an event that has gone down in local lore simply (and with deliberate irony) as "Stalingrad."[120]

In 1998, a hundred "extracomunitari" occupied the Basilica di San Petronio in Bologna to proclaim their right to housing.[121] Across the peninsula in Veneto, twelve immigrants – six with legal papers and six undocumented – after being evicted from their over-crowded apartment in Mestre and having the premises sequestered, staged a sit-in at the office of the neighborhood council. In Pisa, thirty mostly Senegalese immigrants slept in the streets to protest their lack of housing. The city had condemned their basement living quarters with two rooms and no bathroom, and they had sent a formal petition requesting alternative lodging. Receiving no answer, and in a city notorious for landlords who refuse to rent to "extracomunitari," the Senegalese set up camp in the streets.

In addition to these spontaneous acts of protest on particular issues, immigrant associations in every major city in Italy and Spain act as advocates and lobby the government for better housing, more access to health care, more liberal legalization, and a greater voice in policy-making. The Metropolitan Forum of Non-EU Immigrant Associations in Bologna, an umbrella group of fifty immigrant associations, has an informational website, offers free consultation by internet, accompanies people to the police station to process their documents, and helps locate housing and health care. But, their primary function is to lobby the government on behalf of immigrants to improve both formal law and its interpretation. Regarding the latter, as a staff member of the Forum told me: "Administrative officials dictate the law as they interpret it. If they are not informed, you can take it and go, or you can contest it."[122]

Women's associations are at the vanguard of these efforts. Orsini-Jones and Gattullo describe the reaction of immigrant women in Bologna when they discovered that there was a "discrepancy between ideology and reality" when it came to officials' support of integration, and that the City of Bologna did not always deliver on the reality side of the equation:

> The evidence collected shows that migrant women do not want outside assistance from the City Council anymore, they want to participate directly in the creation of the bodies or associations that will help them to live in Bologna. The first written evidence of this new drive and determination is the Manifesto they wrote on the occasion of the *Primo Incontro Nazionale tra le Associazioni di Donne Immigrate* ("First National Meeting of Associations of Migrant Women") held in Rome on 15 June 1995. This document was the first one at national [sic] level in which migrant women were proposing their own "agenda for living."[123]

The agenda prioritized legal status, social security protection, health care, family unity, stemming violence against women and children, and improvements in the labor market. According to Orsini-Jones and Gattullo, it has had some beneficial effects, including spearheading changes in the way immigrants are perceived and talked about – changes that are revealed in the language used in City Council literature.[124]

Another ethnographic study of Moroccan women in Bologna found that among their many strategies, these women consciously use the presence of the family unit, especially children, as a way to gain access to public housing and other social goods that allow them to

a "solid domestic stability" despite many deprivations and
ies.[125] Noting that Moroccans have been the protagonists
of the squatting movement, Decimo argues that Moroccan women's
strategic use of laws permitting family unity has had profound political effects, in part because Italians are reluctant to evict entire families
and throw them into the streets.[126]

In her study of Somalian women in Naples, Decimo reports that
they use "networks of solidarity" and "ethnic resources" not only for
their initial emigration, but for their survival in Italy and the success
of their immigration project, a project that includes, above all, remit-
tances home. Their collective action is less about political resistance
than it is about painstakingly garnering the resources and constructing
the networks necessary to defeat the long odds against them. As the
author describes it: "In this way there emerges an elaborate and informal network of relations that link Somalia with neighboring African
countries; Africa with the Arab countries; and, then, with Italy, Europe,
the United States, Canada, tracing a voyage that from the 'periphery'
leads to the 'center' of our 'world-system'. [In this way] a network of economic ties comes into being that is altogether invisible to the naked eye
of official statistics."[127]

It should be noted that not all immigrants are interested in integrating into these host societies. While they need access to basic social
services and amenities, many are less concerned with full insertion.
Like the Mexican "sojourners" in the United States described by Leo
Chavez,[128] many are there temporarily – or expect to be so – shuttling back and forth from their home countries like long-distance commuters, or making a one- or two-shot sojourn, and returning home,
or migrating elsewhere. For many, the stint in Southern Europe is
just as much about economic realities and juggling options without
over-committing, as it is for the local policymakers who only grudgingly welcome them and rarely commit to them permanently. The
"immigration shopping" among potential destinations some migrants
do might be thought of as the counterpart of the host societies' reluctance to give them a permanent home. Recounting the experience of
Cape Verdean women working as domestics in Italy, Jacqueline Andall
describes their efforts to "find a way around" abusive employers, with
their mobility (originally from Cape Verde, then from particular Italian employers, and sometimes from Italy) being their principal tool of
resistance.[129]

These myriad activities of resistance — large and small, organized and spontaneous — above all reveal the determination and agentive power of people who have journeyed across several borders already and who reject their assigned position as outsiders or outlaws. Some of these actions yield tangible results – new contracts, legalization, a better employer – and in the aggregate and long run, they no doubt will alter the way these "flexible," and only grudgingly welcomed, guests are perceived. In the meantime, as we will see in the next chapter, powerful cross-currents are at work.

DISCUSSION, AND A CAVEAT

Immigrants' illegality (and vulnerable legality), economic marginality, inadequate housing, and lack of access to health care, are each markers of social exclusion, and themselves compound that exclusion. Overcrowded and dilapidated housing, for example, both flags immigrants' Otherness and reinforces racialized fears. Further, these symptoms (and generators) of Otherness are interconnected, as institutionalized irregularity contributes to economic vulnerability, inadequate housing and health care. Illegal immigrants by definition must find work and housing on the black market where they are vulnerable to exploitation and extortion, and while they might have a right to health care in the abstract (through registration in the municipality), their lack of standard housing, their work in the underground economy without a social security number, and the whims of street-level bureaucrats, often nullify that right in practice.

Institutionalized illegality is in many ways a pivot here, but we should not overstate its significance. It is telling, for example, that *anyone* in the underground economy in Spain is at a disadvantage in the public health system where assignment to a physician depends on having a social security number. Rental housing in Italy is exorbitantly expensive and out of reach of *all* low-income earners. Wages are so low in the booming industries of northern Italy, and housing so expensive, that unemployed southern Italians remain home, unemployed. And, the infamous, post-Fordist hothouses around El Ejido employ Andalusian farmworkers as well as North African immigrants. Clearly, it is not only immigrants who are denied the vaunted entitlements of denizen status; they are joined in their journey to the margins by some with formal citizenship.

123

Donald Carter, in *States of Grace*, argues that in Italy certain "social problems...have come to national awareness through means of the arrival of newcomers, such as housing, health care, and abuses of labor practices."[130] In other words, the influx of immigrants has exposed social inequalities and wide gaps in the safety net that pre-date their arrival and continue independently of the immigrant presence. Before exploring fully the implications of this argument, one more piece of the picture must be filled in.

CHAPTER SIX

FUEL ON THE FIRE: POLITICS, CRIME, AND RACIALIZATION

Discourse on what we want them to be

Tahar Ben Jelloun begins the memoir of his immigration to France: "Often with immigration it's the aesthetics that cause problems. Immigrants are not photogenic, except in cases of tragedy, when their image is all over the newspaper. Their looks are not reassuring."[1] Integration programs partly constitute an effort to stave off the backlash against those who are not "photogenic," but who are nonetheless useful. The "aesthetic" problem *derives* from that utility, since by definition cheap and flexible labor bears the ugly stigma of poverty, a stigma that the social and spatial segregation described in the previous chapters draws attention to and enhances.

In this chapter, I follow through the logic of this disfiguring stigmatization and its unseemly consequences. For, immigrants are not just excluded, they are criminalized; they are not just different, they are dangerous. Above all, they are racialized. And, that racialization is part and parcel of the economics of alterité,[2] as those who at other times and in other places were themselves declared racially inferior now construct others in that role. The dynamic is at once structurally driven and fueled by politicians and a media that are drawn to, and make careers from, the frightening and the macabre. Tahar Ben Jelloun may be right, immigrants are only photogenic in cases of tragedy. But, given the saturation of the Spanish and Italian media with images of boat people, human smugglers, and African prostitutes, the tragedy is in part constituted by the images themselves.

I

R

PUBLIC OPINION POLLS AND ATTITUDES TOWARD IMMIGRANTS

It has become conventional wisdom in some quarters that Spaniards and Italians are more tolerant than their Western European neighbors. Sometimes attributed to their own historical experience of emigration and sometimes to the mellowing tonic of the Mediterranean climate, their relatively low xenophobia is consistently affirmed in surveys. In one study of attitudes toward immigrants conducted by a major Italian research foundation, Italians and Spaniards had lower anti-immigrant attitudes than citizens of any of the other participating EU countries (France, Germany, and Great Britain).[3]

But, beyond this broad-brush, relative tolerance revealed in polls, a number of interesting patterns can be discerned. For one thing, the low xenophobia levels displayed in such polls are *relative*. *Absolute* levels are fairly high, with almost one-third of Spaniards and Italians saying they "strongly agree" or "very strongly agree" with statements characterizing immigrants as threatening, harmful, or dangerous.[4] A Spanish study in 2000 under the auspices of IMSERSO developed an "index of xenophobia," and concluded from its survey that there is "a low level of xenophobia among the Spanish population."[5] But, there was an increase in 1999 and again in 2000, a trend the researchers note was associated with a rise in anti-immigrant violence and which they ascribe to political and media discussions surrounding reform of Law 4/2000 by the Aznar Administration. Indeed, the number of Spaniards who said there were "too many" immigrants in Spain shot up from 27 percent in 1999 to 40 percent just a year later.[6] "Constant references in the media to political discussions of reform," the authors argue, "together with continual media coverage of the arrival (massive?) of undocumented immigrants, produced a fertile breeding ground that . . . stimulated the verbalization of more xenophobic attitudes over the last two years."[7]

The EU study cited at the outset confirms this increase and shows that it exploded in 2001 and 2002. In 1999, only 10.6 percent of Spanish respondents agreed with the statement, "Immigrants are a danger to our culture and identity," less than half as many as among Italians, Germans, or French, and only one-third the number of English respondents who agreed. Three years later, the percentage of Spanish respondents agreeing with this "cultural threat" statement jumped to 25.8 percent, surpassing the percentage of Italian or German respondents who agreed (which in this same period declined), and narrowing the gap with the French and English. The percentage of Spaniards who b immigrants posed a threat to job security and to public safety *tripled* during this same period.[8]

Not all immigrants are equally worrisome of course, and not all of the socially rejected are immigrants. When respondents were asked to rank immigrants of various ethnic groups and nationalities on a scale from 1 ("very good") to 10 ("very bad"), Arabs and Muslims scored highest (that is, worst) on a par with Roma (who are usually not immigrants but are often included in such studies and always rank at the bottom). Russians were next, followed, curiously enough, by North Americans and Jews (the latter of whom are also not usually immigrants). "Black Africans" and Asians, in that order, were in the middle of the pack, with Eastern Europeans, South Americans, and EU members, respectively, thought of most favorably. As one person in the Andalusian province of Almería told an ethnographer: "Look, nobody would want to have immigrants as neighbors . . . one would always prefer Spaniards . . . but if you had a choice, better they be Latin Americans, who are more like us, or black Africans, who are good people, better than Moroccans or Algerians who are the dirtiest and most problematic . . . this is not just my opinion, it's the facts."[9]

Polls in Italy show roughly similar patterns. In a 2001 survey, 15 percent of the Italian respondents considered themselves "actively tolerant" of immigrants and diverse cultures, 54 percent were "passively tolerant," and 21 percent ambivalent, with 11 percent rating themselves "intolerant" (compared to an average 14 percent for other countries in the study).[10] In the EU study conducted by Diamanti and Bordignon, Italy ranked just above Spain on xenophobic attitudes overall, and Italian respondents scored lowest of all countries in the study on the two central questions of whether "immigrants threaten our culture and identity," and whether they "are a threat to job security." Italians also were the most "trusting" of people from "the third world." And, a higher percentage of Italians (72.5 percent) thought legal immigrants should have the right to vote in local elections.[11]

Furthermore, the level of Italian xenophobia, as measured in polls, has decreased since 1999, although the trend may be reversed in the wake of the Bossi-Fini law of 2002, as happened in Spain following Aznar's Law 8/2000. In the Diamanti and Bordignon study, Italian responses to *all* items showed a decline in xenophobia from 1999 to 2002 – that is, just after the liberal Turco-Napolitano Law was passed – a period during which scores for every other country in the study showed increases.[12] By 2002, immigration had fallen to seventh place among social problems cited by Italians as the most important (with just 18.7 percent calling it the major problem), down from third place in 2000.[13] But, even the relatively low 18.7 percent who call immigration the nation's major problem represents a significant level of alarm in a country where less than 4 percent of the population is foreign-born.

As further indication of this alarm, a study of 800 residents of notoriously progressive Emilia-Romagna found that while only 28 percent of respondents could mention "something they liked" about immigrants, 49 percent mentioned "something they did not like," including "their insistence and overbearance, their refusal to adapt to local customs, [and] their apparent connection with crime and various social problems."[14] Asked how many immigrants they thought were in Italy, respondents over-estimated by a multiple of six or seven. And, in a poll that questioned Italians on what should or could be done to keep immigrants out, 70 percent supported using the Navy for that purpose.[15] In another study, almost half of Italian respondents agreed with the statement, "The behavior of some immigrants can sometimes justify racist opinions" (another 20 percent shunted the question, choosing the diplomatic, "I don't know").[16]

When Italians were asked to rank eight groups on a scale from 1 to 4, with 1 indicating "not at all likeable" and 4 "very likeable," Filipinos/as (who in Italy are almost always domestic helpers) ranked highest, with 75.7 percent of respondents giving them a 4. The Senegalese came next, followed in order by Egyptians, Sri Lankans, Chinese, Moroccans, Albanians, and "gypsies," with the last two groups rated "not at all likeable" by 80.7 percent and 89.5 percent of respondents, respectively.[17] It is interesting to note that while Moroccans and Roma fare poorly on such scales in both Spain and Italy, Albanians – directly across the Adriatic Sea from Italy and the source of many refugees and so-called "boat people" – regularly join them at the bottom of the scale in Italian polls.[18] Also notable is the fact that this hierarchy – as in Spanish polls – does not consistently coincide with skin color, which is not to say that no racialization occurs, a point we will return to in a moment.

Answers to telephone surveys and other such polling devices are of course not straightforward or linear conduits through which to tap attitudes, compounded as they are by methodological issues of timing, format, and question bias, as well as by more fundamental factors such as respondent equivocation and self-censorship. But, at a minimum such polls indicate the number of people who at a given moment are willing to express particular sentiments. While Italians and Spaniards seem less likely to express intolerance than some other nationalities, one exception stands out: they consistently articulate a view of immigrants as prone to criminality and deviance.

In the Diamanti and Bordignon study, the percentage of Spanish respondents who agreed that, "Immigrants are a threat to public safety and personal security," went from just under 14 percent in 1999 to over 34 percent three years later, registering the largest increase, and the highest score, of any survey item. Italian respondents also ranked the threat immigrants pose to public safety above all other perceived threats, actually surpassing the Spanish, English, and German respondents on this item, and almost on a par with the (at least on this issue) fearful French.[19]

In a May, 2002 poll carried out by the research firm Opina, 60 percent of Spanish respondents said they believed immigrants were causing increases in the crime rate.[20] A Gallup poll the previous month found that 77 percent of Spaniards thought immigrants were a public safety problem.[21] And, in the IMSERSO study of Spanish xenophobia, 59 percent of respondents said immigrants increased crime.[22] Similarly, over 57 percent of Italians in a 2002 study agreed that "the presence of immigrants increases crime and delinquency," and when asked which categories of people pose a safety threat in their own neighborhoods, 21 percent said immigrants do (compared to less than 10 percent for "youth gangs," and 8 percent for "organized crime").[23] Independent research confirms that Italians connect immigration with increasing crime rates, and that they consistently view immigrants as potential delinquents.[24]

The notion that immigrants increase the crime rate persisted through the late 1990s at a time when immigration was increasing and the crime rate was declining, quite significantly in Italy and to a lesser extent in Spain.[25] Whatever the reality of the link between crime and immigration, the symbolic criminalization of immigrants is fueled by hot political rhetoric and a media that thrives on the heat, as we see in the next sections.

"RIDING THE TIGER" OF IMMIGRATION IN ITALY: POLITICS AND THE MEDIA

When nearly 1,000 Kurdish refugees made an emergency landing on the coast of Sicily in early 2002, it was called "manna from heaven" for the

Berlusconi government. Berlusconi had been advised to "ride the tiger" of immigration to win the elections of May, 2001, and the advice is widely credited as playing a part in his victory.[26] Local politicians from the Northern League and the National Alliance party had successfully used their anti-immigrant rhetoric in regional elections the year before, with the National Alliance candidate winning the provincial governorship in Lazio (the region where Rome is located) with his warnings about "wild clandestine immigration" and the "social deviance" he said it produces.[27] According to Loic Wacquant, "When a series of murders in Milan in 1999 set off a media panic over 'the criminality of immigrants', Mayor Gabriele Albertini and his Deputy Riccardo Decorato (from the National Alliance Party) went off to New York," to consult with Rudolph Giuliani.[28] Thus was born the Italian right's commitment to "zero tolerance," and electoral victory for Albertini and Decorato.

The Prime Minister continued to "ride the politics of fear,"[29] when the latest shipload of refugees landed. Announcing a decree that would allow the government to destroy vessels used for immigrant smuggling, he told Italians that they were on the verge of being pushed from their own country "by a wave of immigrants." "Nobody is thinking about firing cannons at a ship full of people," he told an interviewer, his words bristling with such antagonism it left people speculating that he had indeed thought of that, "but something has to be done."[30] Even the figurehead President of the Republic, the moderate Carlo Ciampi, got into the act, traveling to Morocco to deliver the message, "Italy is not America. It has a limited capacity to receive immigrants," words that probably had little effect on prospective immigrants but made headlines back home in Italy.[31]

Umberto Bossi and his Northern League (colloquially, "The League") are the unrivaled "political merchants of fear." As one journalist put it: "He [Bossi] aspires to a monopoly on a political product for which there will always be great demand. The Minister of Reform [Bossi] needs Italians' fear of the 'other' like the air he breathes . . . Fear is the resource he cannot do without."[32] Exploiting that resource to its fullest by referencing Albanians – one of the most demonized of all immigrant groups in Italy – The League plastered Milan before the 2001 elections with posters promising, "One more vote for The League, one less Albanian in Milan."[33] At the landing of the Kurds, Bossi exploded, "Enough immigration or it's all over!" And, "We cannot continue to tolerate disrespect for our laws." "The church criticizes us? Let them not forget that there are already people here who are making us take the crucifixes out of our schools."[34] "If I had my way, we would sink these smugglers' ships, blow them out of the water," he famously declared, conspicuously omitting the question of whether people would be on board.[35] Even before the Kurdish landings in 2002, Bossi could hardly contain himself: "We will make illegal immigration a serious crime . . . Stop treating illegal immigrants like normal people [*sic*]. Only people who have got work contracts can come in. And we need more cops on the borders, helicopters. *In America they shoot at illegal immigrants*."[36] On the issue of multiculturalism, Bossi was as usual sound-bite savvy: "Immigrants," he said, "bring with them a lot of cultural baggage that nobody can confiscate at the border."[37]

So inflammatory was Bossi and his Northern League during the period of the 2002 refugee landing that it was said to cause problems for Berlusconi. After all, while the politics of fear is a valuable product during elections, its shelf-life may be limited. As one journalist put it: "It is one thing to be the opposition or to be in an electoral campaign, and another to be the government. If you are governing, you can't continually fatten fear. You need normalcy to govern . . . A state of 'continual emergency' threatens the government's legitimacy." One way out of this dilemma was to let Bossi do the rhetorical iron-fisting, and then call him to task for it.

Whether they reflected a joint political strategy or a genuine rift between leaders trying to save their own skins, tense meetings were reported between Bossi and Berlusconi, with the former ridiculing the "crocodile tears" of his more moderate allies, and the latter making a loud point of trying to get the former to "lower [his] voice."[38] Lest anyone misinterpret Berlusconi's discomfort with Bossi's outbursts as disagreement, a Cabinet minister of Berlusconi's own Forza Italia party entered the fray, apologizing for Bossi's blunt language but not its substance: "True, sometimes his language is a little harsh, but he is basically right about immigration."[39]

Sometimes in the "harsh" language of Bossi and the Northern League, and at other times in the slick rhetoric of the tycoon Premier, the theme of immigrant criminality is returned to again and again. A League official wrote in the party's daily newspaper, *La Padania* (Padania is the name Bossi had given to the northern regions of Italy that at one period in his career he had urged to secede): "We Padanians are no longer having children, while immigrants, besides running prostitution rings and drug pushing . . . procreate at an exponential rate . . . This is not a xenophobic concern, but a real and spontaneous one."[40]

In May, 2002, Berlusconi held a high-profile press conference to announce a series of round-ups of petty criminals and immigrants, and in the process conflated the two. He labeled the initiative, as if it were a military exercise, "Operation High Impact." Eerily reminiscent of the "axis of evil" State of the Union Address by US President George W. Bush a few months earlier, Berlusconi called street criminals and undocumented immigrants "an army of evil . . . that lays in wait for citizens, who will be defended by the army of good." On May 15 and 16, 2002, thousands of police stormed designated neighborhoods in nineteen cities across the country, entering private homes, bars, restaurants, and pensions, and making 240 arrests, 166 of whom were immigrants. Most of the arrests were for suspected drug dealing and prostitution, or simply for being a "clandestino."[41]

With municipal elections scheduled for late May and early June, Operation High Impact was timed for high political impact. As the *International Herald Tribune* put it: "[A]ides to Berlusconi made no secret of the political nature of the anti-crime and anti-alien drive."[42] A cartoon in the Rome daily, *La Repubblica*, featured two fanciful creatures in front of a television, with one saying to the other, "The police have arrested some drug-dealers, a few prostitutes, and several clandestini," and the other responding, "I don't know about the citizens, but the exit polls are now safer."[43] Whatever its impact on the polls, the broader ideological significance of such a well-publicized initiative aimed generically at "criminals and immigrants" should not be missed. Besides putting hundreds behind bars and thus literally criminalizing them, Operation High Impact symbolically criminalized millions of others with its sweeping rhetoric.

Among the many verses to the steady "immigrants = crime" drumbeat is, predictably, one that links immigrants to sexual violence. The Governor of the Piedmont region, for example, declared unequivocally: "The reality is that besides problems that immigrants pose for our culture, there are also serious security difficulties, such as the increase in crimes of sexual violence . . . The exponential increase in prostitution is also testament to a grave social evil connected to immigration."[44]

Other verses imply that immigrants are either workers or criminals, justifying the Bossi-Fini connection between residence permits and work contracts and thus scoring two political points at once. The Minister of Social Affairs from the Northern League argued: "Those who come to Italy to work and not to commit crime, have a work contract."[45] In another context, he went on: "The clandestini are a threat to public order . . . Once a person's work contract has expired, he's got to leave."[46] (The most controversial requirement of the Bossi-Fini law – that all immigrants be fingerprinted – drew from, and not so subtly reinforced, this cognitive association of immigrants with criminality.) When robberies increased in a hill town north of Milan, local League politicians lost no time tying it to immigration: "This wave of crime began a few years ago with the flood of immigrants from the Slavic countries, the Balkans and Kosovo . . . We need to eliminate this wildfire influx and let in only those who come to work, not those who come to commit crime." The Northern Leaguer who planned to run for mayor of the town concurred: "It's not as if this influx of illegal immigrants has been a good thing for us . . . When it comes to crime, often they are armed and we are just defenseless citizens."[47]

Yet another verse draws from the September 11 terrorist attacks in the United States. The Interior Minister took the lead, linking immigration to the "destabilizing" effects of terrorist attacks.[48] A rally was organized by the Northern League outside a mosque in Milan, with a placard prominently displayed: "Get the Terrorists out of Milan."[49] A League leader attended the press conference accompanying the opening of a mosque in Rome, contending that it would be "the headquarters of Islamic expansion in Europe," while a Parliamentary ally joined a group of conservative Catholics to pray for "protection" from the Mosque.[50] As one journalist observed of the scene throughout Europe in this period following September 11: "The Pat Buchanans of Europe are having a field day."[51]

There are of course alternative political visions. The Secretary of the new Communist Party announced that party officials would march against the Bossi-Fini Bill, and expressed his solidarity with immigrants: "We Communists will use all means that Parliament allows to keep from insulting [with this Bill] all the thousands of immigrants who live and work honestly in our country."[52] The leftist mayor of Rome joined demonstrators condemning the Bossi-Fini law and supporting the "anti-racism" of the rally; the governor of Campania was there too, declaring it his "institutional duty" to show solidarity with immigrants and others protesting the law.[53] But, these quiet voices are barely heard over the bombastic sound bites of Umberto Bossi and his ilk. Not even Berlusconi himself gets the media coverage of Bossi and The League on the subject of immigration.

The powerful allure of Bossi for the mass media is not surprising given the latter's ineluctable attraction to the perverse, the scary, and the hyperbolic. Indeed, the mass media in Italy – including the few major outlets not owned outright by the billionaire Prime Minister – are witting or unwitting coalition partners on this issue, helping fuel the fear on whose back Berlusconi and Bossi rode into office. The media appear to be obsessed with the topic of immigration, probably helping account for the over-estimates of the size of the immigrant population that Italians consistently give to pollsters.

Despite its frequency, media coverage of immigration rarely touches the daily reality of immigrants. Instead, the images lean toward "boat people," "clandestini," smugglers, prostitutes, drug traffickers and other criminals, and, especially since September 11, the rise of Islam in Italy. As an Italian scholar of the mass media has put it, the media deal not in the "normalcy" of "the everyday," but in "the exceptional, the abnormality of the real."[54]

It is true that many immigrants enter Italy clandestinely by boat. In the first half of 2002, more than 50,000 people were intercepted trying to enter Italy by sea (compared to under 17,000 in the first half of 2000), and another 14,000 were successful.[55] Italy's vicinity to Albania, just seventy miles across the Adriatic, makes it a particularly tempting destination. Many do not survive the hazards of the crossing, the ruthlessness of some smugglers, and the increasingly aggressive tactics of Italian law enforcement. One journalist described the perils:

> The operators of high-speed boats transporting migrants to Italy have become more brazen about ramming Italian naval and police boats and dumping migrants overboard – at least 200 migrants have died at sea off Italy, either in collisions or after being thrown overboard by traffickers. In August, 2000, Albanian traffickers reportedly threw overboard between 40 to 60 Chinese to protect the glass-fiber hulls of their dinghies from the rocks; two drowned.[56]

In June, 2003, approximately 200 Africans headed for Italy drowned when their over-crowded boat sank near the coast of Tunisia, in one incident doubling the year's mortality estimates for these treacherous sea-crossings.[57] Months later, twenty-one Albanians who had paid the equivalent of $2,300 each for the short trip across the Adriatic, drowned when their boat sank in stormy weather and twenty-foot waves.[58] It is easy to understand the media's attraction to such modern-day morality plays, with their compelling components of excitement, fear, cruelty, and death. But, continually dwelling on these "photo-genic" tragedies,[59] to the exclusion of the more mundane realities of immigrants' lives, paints a grossly distorted picture. While most undoc-umented immigrants enter Italy through airports as tourists and over-stay, or come with work contracts and end up in the underground econ-omy, the relatively few "clandestini" who slip across the border at night or come ashore on speed-boats and fishing vessels, are portrayed as the prototypical undocumented immigrants.[60] The Italian Commission for Integration Policies summarized the effect of this focus:

> Probably the mass landing of "clandestini", who, however, represent only the tip of the iceberg are one of the elements of foreign immigration that most strikes a nerve and grabs the collective imagination, especially for the resonance that it gets in the mass media: It will be difficult for several generations of Italians to forget the image of dilapidated boats bringing hundreds of desperate refugees to our shores.[61]

Indicative of this single-minded media focus, a search of the Inter-net revealed 66,400 entries for "clandestini" and a paltry 763 for the far more numerous "immigrati illegali."[62] Indeed, the word "clandes-tini" – with its evocation of secrecy, deceit, and intrigue – has become the generic term for all illegal immigrants. In this semantic slippage, undocumented immigrant and scary deviant become synonymous.

Quantitative research on immigrants in the Italian media confirm this reading. Massimiliano di Massa conducted a content analysis of daily newspapers in Genoa in 1989, and, based on that analysis as well as on an overview of academic studies throughout the 1990s, concluded that a "vicious circle" of media representations and public opinion shores up stereotypes of immigrants. Alberto D'Elia's content analysis of the two major newspapers in the southern Italian region of Apulia over a four-month period in 1996 found that, of the more than 200 articles about immigration, 78 percent dealt with crime, with the next most common theme occurring less than 15 percent of the time.[63] The most systematic academic study to date was carried out under the auspices of the research group, Censis. In an exhaustive content analysis of television programming from January to Septem-ber, 2001, the researchers found that by far the most common topic involving immigrants – representing 56.7 percent of the coverage – was crime (compared to a mere 13.3 percent for the second most com-mon topic, "welfare/solidarity"). Of the 1,230 articles about immigra-tion or immigrants in the sixteen major national and local newspapers in the same study, crime was "by far the dominant topic."[64] The authors conclude that the media "play mirror games with the supposed 'moods' of the masses . . . In the mirror game . . . a journalist is on the one hand in the position of interpreting feelings of fear and social mistrust and on the other – sometimes against his or her will – of stoking them up."

As we have seen, this simultaneous "interpreting" and "stoking up" applies not just to the media but to political rhetoric as well. And, of course, Italians have no monopoly on the game.

"AZNAR SPEAKS: 'TOUGH BATTLE AGAINST THE CLANDESTINES'"[65]

The Spanish are fond of saying that they have no extreme right-wing national political party, or xenophobic spokesmen like Umberto Bossi in Italy or Georg Haider in Austria. But, Prime Minister Aznar and his Popular Party, and various local and regional parties, easily rival Berlusconi's anti-immigrant rhetoric, and indeed some sound like the extremists whom Spaniards presumably eschew. At the head of the list is Mikel Azurmendi, director of the national agency for immigrant integration. An Aznar appointee, Azurmendi routinely denounces multiculturalism, and has authored a controversial book about the El Ejido riots that many experts contest as anti-immigrant propaganda.[66]

At the local level, Jesus Gil takes up the mantle of xenophobia in Andalusia, where he is mayor of the Costa del Sol tourist town of Marbella. An entrepreneur and ex-president of the Madrid soccer team who has been plagued by a variety of financial corruption scandals and only relatively late in life turned to politics, Gil is frequently compared to Berlusconi. His new-right party, the Gruppo Independiente Liberal, won local elections in Ceuta and Melilla in the summer of 1999 and has since extended its popularity into Malaga and Cadiz.[67] Gil's political success is attributed to his name recognition in soccer circles and to his undisguised disdain for immigrants, whom he refers to unapologetically as "wetbacks."

Gil's counterpart across the sea in the Canary Islands, the Popular Party mayor of Las Palmas, says that locals have been "infinitely patient" but that the immigration situation is "unsustainable." He told the reporter: "If you tell me I am a xenophobe for saying it is not the same whether they come legally or illegally, I will answer that there are 500 million sub-Saharan Africans who want to come to Spain."[68]

But, it is Aznar himself who sets the tone. Like Berlusconi, Aznar has used the issue of immigration to considerable political advantage, and in turn has used his office to amplify the debate. In one of his first speeches to Parliament after his re-election, Aznar emphasized the limited capacity of Spain to receive immigrants, and stressed the need to give the government free rein to deport criminal aliens. It is necessary, he said, to establish "respect for the discretion needed to control these mafias and certain illegal aliens in Spain."[69] The hyperbole surrounding Aznar's campaign to reform the immigration law is widely thought to account for the abrupt shift in Spaniards' attitudes about immigration from 1999 to 2000 and beyond. As an official at IMSERSO told me: "Immigration used to be considered a 'phenomenon.' This government has convinced people it is a 'problem.'"[70]

Aznar, together with Berlusconi, formed a block at the Seville EU Summit in June, 2002, against what they alleged were the "permissive" immigration proposals of their neighbors. On a trip Aznar made to Rome just before the summit meeting, he and Berlusconi declared themselves in "full harmony" with regard to fighting "clandestine" immigration. Aznar told the Italian press that illegal immigration must be "combatted decisively," because "illegal immigration generates criminal networks and mafia rings that traffic in human beings."[71] As usual, he drew a sharp distinction between legal and illegal immigrants, hailing the former and demonizing the latter. It is wrong, he said, to think of "legal immigrants and clandestini" as in any way the same. "These masks have to fall [because it is] absolutely unacceptable that legal immigrants have to pay for [the problem of] clandestine immigrants and the mafias that profit from them."[72] Playing on fears generated since September 11, he declared: "Immigration and terrorism not properly dealt with, have generated radicalism."[73] The following month, in his annual state-of-the-union debate with the opposition, Aznar dedicated a large portion of his remarks to a further toughening of the immigration laws, a theme he peppered liberally with references to immigrant criminality and the presumed link between illegal immigration and various "mafias."[74]

The media concentration on "boat people," their crimes, and the tragedies that beset them is even more pronounced in Spain than in Italy. With the Strait of Gibraltor separating Spain from Morocco by just nine miles, and with two Spanish enclaves – Melilla and Ceuta – surrounded by Moroccan territory, the trip across the Strait is a common way to enter Spain from North Africa. Another common

ırticularly since Melilla and Ceuta have been equipped with
ınology surveillance and fortified with intimidating walls and
....y weaponry,[75] is from Morocco to the Canary Islands across
seventy miles of Atlantic Ocean. In both cases, immigrants cross on
flimsy rubber "pateras" built for eight people, but often weighed down
with forty. Between 1997 and 2002, over 4,000 people died or disappeared trying to make the journey across the Strait of Gibraltor or to the
Spanish Canary Islands.[76] With up to a thousand bodies washing ashore
each year in southern Spain, and many more unaccounted for, immigration scholar Wayne Cornelius points out that this crossing exacts a
death toll more than twice as high as the treacherous mountains and
desert of the 2,000-mile US–Mexican border.[77]

The crossings, the captures by law enforcement, the militaristic forti-
fications of Ceuta and Melilla, and the deaths, make for high drama, and
provide the most common images of immigrants and immigration in
the Spanish media, despite the fact that far more immigrants – including illegal immigrants – arrive through Spain's busy airports.[78] Indeed,
the "patera" has become the iconic symbol of immigration in Spain.
The images are at once horrifying and, by now, numbingly recurrent.
Under the headline, "No One Wants to Live in Morocco," and with
a large photograph of a dead North African washed up on a Spanish
beach, the national daily, El País, ran a three-page story in its Sunday
edition detailing the perils of the trip and the desperation of Moroccans to make it anyway.[79] Each capture brings its own story, more
often than not replete with wrenching photographs of the dead and
dying.[80]

Biological metaphors abound. Articles in El País speak ominously of
a "rising tide of immigration."[81] As a number of Spanish social scientists have pointed out, the use of terms like "'currents', 'avalanches',
'floods', and 'waves', suggests that immigration is irrational and uncon-
trollable," and certainly dangerous.[82] Referring to immigrants as human
"merchandise" and "cargo," race is often a sub-text.[83] The entire front
page of a Catalan weekly featured an inflammatory cartoon drawing
of a smuggler breezing by Customs agents in an oversized trench coat
under which, besides his own well-shod feet, could be seen several
pairs of bare, black feet. The headline screamed, "CARAVANS OF
SLAVES."[84]

As in Italy, crime and public safety are prominent themes, and are
often transparently racialized. Photographs of a North African lurking

behind a doorway holding a long knife, or bedraggled sub-Saharan Africans standing beside their "patera" in handcuffs, are ominous images to people already predisposed to fear immigrants as criminal.[85] When Aznar, like Berlusconi before him, announced a crackdown on – in one breath – "crime and illegal immigration," it made the headlines of *El País*, the independent newspaper once associated with the Socialist Party: "Aznar Proposes Tougher Laws against Delinquency and Illegal Immigration."[86] Even articles that criticize the stereotypes of immigrants as criminals sometimes carry headlines that send quite a different message. Above a picture of North Africans handcuffed on a beach, the headline of one article *condemning* the stereotypes read, "An Increase in Delinquency: Perpetrators and Victims of Violence."[87]

To recap, at the same time that official policies in Spain and Italy talk of the need to integrate, immigrants are marginalized in the national discourse through political rhetoric and a mass media that associate them with chaos, drama, and, above all, crime and illegality. Thus, not only are immigrants excluded from basic services as we saw in the last chapter, but their criminalization sets them apart symbolically, amplifies their Otherness, and invigorates the structural forces working against their integration. As we will see in the next section, their criminalization is not confined to perception or discourse alone.

CRIMES OF THE OTHER

Plenty of evidence seems to validate fears of immigrant crime. In Spain, the proportion of the prison population who are foreigners is over *twenty-five times* higher than the proportion of immigrants in the population.[88] And their ranks continue to swell, with the number of immigrants detained by Spanish police jumping by more than 42 percent between 2001 and 2002.[89]

But, these statistics need to be carefully unpacked. For one thing, the 8/2000 immigration law for the first time provided for the incarceration of undocumented immigrants for the sole offense of not having residence permits, and by 2002 almost half of all immigrant detentions were for such administrative violations.[90] More subtle than this criminalization of illegal status is the general stigma attached to third-world migrants. Manuel Delgado, a professor of cultural anthropology at the University of Barcelona, explains that this stigma produces a heightened visibility. Arguing that immigrants are not accorded the privilege of fading into the background, Delgado contends that even those who want to be "tolerant" think:

> Look at him! He is over there, let's watch him closely and let's try hard to understand him . . . to open ourselves to him, to tolerate him, to accept him . . . But . . . be careful, never take your eyes off him.[91]

This cognitive phenomenon by which our attention is drawn to those who are constructed as different, results, says Delgado, in disproportionate police activity and subsequently in criminalization, particularly in a context in which some nationalities are already thought to be predisposed to crime. It should come as no surprise that Moroccans are particularly susceptible to the law-enforcement gaze. In the late 1990s, investigations were launched in the cases of several Moroccans imprisoned for serious crimes who, it now seems, were falsely convicted. In one case investigated in 1997, two Moroccans had been in prison since 1991 on 150-year sentences for a series of sexual assaults, despite contradictions in victims' testimony and identification problems.[92] The newspaper editorial on the case's reopening – and the xenophobia that the editor suggests contributed to the original convictions – ran the headline, "Moroccans Under Suspicion."[93] Since then, Moroccans and other Muslims have come under even more suspicion, as the Spanish police carry out mass arrests of suspected terrorists.[94]

In Italy, immigrants – representing less than 4 percent of the population – comprised 30 percent of the 57,000 people in prison in 2001,[95] and, in some regions, over 50 percent of prisoners were immigrants.[96] But, few believe that such statistics draw an accurate picture of immigrant criminality. Even the Minister of the Interior (responsible for law enforcement) warns that incarceration statistics provide "an overestimate of the relative rate at which immigrants commit crime." "All else being equal," he says, "foreigners end up more frequently in our prisons than Italian citizens."[97] He points out that most prison inmates are there under preventive detention, and that a far larger percentage of immigrants than Italian citizens fall into this category, because they are more likely to lack the community roots and family networks that are assumed to reduce pre-trial flight risks.[98] And, in a country that makes heavy use of house arrest as an alternative to prison, many immigrants are imprisoned because of the absence of housing or a fixed address to which they can be confined as an alternative to incarceration – exposing the concrete connections between economic marginality (resulting in exclusion from the housing market) and criminalization, with its attendant forms of moral stigma and social exclusion.[99]

Looking at arrest statistics, the discrepancy is even more pronounced, at least for certain categories of crime. Nationally, immigrants make up 56 percent of those accused of prostitution (and 62 percent of the women), 44 percent of those accused of carrying contraband, 40 percent for theft, 29 percent for drug offenses, 28 percent for robbery, and 21 percent for sexual violence.[100] Immigrant children under the age of 14 make up approximately half of all police stops of juveniles in that age category; and, for youth between the ages of 14 and 17, they comprise about 20 percent of police stops.[101]

As Giovanna Zincone suggests, these statistics too "need to be interpreted with extreme caution."[102] Dal Lago speaks of the "hostility against foreigners reflected in the daily practices of the . . . justice system."[103] Melossi summarizes data that suggest that, all else being equal, the police in Emilia-Romagna stop and question immigrant men far more often than they do Italian men.[104] Lagazzi *et al.* conclude an empirical analysis of law enforcement against suspected drug-dealers in Genoa, arguing that a bias against immigrants leads to their disproportionate arrest and prosecution.[105] A police officer interviewed by a reporter suggests that this bias is the same that pervades the culture at large. In his words:

> From the newspapers, one learns that immigrants are all criminals. To this, one should add the fact that the police officer categorizes the world between suspects and non-suspects; and that for him [*sic*] to find a foreign drug dealer in the street is the simplest thing of all. Then we can start to understand why the courts are replete with foreigners.[106]

Once in court, immigrants are as much as five times more likely than Italian citizens to be convicted.[107] Dal Lago quotes lawyers and magistrates who speak to the processes that produce these discrepancies, including stereotypes, language difficulties, immigrants' lack of resources, and their reliance on public defenders. In the words of a lawyer in Genoa, eventually the bias gets routinized and normalized:

> At a certain point the foreigner has become objectively criminal . . . What I want to say is that at a certain point the immigrant, foreigner, "extracomunitario," came to be associated with the idea of latent criminality [and] the "foreigner" and the "deviant" in that moment became one and the same.[108]

Dal Lago concludes: "[T]he statistics that indicate an increase in the number of immigrants stopped, arrested, convicted, and imprisoned, do not reveal a greater propensity for crime, but a real and true 'penalization' of immigrants." He rues: "Many immigrants, *as such*, have found prison the inevitable destination of their migratory experience."[109]

Of course, the existence of bias does not mean that immigrants do not commit crime, nor even that they do not commit a disproportionate amount of crime. The Commission for Immigrant Integration reports that, in northern Italy, criminal activity by immigrants does appear to be higher than for Italians.[110] Dario Melossi points out that some people may immigrate for the purpose of committing crimes much as others come for the conventional labor market.[111] Others may be induced into crime by desperate circumstances after they arrive. As the Commission for Immigrant Integration says: "Deviance may represent one of the only avenues open to immigrants in the absence of the possibility of integration into society."[112] Interestingly, it appears that even in the realm of crime, immigrants are not thoroughly "integrated," in the sense that "just as in the regular economy they tend to cover the lower ranks, being willing to take jobs at the base of the 'legitimate pyramid', they are also disposed to substitute for Italians at the base of the 'penal pyramid' . . . in the lowest ranks of urban delinquency."[113]

With regard to high official rates of juvenile delinquency among young migrants, "Psychological distress [associated with immigration], social insecurity and the precariousness of the economic situation in which many foreign youths live seem to bring a considerable risk of falling into criminal behavior."[114] As Roberto Bergalli puts it, in this context the criminal justice system acts as a kind of "sponge" absorbing more "profound social problems."[115]

Melossi cautions too that the "somatic markers" associated in the public mind with drugs and prostitution may exert a gravitational pull on some groups and, through this labeling process, produce a "vicious circle." A Moroccan youth interviewed by Melossi tells this story:

> Last Saturday I was at the IPERCOOP [supermarket] all dressed up with my friends and a young guy approached me and said: "I want to ask you something, I am looking for a job in the black market"; I tried to tell him that he would only be exploited, and he said: "No, I am talking about dealing drugs." He saw me well put-together and well-dressed and he deduced the wrong thing.[116]

Asher Colombo collected oral histories of young Algerian men in Milan who were involved in a variety of petty crimes in 1993 and 1994, and found that one self-narrative of the entrance into crime had to do with dashed hopes and anger at mistreatment. The following story of one of these young men reveals the interaction of stereotypes and legal status and its precariousness, and affirms the "vicious circle" described by Melossi. The story is worth quoting at some length:

> In the summer of 1991, together with seven or eight other Algerians, we moved back to Greco's dairy farm, where we had lived between 1989 and 1990. One day, towards evening, a police patrol arrived in order to make a search, thinking they were going to find drugs, which of course they didn't. They asked us for our papers, identity cards and residence permits, and we were all thoroughly examined. It was then that I exploded in exasperation. I said that we were already penniless, jobless and homeless; now we couldn't even sleep in peace because they wanted to come and bust our balls. So one of these cops, who I'll never forget, and who I've seen several times since, took me aside, brought me into another room and said, "You have your residence permit?" [I said] "Yeah," [He said] "Well, you can stick that permit up your ass." And saying that, he tore up the paper right in front of me. Then he went back and said to us: "Anyone here without a residence permit?" Whoever said they didn't have a permit got a piece of my ripped-up document. From that moment I said: "OK. You want me to be illegal? You don't want me to have a residence permit? OK, that's the way it will be." And from that moment on I began stealing for real![117]

Narratives like this may of course be self-serving or rationalizations, but they nonetheless underscore the prominence of legal status and "papers" in migrants' daily consciousness, the perceived hostility with which they are treated by law enforcement, and the subjective link between those perceptions and subsequent crime. Having been "written off" or "expunged" from legitimate social existence by the withdrawal or withholding of validating papers, these immigrants retaliate by fulfilling their assigned role as outlaws.[118]

Of course, too, immigrants are usually young men (with women now beginning to close the gender gap), a category that is more disposed to crime in every population. Whatever the causal factors that produce immigrant crime – demographics, labeling, hostility over mistreatment, economic desperation, or psychological distress – one thing is clear: it draws a disproportionate response from law enforcement and in turn reaffirms collective stereotypes of the immigrant as a potential criminal. As Melossi has put it:

> The stranger, being already at fault for his strangeness . . . will easily be the target for suspicion of all kinds of deviant and criminal acts. If only some stranger will engage in such acts . . . the viciousness of the circle will be perfect and the stranger will be found doubly guilty, for his strangeness and for his deviance.[119]

A rich literature traces the use of the criminal justice system to mark off a group as Other and in the process define our own identity. Young and Simon, for example, have both discussed the "outlaw as other." And, Young describes the social exclusion of these Others as a counterproductive effort at community building.[120] Similarly, Chia-Wen Lee situates the current American "war on terrorism" within a history of "making America [American national identity] through crime and justice."[121] In the context of immigration, this mutual constitution of the criminal, the "Other," and "us," is particularly potent, and, as we will see, is inevitably shot through with race.

RACE, EXCLUSION, AND AESTHETICS

I began this book with descriptions of mob violence against immigrants in the small towns of El Ejido, Spain, and Salandra, Italy, and suggested that racism lies at the heart of such anti-immigrant frenzies. It not only fuels the outbursts, it rationalizes them after the fact and mitigates official sanctions against the perpetrators. At least as important, racism fuels, rationalizes, and mitigates reactions to the kind of everyday exclusions described in the previous chapter.

Critical Race Theory explains that race – or perhaps more accurately racism – is socially constructed.[122] While there are all kinds of phenotypical differences among us, the social meaning of those differences, their groupings, and their hierarchical arrangement – their racialization – are constructed through the interaction of social, economic, political, and ideological processes, comprising "sociolegal webs of domination and subordination."[123] Ian Haney Lopez describes race thinking as akin to "common sense" in that "most people treat racial beliefs as timeless truths."[124] As Omi and Winant say in their discussion of race in the United States, "Race is not an essence. It is not 'something fixed, concrete, and objective'." Instead, it is "a set of social meanings," woven from the fabric of social and economic life.[125]

These social processes are so powerful that phenotypical rationales for the groupings often disappear altogether, exposing the arbitrariness of the labels, or at least their independence from any objective or natural reality. Ignatiev highlights this arbitrary quality of racial categories in his study of Irish immigrants to the US: "No biologist has ever been able to provide a satisfactory definition of 'race' – that is, a definition that includes all members of a given race and excludes all others." Noting that Catholics in nineteenth-century Ireland were considered a distinct race (Celts or Gaels) and that Irish immigrants to America were called "niggers turned inside out" (and African Americans were "smoked Irish"), Ignatiev traces Irish immigrants' simultaneous social and racial upward mobility.[126]

Contemporary immigrants in Italy and Spain are racialized through several interrelated processes, the broad outlines of which are similar to those of previous times and places – including those that applied to Spanish and Italian migrants to America and northern Europe less than a century ago. Among these processes is the criminalization described above. Citing Goffman, and turning on its head Dal Lago's critique of the treatment of immigrants as "non-persons," Delgado notes: "The vast majority of people we come in contact with in public spaces are . . . 'non-persons,'" in the sense that they are merely "extras" on a set and thus enjoy the absence of scrutiny.[127] But, the stigma of difference marks non-EU immigrants as highly visible Others who are not only suspicious by virtue of their difference, but *conspicuous* in their strangeness. According to Delgado, "This is the primordial act of racism of our day, denying certain people . . . the possibility of passing unnoticed."[128] Subject to economic marginality and its myriad deprivations, assumed to be prone to crime, and always in the spotlight, immigrants' criminalization is over-determined by a factor of three, with the common denominator being their racialization.

The racialization is sometimes transparent, as when the news media link African immigrant women with the sex trade. One Italian newspaper article, complete with photographs of African women walking the streets of Rome in mini-skirts, begins: "Slaves. To find them you do not have to look in history books . . . Because in Rome in 2002, in front of our houses, 3,500 women live in conditions of slavery . . . They have a price, they are sold at auction . . . In Rome the majority are Nigerians, more than 15 percent [sic], at least 600 women."[129] More often, it is subtle, hovering beneath the surface of the collective stereotypes and attendant exclusions that lead to prison for so many and that symbolically criminalize so many others.

Criminalization is a symptom of immigrants' racialization, and at the same time feeds it. But, the building blocks of racial construction are more generic, and are alternately located in perceived somatic markers, definitions of non-Western culture, and objectification. Somatic markers have long been thought of as the defining components of race. As Omi and Winant put it: "Racial beliefs operate as an 'amateur biology,' a way of explaining the variations in 'human nature.' Differences in skin color and other obvious physical characteristics supposedly provide visible clues to differences lurking underneath."[130] So it is that a regional deputy in Aznar's Popular Party speaks generically of immigrants as "moros" (a perjorative word for Moors/Arabs) and "morillos" (little Moors); the owner of a television channel in the Canary Islands remarks: "The blacks bring in drugs and trash . . . We will get rid of these people, even if we have to stone them"; and, the police in Spain routinely use skin color as a criterion for identity checks, a practice that has been upheld by the courts.[131] A personnel officer for a chain of supermarkets in Madrid rejects 250 applicants on the grounds (specified in written memoranda) that they are "ugly," "fat," "Cuban and with a mustache," or "Foreigner" – to which is added in one case: "He's scary. He seems Indian."[132] A Moroccan in Spain says that when he calls about an apartment for rent, he is turned down because they can tell he is Moroccan: "They haven't even seen me yet . . . but they know I am an immigrant by *the color of my voice!*"[133]

In Italy, sub-Saharan African immigrants are known universally as the "Vu Comprá," a derisive label based on the similarity of skin color with early immigrant street vendors from Nigeria who were said to approach people with this broken-Italian version of "Vuole comprare?" ("Do you want to buy?"). Harking back to the days of apartheid on other continents, a Northern League official recommends separate train compartments for African immigrants along one particular route, where he says second-class compartments have been reduced to "a situation of civil degradation due to the presence of many 'extracomunitari.'"[134] Even Italian citizenship does not protect those who bear a somatic resemblance to immigrants. A second-generation immigrant woman whose family had come from Eritrea and who had since gained citizenship told the following story about the racist association of African women in Italy with prostitution:

> There were three of us, three Eritrean girls and by mistake . . . we did not have our papers on us. They stopped and took us to the police station. I can even comprehend that they did this to check out our status, but don't keep me there for five hours and don't take my finger-prints and don't treat me as if I were the last of the prostitutes. Then, can you believe it . . . in the end they realized that they had arrested completely the wrong people and they brought us breakfast.[135]

Jacqueline Andall quotes others in her ethnographic study of African-Italians in Milan who recount their numerous experiences of racism at the hands of potential employers, the police, and the public at large. One Senegalese-Italian reported: "As I am black, it's extremely difficult to get work in a bar [café]. I have gone along to so many interviews. Sometimes they have told me that if I were a little fairer then I would have been suitable."[136]

Andall suggests that "Black and Italian [are] mutually exclusive categories" in people's minds. One young woman described what it was like to arrive at the airport in Italy: "I had just come back from London and the guy . . . was checking my identity card, he looked at me, looked at it, looked at me, looked at it, as if to say it just cannot be that this girl is from Italy." A young man who was seeking employment at a warehouse tells of his experience with Italians' deep-seated stereotypes and their inability to fathom the reality of black Italians:

> I brought along my CV where everything is written down – where I was born, how old I am, what I have done. He [the employer] looked at me and said, "But were you born here?" And I said . . . it's written there. Then he said, "But are you an Italian citizen?" and I said, again, yes, it's written there, I was born here. Then he said, "So you speak Italian?" At that point [after an entire interview in Italian] I just looked at him and said no and left.[137]

As Mary Waters describes in her study of West Indian immigrants in the United States, race is a "master status defining the person to others."[138] As such, it suppresses all other qualities and blinds the observer to even the most blatant inconsistencies with the stereotypes (such as the ability to speak Italian).

Somatic markers and "the differences lurking underneath" that they are thought to encode are arranged hierarchically in a nuanced ordering, the detailed gradation of which is remarkable particularly

.he recency of immigration to these southern European countries. ᾿ saw earlier, the ordering does not always follow skin color. Arabs Roma form the bottom rung of the race pyramid, joined by Albanians in Italy, with black Africans faring better in the rankings. The placement of North Africans at the bottom is so consistent, they approximate blacks in the "racial triangulation" that Kim discusses in the context of race relations in the United States, where African-Americans anchor the point of the triangle and other minorities are positioned relative to them.[139] Less than two decades after significant numbers of immigrants began arriving in Spain, a shopkeeper in a small town in Catalonia knows the ordering well: When central African farmworkers were living on the street in his town after hailstorms had destroyed the fruit harvest, he could proclaim with confidence: "They [black Africans] are not conflictual. They are good workers and better clients than the North Africans ['Magrebíes']."[140]

While the markers of such racial distinctions are often somatic, it is increasingly unfashionable to justify racial rankings on the grounds of biology. Instead, culture – essentialized and suffused with biological insinuations – has become its proxy. In this "neo-racism,"[141] cultural differences are pointed to as the reason for social exclusion – or different levels of inclusion – just as biological differences once justified the unequal social and economic position of African-Americans and other minorities in America and elsewhere. This "racism without race," as Balibar has called it, is grounded in and draws its power from three extant conceptualizations of culture. The first is a cultural essentialism in which cultures are thought of as packages of discrete and static elements that inhere in various ethnic and national groups. As one Spanish politician told an interviewer:

> Of course culture is extremely important [in whether immigrants can integrate]. See, I believe that it is at the base of everything . . . Each person is like he is because of his culture, no? One cannot change it because that's how it is. If you are used to doing things one way, you can't change overnight. So, the problem is that people come here and they are very different, and they are shocked by some things about us, and – this is where sparks really fly – they do things that seem strange to us and that we don't like.[142]

In an illustration of how ingrained and intrinsic culture is presumed to be – and how racialized its association with particular ethnic groups – the massive campaign launched by Venetian officials to encourage the "return" migration of descendants of Italian emigrés presumes that they share a cultural heritage with Venetians despite many decades or even generations of absence.

The second perception about culture that is relevant here is that it can act like a virus. In apparent contradiction to its presumed discrete, packaged nature, it is thought to be capable of invading and weakening the cultures and cultural identities of others. Hence, Mikel Azurmendi's comment about multiculturalism being a "gangrene" that threatens Spanish democratic values.[143] A National Alliance official in the Italian Parliament urges his compatriots to control immigration, to "safeguard the security of our citizens, but also – and it is right to say this – our cultural roots and the patrimony of ideas, past and present, that characterize our national Italian identity."[144] This portrayal of foreign cultures as akin to a contaminating virus helps explain the concerns of Catalonians who for generations have defended their distinct cultural identity within Spain, and who perceive their immune system already to be under siege. As a Catalan official told a radio audience: "Our collective identity" is at stake in the immigration debate, and "immigrants must understand . . . that they have come to Catalonia . . . a country that has its own collective identity, its own way of thinking, its own way of acting, and they must respect that fully."[145]

Verena Stolcke calls the conviction that foreigners are "culturally distinct from nationals, who are presumed to share an organic cultural identity in the heart of the body politics," "cultural fundamentalism."[146] Putting aside the fact that the Catalan, Basque, and other Spanish and Italian regions' local identities problematize such notions, this fundamentalism helps account for the concerns about cultural integrity that underlie many fears about immigration. Illustrating these fears of cultural contamination, and at the same time highlighting the diversity of cultures *within* Italy (where most people would assume pasta is the prototypical national food), one anti-immigrant protester in polenta-eating, northern Italy held high a sign that read: "Polenta Si! Couscous No!"

Thirdly, and threading through these conflicting constructions of culture is what might be called "Orientalism" from within. As Edward Said describes it: "Orientalism is never far from . . . the idea of Europe, a collective notion identifying 'us' Europeans as against all 'those' non-Europeans, and indeed it can be argued that the major component in European culture is precisely what made that culture hegemonic both in and outside Europe: the idea of European identity as a superior

But is also cultivated in new envir. as well as brought from home

one in comparison with all the non-European peoples and cultures."[147] (In this regard, the terms "extracomunitari" or "non-EU" migrants are particularly evocative, because they have come to mean not just non-European, but, more narrowly, third world. And, the concept of "European" is not straightforward either, as until recently southern Spaniards and southern Italians were themselves Others whose cultures (and race) were disdained by their own northern compatriots. An old northern Italian saying has it that, "Africa begins in Rome.") Just as people were once divided into races based on biology, with one race "progressive" and the other "primitive," so the "barely reworked variant" ascribes the difference to culture,[148] with "European civilization the universal and legal, the ordered, the dynamic and progressive . . . set against . . . the particular and lawless, the chaotic, static and backward."[149]

As people from the third world move into Europe, the work of Orientalism goes on internally as well as from afar. Sometimes it is explicit, as when Cardinal Biffi of Bologna declares the moral superiority of Christianity over Islam whose members in Italy, he says, remain "strangers to our humanity";[150] or when the Northern League puts up electoral campaign posters featuring degrading and infantilizing cartoons of immigrants;[151] or when Mikel Azurmendi turns the logic of prejudice on its head: "Our moral superiority [to Arabs] consists in our recognition of human dignity. We consider all individuals are worth the same and that [human dignity] is not confined to any particular tribe."[152]

Sometimes it is more subtle, as when immigrants' cultural practices are blamed for their inferior health care (see Chapter 5); or when a public administrator in charge of immigrant integration suggests that Arab immigrants are difficult to integrate because of their (read, "backward") culture: "I have come to understand," this administrator told me, "that there are forces I can't control. I can't force Muslim women to come to our Italian classes. I can beat my head up against the wall, but they won't come";[153] or when a housing official in Almería, Spain, tells an interviewer: "People [immigrants] live in very bad conditions. In the field, without water or electricity or bathrooms . . . It's all very bad and must be changed . . . but . . . they are accustomed to it because they come from countries where it is much worse."[154]

Even those who pride themselves on being tolerant and supportive of multiculturalism may engage in Orientalism, to the extent that they perceive immigrants as "objects to be governed." Ghassan Hage deconstructs the pro- and anti-multiculturalism debate represented in graffiti on the campus of the University of Western Sydney in Australia, and argues that, whatever the differences, the authors of the graffiti have one thing in common:

> Those who wanted the "ethnics" to stay and those who wanted them to leave were divided as to who and what should be allowed into the national space. [But] they were united . . . [in] their conception of ethnics as people one can make decisions *about*: objects to be governed.[155]

In what Hage calls "internal Orientalism," "[w]hat is most evident is the naturalness with which they both assumed that it was up to them to direct the traffic."[156] This objectification of immigrants as "objects to be governed" helps explain the hostility aroused by *uncontrolled* immigration. Indeed, the apparent inability to control immigration is probably as upsetting to many as is the actual presence of immigrants, and accounts for natural disaster metaphors like "floods," "avalanches," and "tidal waves."

Finally, these conceptualizations of culture are infused with, and form the basis for, racial meaning. Biological hierarchies may have been replaced by cultural fears as the stated rationale for differentiation, but the Other is no less racialized, nor do somatic markers become irrelevant. As Aihwa Ong has put it, in light of the mutual permeation of race and culture in popular understandings, the "race-versus-culture construction of exclusionary discourses is . . . a red herring."[157]

The convergence of these aspects of immigrant Othering – criminalization, cultural racialization, and the internal Orientalism that they constitute – was highlighted for me on a visit to an immigrant shelter operated by a Catholic NGO outside a major Italian city. I use this anecdote not to suggest that the shelter is in any way typical, but to provide a vivid illustration of these processes of criminalization, racialization, and objectification as they operate in everyday life. This relatively small shelter housed twenty-five Albanian, Moroccan, Algerian, Kurdish, and Nigerian men who worked in the surrounding countryside and nearby towns. While it was a shelter and not a detention facility, the men (all of whom were legal immigrants) were allowed out only during the day to work, giving the whole operation the air of a halfway house. The front and back doors were equipped with security cameras, and the several refrigerators in the kitchen were padlocked. Graciously accommodating to me, the director insisted on giving me a tour of this all-male facility, unceremoniously opening doors without notice to show me the sleeping quarters. When we encountered some-one walking down the hall, or in the living area, he barked, "Don't wander around the house!" Then, "Who put something on the stove to cook?!" A staff member added, "I've told you to put the fan on when-ever you put something on the stove!" (with an aside to me that the foods these men cooked were pungent and required extra ventilation). I was told that "fundamentalists are a real problem" at the shelter, and that there is a rule against Muslims praying in the house, as it is con-sidered disruptive. Technically, the maximum stay in the shelter is sixty days, but many stay longer because they often have nowhere else to go. A modest rent is charged. As the director explained: "It is not only a matter of cost. It is also educational. They have to learn we don't owe them anything."

We might define racism as the systematic subordination, exclusion, or domination of one group by another, that is justified by prejudice against that group as inferior, and that is accompanied by perceived physical inscriptions. It thus has a structural/material dimension (sub-ordination), an attitudinal one (prejudice), and a physical one (per-ceived bodily inscriptions). In the past, somatic markers were thought to be the *cause* of "differences lurking beneath," or at least part and par-cel of the biology of difference. Those markers have increasingly come to be seen as just that – *markers* of difference, not its cause – but the process of Othering is no less a racializing one, nor is the subordina-tion and justification that now relies on cultural explanations any less powerful.

That said, and as useful as Said's concept of Orientalism is in unpack-ing these cultural explanations of immigrant exclusion, it seems that there is more going on here. Balibar offers us a hint when he warns:

> The object (the target) of current European racism is not by any means just the *black*, the *Arab* or the *Muslim*, though they doubtless bear the main brunt. This point is . . . important because it forces us once again to go beyond abstract interpretations in terms of *conflicts of identity*, or *rejec-tion of the Other* and of "otherness" as such – as though otherness were something constituted *a priori*: explanations which, in reality, merely reproduce part of the racist discourse itself.[158]

If we are to avoid essentializing cultural difference and reproducing the "racist discourse," we have to locate some more fundamental source of Otherness upon which cultural difference is cognitively superimposed.

152

In other words, just as race is socially constructed, so is the cultural difference on which it is now thought to depend. Empirical evidence of the social construction of cultural difference – or at least its parameters and their meanings – abound. Decades before the unification of the European Community or enactment of the first Spanish immigration law in 1985, North African farmworkers – at the time not even officially defined as "immigrants" – worked side-by-side with Andalusian peasants in the fields of southern Spain. Only with the new images of citizenship and belonging that Spain's entrance into the EU and passage of restrictive immigration laws brought, were these North African workers – with whom their Andalusian counterparts had heretofore bonded – highlighted as Others with intolerable cultural differences and dangerous proclivities.[159] In another example of the problem of essentializing culture as the building block of racialization and difference, most Latin American immigrants, with whom Spaniards share linguistic and religious traditions, fare little better legally, socially, and economically in Spain than other third-world immigrants, and far worse than northern Europeans who arguably share less culturally. In a final example from the European experience, southern Italians and Spaniards have relatively recently been incorporated into the idea of Europe, after many decades of racial and cultural exclusion.

Recent immigration literature in the United States reveals that things are even more complicated in the heavily racialized American context, where immigrant children often do better when they are *less* identified with American culture.[160] Mary Waters, in her study of West Indian immigrants, found this to be particularly the case with immigrants of color. In the US context where "black identity" is so heavily freighted, Waters explains, West Indian immigrants who maintain their ethnic roots, self-identify as *immigrants* rather than black Americans, and retain their cultural traditions, often do better than those who Americanize.[161] Clearly then, the recognition of cultural distinctions as meaningful differences in the first place *and* the practical implications of that differentiation, are socially constructed and context-contingent.

Race – and the cultural difference upon which it now is said to be constituted – are not just socially constructed; they are more precisely economically and materially constructed. That is, the social meaning ascribed to both somatic difference and cultural Otherness is in large part grounded in material conditions, constituting "the economics of alterité." I mean this in two senses. First, immigrants are racialized, and their cultures highlighted as problematically distinct, to the extent that they are economically distinct. In his moving account of immigrating to France, Tahar Ben Jelloun makes this point with poignance:

> Poverty has never been well-received . . . At most, difference is accepted under condition that the person be rich, under condition that he has the means to disguise it and pass unobserved. Be different, but be rich! Whoever has no other riches than their ethnic and cultural difference are consigned to humiliation and every form of racism.[162]

Remember, not all foreign residents in Spain and Italy are considered immigrants. This appellation of Otherness is reserved for foreign residents from the third world who are mostly confined to jobs that locals shun, and connotes a level of exclusion and difference from those of the affluent first world, including other foreigners. So pronounced and taken for granted is this distinction that an acquaintance of mine – an expatriate of the United States who has lived in Spain for more than twenty-five years as a freelance writer – reports that he is regularly corrected if he refers to himself (playfully, because he too knows the distinction) as an "inmigrante." He is politely but firmly told he is an "extranjero" – "los inmigrantes" are those who toil in the fields and factories, even if, unlike my American friend, they remain for only a few weeks or months and have no intention of "immigrating."[163] It is their poverty that distinguishes them, their economic need that racializes them as "inmigrantes," not simply "extranjeros".

As we saw in previous chapters, law plays an important supporting role, as virtually the only way for immigrants from the third world to enter Italy and Spain legally is through the quota systems that channel immigrants to what might loosely be referred to as "non-EU jobs," thus shoring up the economics of alterité through law. Conversely, those who do not enter through these channels are by definition illegal, and subject to even greater degrees of economic marginality. The point here is that this institutionalized economic marginality is integral to the racialization of immigrants (indeed, their very nomenclature as such), much as the economic function of African-Americans and other minorities in the United States over the last several centuries cannot be disassociated from *their* racialization.

Secondly, immigrants' position in the economy inevitably *reproduces* the visible markers of poverty, and further generates the kinds of material and social exclusion (from housing and health care) that we explored in Chapter 5. These unseemly markers of poverty are what make immigrants, as Tahar Ben Jelloun would say, not "aesthetic."

Many theorists have pointed out that immigration plays a "mirror function," in that it "clarifies that which is latent . . . in the functioning of the social order, it unmasks that which is masked to reveal what many prefer to ignore and leave in a state of 'innocence' or social ignorance."[164] Following this logic, immigrants' poverty is not just unseemly; it forces us as a society to look in the mirror, and it is the ugly image we see there that is "not reassuring."

Spatial segregation represents one attempt to deal with this problem of aesthetics, but often results in ethnic ghettos of impoverished immigrants that are even more of an eyesore. The mayor of El Ejido, when offered help in providing immigrant housing by IMSERSO officials after the riots, solved the aesthetics problem by mandating that all immigrant housing must be at least three miles from everyone else. When a Madrid government official proposed a community for 200 immigrants (at the required three-mile distance from locals), the mayor instead installed them in forty container-trailers dispersed throughout the countryside.[165]

Immigrants' stigmata of poverty is every bit as conspicuous and consequential – as racialized – as somatic signs inscribed in bodies, and are at the heart of the social interpretation of those signs. I do not mean that this racialization of poverty is always more important than traditional forms of racism based more directly on somatic markers; in the context of immigration, the two usually go together, and understanding their mutual constitution can help us better to decipher the volatile dynamics of this brand of exclusion. It should be pointed out, however, that while somatic distinctions may be neither necessary nor sufficient for racialization to occur – witness the racialization of Albanians in Italy – the *sine qua non* of immigrant racialization may be their status as members of the third world, their poverty, and their need.

This material base of race and racism is underscored by SOS Racismo in their report on the El Ejido riots. The report points out that racial hostility was triggered not just by the economic insecurities of locals and their related worries about immigrant competition – the conventional materialist approach to such incidents. Although these concerns were not altogether absent, the report concludes that the super-exploitation of immigrant labor in the hothouses, the illegal status of the immigrants that facilitated and enhanced it, and living conditions barely suitable for farm animals, contributed to the racism unleashed in the riots. Emblematic of this economic exploitation and the de-humanizing racism it both fed and thrived on, the mayor of El Ejido during the period of the riot famously quipped: "At eight o'clock in the morning there are never enough immigrants. At eight at night, they are everywhere."[166]

DISCUSSION

We saw in previous chapters that despite a focus on integration in Spanish and Italian laws and policies, and in the political discourse, immigrants experience systematic exclusion at a number of levels, including such basic amenities and markers of belonging as housing and health care. I argued that this exclusion is an inevitable by-product of immigrants' poverty, and immigration laws that are contoured to their function in the economy as contingent and cheap labor and that inevitably reproduce that poverty.

As we have seen here, this racialized process of exclusion is further fueled and enhanced by their criminalization, another form of "institutionalized irregularity." And so, institutionalized irregularity has achieved symmetry, as immigrants are not only illegalized by virtue of their always precarious legal status prescribed in law; they are also criminalized both literally and symbolically by virtue of that outsider status. They are in effect doubly "down by law."

To the extent that law and legal discourse play a central role in immigrant exclusion, criminalization, and racialization, they sabotage integration efforts and at the same time intensify their urgency. For, while immigration law is crafted to admit immigrants specifically for their Otherness – most conspicuously codified in quotas designed to bring in immigrants who will do domestic work, farm labor, and low-end construction work that locals shun – it confronts the fallout of this strategy as the poverty, racialization, and criminalization to which it leads fuel anti-immigrant backlashes.

Politicians who exploit anti-immigrant sentiment neatly embody this contradiction. On the one hand, the immigration issue is a tempting "tiger to ride" and easy to exploit for political advantage. On the other, stirring anti-immigrant passions leads not just to violence but to popular demands for effective immigration controls that are both logistically impossible and economically undesirable. As a journalist said of Berlusconi's precarious tightrope walk on the edge of this contradiction: It is not easy to use an iron fist against immigration without also hitting the interests of employers . . . and without mortgaging the interests of the country."[167]

CHAPTER SEVEN

CONCLUSION: IMMIGRANTS AND OTHER STRANGERS IN THE GLOBAL MARKETPLACE

Enjoying an espresso on an early summer afternoon in elegant Bologna, I listen to a young Neapolitan woman who has just finished her dissertation on Moroccan and Somalian women in Italy, and who has graciously agreed to meet with me. As she tells me of these women's experiences and the hostility they encounter despite their hard work and often ingenious efforts to "integrate," she muses, "Poverty is Italy's last taboo."[1] She adds that, having only in the last few generations escaped the grinding poverty that induced their own emigration, Italians are repulsed by the sight of poverty. Probably that is why its "aesthetics" are so disturbing. It is not just that poverty is an eyesore that causes us to avert our gaze or spatially remove ourselves in gated enclaves. The real fear that fuels our passions is that it might be contagious.

We saw in the last chapter that the stigma of poverty is a core component of immigrants' racialization. But, poverty and economic marginality are more than unseemly markers of difference that trigger fear and disgust; they are the material axis on which immigrants' exclusion turns. Basic necessities such as housing and health care are often inaccessible to immigrants not just because of administrative ill-will and deliberate discrimination (although, as we saw in Chapter 5, that is not inconsequential), but because of their unaffordability and – in the case of health care – the absence of a fixed address or social security card. The inability to secure housing even reverberates in immigrants' vulnerability to incarceration, producing a "vicious circle" of exclusion from which those caught in its vortex are unlikely to escape.

One of the main arguments of this book has been that this pivot is itself the product of law and policy. With immigrants admitted only to the extent that they will do jobs that most locals shun or will not move for, and with their legal status always up for grabs, their economic marginality is structured in, their Otherness codified. In this context, efforts to offset immigrant exclusion through integration policies are as urgent as they are doomed. The tension between immigrants' utility as a labor force and their social exclusion is not just a matter of them being "wanted but not welcome," as Zolberg put it.[2] Immigrants are wanted for very specific purposes, the nature of which depends on their having limited labor market choice and the inevitable consequence of which is the reproduction of their marginality, despite frenetic efforts to integrate them. Law's failure then – when it comes to integration – can be explained in part by its success at Othering.

In some ways, this importing of workers from the third world, their reconstruction as racially and culturally different Others, and the material utility derived from that Otherness, can be thought of as colonialism in reverse, or doing empire from within. Saskia Sassen has spoken of the "peripheralization at the core" to refer to the third-world labor force that increasingly does the service work required to sustain the "Global City"; Renato Rosaldo similarly refers to "the implosion of the Third World into the first."[3] My point here is that while the outsider status of these third-world laborers is in part the product of longstanding global inequalities of the old colonialisms and imperialisms, these post-colonial subjects (and the "peripheralization" with which they are associated) are *reproduced from within* through law and the economic marginality it helps constitute. The Spanish enclaves on the Moroccan coast, Melilla and Ceuta, serve as potent symbols of the contradictions of this reverse colonialism, as these colonial outposts have become the heavily fortified and chaotic staging centers for much of the immigrant traffic into southern Spain.

REVISITING DICHOTOMIES OF MEMBERSHIP AND EXCLUSION

There is a conceptual tension brewing here. For, if we take seriously the materialist analysis of exclusion and difference – what I have called the economics of alterité – the particularity of these post-colonial subjects' marginality (a central theme of this book) is problematized. Before attempting to reconcile this tension, let us develop it a bit further by interrogating the dichotomy implicit in the concept of citizenship.

We saw in the Introduction that the simplistic dichotomy of immigrant-outsider/citizen-member is increasingly being unpacked by scholars from a variety of perspectives and with a range of goals. It is argued for instance that the distance between citizen and non-citizen has declined as non-citizens have secured more formal rights; that societal membership is more a matter of degree than absolutes, with "citizens, denizens, and helots" constituting points on a continuum; that "transnational citizenship" is on the rise; and that "formal citizenship" is not the same as "substantive citizenship"; to this, we can add that not all non-citizens are treated as non-members, or even as "immigrants," a classification that is reserved for those from the third world. At the very least, then, the dichotomy of immigrant-outsider/citizen-member overstates both the *exclusion* of all foreigners, and the *inclusion* of all citizens.

Extrapolating from the economics of alterité further destabilizes this dichotomy in ways that are consistent with the notion that formal citizenship does not always confer the neat set of civil, political, and social rights of membership implied by T. H. Marshall's classic schema.[4] If economic marginality is a core component of immigrants' exclusion, then it stands to reason that other impoverished groups in highly stratified, market societies like Spain and Italy are similarly denied full membership. As we saw in Chapter 5, immigrants make up a disproportionate number of those using homeless shelters and soup kitchens in these southern European countries, but they are joined by significant contingents of the locally dispossessed. The vast underground economy and informal sectors that continue to expand even as Spain and Italy join the roster of the world's most advanced capitalist nations, thrive not only on immigrant labor but on the cheap labor of millions of citizens as well. Median housing costs are beyond the reach of most young Spanish and Italian workers too, perhaps helping to explain the reluctance of many to marry, their propensity to live with parents well into their twenties and thirties, and their low fertility rates. Finally, poverty and unemployment rates in the southern regions of Spain and Italy are legion. A recent report on poverty in Italy subtitled "The Nation of Inequalities," declares that Italy is a "society at three speeds," with absolute and relative poverty levels stubbornly high in the south and much lower in the north and center.[5] The dire living and working conditions of many southern Spaniards were dramatically brought to public attention in the summer of 2002, when 1,000 destitute day laborers from Andalusia marched on Madrid, calling for job creation and rural development projects.[6]

It is often said that immigration acts as a mirror in which society sees its own reflection. The immigration mirror is unforgiving, shining a bright light on blemishes like the absence of affordable housing, the stretched and sagging safety net, and the ugly scars of the not-so-"hidden injuries of class."[7] Jessika Ter Wal summarizes the discourse of Italian leftist parties in Parliament: "[The] underlying themes of illegality, poverty and anomie which are addressed in relation to immigration are in reality problems...of Italian society."[8] Addressing the issue of immigrants in the underground economy and their alleged criminality, a Green Party representative responded to his colleagues in Parliament: "[I]n terms of black labour and criminal organisations the Italians are certainly not the pupils of the immigrants!"[9]

The mirror of immigration also exposes more fundamental asymmetries such as the contradictions and disconnects between material inequalities and formal rights.[10] Marshall himself recognized that there is an historic tension between the inequalities spawned by capitalism and the promises of equal citizenship under the democratic states that emerged simultaneously with that economic system.[11] Many others have since noted this schism, sometimes arguing that economic equality is a prerequisite for true political equality and the realization of citizenship claims.[12] As the mirror is held up to immigration, revealing the material inequalities that deprive many foreign workers and their families of the most basic amenities for subsistence, the reflection exposes too the limits of membership for all who are similarly materially disenfranchised. Tahar Ben Jelloun prefaces the Italian edition of his memoir of immigration to France, *La Réclusion Solitaire*:[13]

> Whether in Italy or on the border of Mexico and the United States, whether in Spain or in France, wherever we find at this end of the millennium great movements of people...It is not a matter anymore of an opposition between North and South. It is an opposition between the rich and the poor. Every country has its own south...Immigrants and poor people!...The same condition, the same struggle!

Immigration exposes the contradictions of globalization as well. As Sassen and others have argued, immigration in many ways epitomizes the contradictory nature of, and fragmentations within, contemporary globalization.[14] I use the term globalization guardedly here to refer not to the integration of the global economy in general (as much of the world's economy has in fact been marginalized in the process), but more precisely to the increased integration of first world economies, their heightened dominance over world economic processes, their increasing reliance on third world labor, and the contraction of time and space through communication and transportation technologies that make such integration and dominance possible.[15]

The myriad contradictions associated with this globalization make up what Overbeck calls the "dialectics of globalization."[16] He argues that we might have expected that with the reduced importance of space due to advanced technological capabilities, labor migration would be rendered virtually obsolete; instead, it has speeded up, such that today close to 120 million people reside outside their countries of origin.[17] We might have thought that as the ideology of free trade and the free circulation of capital took hold, the time might have come for the notion of the free circulation of human beings; instead, immigration restrictions have been stepped up. And, we might have expected the penetration of first world working conditions and labor rights along with the Westernization (more precisely, Americanization) of global culture; instead, world economic systems and standards of living are increasingly polarized.

Globalization also unleashes a series of crises within relatively privileged countries, exacerbating longstanding inequalities. As the free-market ideology and neo-liberalism characterizing the American political economy are globalized, and the post-Fordist economic model makes inroads in even those Western European countries with strong contingents of organized labor, a number of material and socio-emotional reverberations are felt, reverberations that are exposed, and complicated, by immigration.

At the material level, the protections offered by the Fordist economy are eroded at the very moment that the welfare state and its safety nets begin to shrink. Ambrosini documents the effects of post-Fordist economic developments in Italy beginning in the 1980s when the gap between different categories of workers began to widen. He argues that, even aside from the extensive underground economy, Italy has a class of indigenous workers whose ranks are unmatched in any other country in Western Europe (mostly made up of the young, the less educated, women, and southern Italians) who, when they are not unemployed, are consigned to poorly paid, contingent, and precarious work. This "post-industrial proletariat," this "anxious class," is too preoccupied with its own survival to develop bonds of solidarity with others. Further complicating the issue of labor solidarity, these "outsiders" often work side-by-side with privileged "insiders," e.g. older workers whose job security, benefits, and pay scales far outstrip their own. Remarking on the similarities between this post-industrial proletariat and immigrant workers, Ambrosini concludes: "Immigrants are the prototypical figure of the current contradictions."[18]

Jock Young takes the notion of broad exclusions in late modernity one step further, arguing that the binary of inclusion/exclusion "paint[s] a far too calm and rational picture of the fortunate citizens – the included." Late modernity, he contends, is a world where "the market forces which transformed the sphere of production and consumption [have] relentlessly challenged our notions of material certainty and uncontested values, replacing them with a world of risk and uncertainty, of individual choice and pluralism and of a deep-seated precariousness both economic and ontological."[19] It is a world of fragmentation, inequality, and differentiation, but at the same time one in which virtually all of us – including the "normal majority" – share the "chaos of reward and ... [the] chaos of identity."[20]

At the socio-emotional level, when these uncertainties encounter mass immigration, the latter is blamed for this "chaos of identity." It is not surprising that in this context of threatened cultural identities so much of the debate over immigration in Italy and Spain focuses on the pros and (mostly) cons of multiculturalism. But, the identity crisis allegedly sparked by immigration is part and parcel of the wider crisis of identity in late modernity. Anti-immigrant passions are predictable at the very moment that more immigration is unleashed, not only because locals feel threatened by the "invasion" and must differentiate themselves, but because the same global forces that intensify immigration are also challenging national identity and community.[21] (It should not be missed that if immigrants are perceived as the trigger of the identity crisis, they also are used to shore up identity in this time of crisis. For, as Zolberg has put it, "We are who we are by virtue of who we are not."[22])

This understanding of the material and socio-emotional effects of globalization has further, more radical, implications for the unpacking of the immigrant-outsider/citizen-member dichotomy. It calls into question the very existence of a community to be excluded *from*. In the Introduction, we examined the vast literature that speaks to the erosion of community in late modernity as cosmopolitans shed territorial ties; the underclasses are walled off, closed in, or otherwise segregated; the collective protections of the welfare safety net are shredded; and the middle-classes retreat to individualistic pursuits, epitomized in their "Bowling Alone."[23] *Putnam*

It might be argued that pronouncements of the death of community are premature.[24] Admittedly, they cannot account for enduring enclaves – often geographically bounded – of like-minded people with ties of solidarity and engaged in collective activities that in some places can still pass for neighborhoods. But, the "imagined community"[25] that reaches beyond the boundaries of neighborhood to include a regional or national membership – and that is the basis for discussions of citizenship, belonging, and exclusion – may be on its way to obsolescence.

Roger Rouse has said, in a different context, that in today's postmodern, globalized world, we need "an alternative cartography of social space."[26] In one version of this new cartography, our public or social spaces are above all shopping malls. And, to the extent that it is market logic that brings us together in these spaces, to be a legitimate participant you must be, if not an actual consumer, at least perceived to be capable of consumption. "Citizen" may be a less accurate term than "consumer" to distinguish one's belonging in this public space. Ironically, it is because of the nature of immigrants' participation in the marketplace – as discounted labor – that they can never be full members of this community of consumption. Thus, it is not their exclusion from community in some traditional sense that characterizes their experience of marginality (after all, immigrants sometimes live in the only tangible communities left in our increasingly fragmented and sprawling urban spaces). Instead, it is their lack of standing as unencumbered consumers that defines their – and many others' – status as *de facto* nonmembers. In this post-industrial ordering, Walzer's normative rationale for restrictions on immigration – "Neighborhoods can be open only if countries are ... closed"[27] – seems quaintly anachronistic.

The transnational belonging enjoyed by elites in this context is not entirely new. Indeed, the membership of consumer elites – Zygmunt Bauman's cosmopolitans, discussed in the Introduction – in today's global marketplace parallels transnational modes of belonging in other economic formations. Thus, in colonial times, "'solidarity among whites' ... linked colonial rulers from different national metropoles, whatever their internal rivalries and conflicts," and later the "class solidarity of Europe's nineteenth century aristocracies" provided the basis for extra-territorial membership.[28] Like many aspects of today's global-ization, it is the scale of the phenomenon that inspires new interpretive schemes.

Aristide Zolberg has pointed out that the word "foreigner" is derived from the Latin "foris," which means "outside," and which is also the root of the French word for "fair." "Foris" is the etymological source too for "forum," the Roman term for public space, especially a market-place. "'Foreigners,'" Zolberg says, "were thus outsiders who turned up in connection with fairs" and to sell their wares in the marketplace.[29] Today, most immigrants' "wares" are their cheap labor and it is the dis-counted nature of those wares that defines them as outsiders and that denies them full participation in the consumer market, an exclusion they share with large numbers of citizens. Nor is this exclusion partic-ular to the southern European societies focused on here; rather, as the vast literature reviewed in the Introduction reveals, it characterizes the immigrant experience in other countries of the European Union, the United States and wherever immigrants' cheap labor is simultaneously their greatest virtue and their stigmatizing vice.

To sum up, immigration exposes, and is implicated with, the contra-dictions inherent in late modernity, and in the process reveals the simi-larities among immigrants and the vast numbers of others who are dislo-cated and under siege. But, how can we reconcile this analysis with the notion developed throughout this book that immigrants are a uniquely marginalized population?

RACE AND THE CODIFICATION OF OTHERNESS

It is one thing to recognize immigrants' similarities with the indige-nous "post-industrial proletariat" and other "anxious classes" in this age of material uncertainty and declining community. But, the *meanings* attached to their status should not be ignored, and indeed are critical to understanding both the immigrant experience and the kind of vio-lent outbursts by local citizens with which this book began. One central component of this set of meanings is the racialization of immigrant dif-ference.

Immigrants who are marked both by their economic marginality and, relatedly, by perceived racial difference are not just excluded but stig-matized as not "suitable" for inclusion.[30] Aihwa Ong's analysis of the racial classification of minorities of color in the United States based on their consumer power makes the points both that class and race are largely interdependent constructions, *and* that the markers of race still matter.[31] Second-generation African immigrants to Italy who have secured citizenship and linguistic fluency are still denied jobs; and those with jobs still elicit stereotypes from their co-workers, in one case incredulity that the African-Italian factory worker recounting the story would not be selling wares on the beach over the coming summer.[32] Similarly, the racism that criminalizes North African immigrants in Spain or Albanians in Italy is both ultimately an economic construction and carries implications far beyond the economic arena.

This racialization and its implications are inextricably linked to the dislocations associated with globalization. For, racialized immigrants, denied the economic rewards of late modern society and excluded from socio-cultural belonging, are scapegoated for the denials and exclusions experienced by others. It may be then that immigrant poverty is "taboo" not because these southern Europeans have only recently escaped that state, as my informant in Bologna surmised; it may be precisely because material uncertainty remains a reality that the racialized face of immigration is so scary.

Law plays a central role in this alchemy of economics, race, identity, and exclusion. As we have seen, immigrants' Otherness is shored up by laws that formally codify them as different at several levels. In the most obvious sense, immigration laws construct some people as noncitizens with a limited set of rights and privileges; others are declared unwelcome altogether and effectively illegalized; and those who do achieve legal status find that it is contingent and unstable, thus enduring episodes of illegality and a vulnerability that bleeds into their periods of legality. Equally importantly, Spanish and Italian laws make it virtually impossible to gain admission as legal residents outside of the quota system that is largely confined to those willing to work in agriculture, domestic help, and construction, i.e. those sectors where wages and working conditions are inadequate to attract sufficient local workers. These laws thus *guarantee* that immigrant workers labor under conditions that are shunned by most of the indigenous working class, an arrangement that reproduces their economic otherness and their exclusion from adequate housing, health care and other basic necessities and accoutrements of belonging. Confronted with this powerful economics of alterité, and the legal infrastructure that supports it, even the most ambitious policies of immigrant integration are doomed, sabotaged not just by racist fearmongers but by the law itself.

Beyond this instrumental role, law plays an important symbolic/ideological part in constructing immigrants as a special population of Others. For these immigration laws – including policies of immigrant integration – send powerful messages about the nature of immigration as a potentially invasive force, the threat posed by cultural differences, and the unquestioned sovereignty of the state in determining who is admissible and under what conditions. Much as Gusfield revealed the temperance movement in the United States to be a symbol of the cultural dominance of white, Anglo-Saxon, Protestants during the industrializing age, so immigration restrictions in this post-industrial period can be seen as a "symbolic crusade" by states experiencing the decline of their national sovereignty and territorial integrity, joined by citizens who face the demise of community and their own threatened identities.[33]

The instrumental effects of these laws have symbolic consequences too. For example, law, through its codification of immigrants' poverty, is complicit in their racialization. Further, the "institutionalized irregularity" embedded in the law gives birth to a litter of ideological offspring, among them the symbolic (and literal) criminalization of immigrants. Identity itself is reshaped in the process, as Italians and Spaniards – even those in the poor southern regions – come to think of themselves as citizens of Europe, belonging to a different cultural and symbolic universe than those immigrant Others with whom they once shared a class identity.[34]

Sarat and Kearns make a distinction between an instrumental approach to law and a constitutive approach, with the latter positing that "social life is run through with law, so much so that the relevant category is not the external [instrumental] one of causality ... but the internal one of meaning."[35] What we have seen here, however, is that the instrumental effects and the "internal one of meaning" are not distinct; rather, they are recursively related, with law's effects injecting meaning into and through daily life.

We have seen too the ways that law's meaning – both material and symbolic – is constructed in the ordinary and not-so-ordinary actions of bureaucrats, police, employers, ordinary citizens, and immigrants themselves. Formal rights are eviscerated, informal rights invoked, legal strategies improvised, and policy decided by the authoritative fiat of practice, as what it means to be an immigrant in these societies is built from the ground up, not just by law, but by "social life ... run through with law."

POSTSCRIPT

Immigration scholars increasingly recognize that the immigrant-outsider/citizen-insider binary is inadequate, and have proposed instead a continuum of belonging (e.g. "citizens, denizens, and helots"[36]). But, confronting the tension between the notion that immigrants are a unique class of excluded others versus the idea that they are merely the embodiment of late modernity's vast precariousness, exposes the limitations not just of this dichotomy, but of a continuum as well. The numerous levels of immigrant exclusion discussed here, and their tangled sources, suggest the need for a more complex model that recognizes the multiple axes of inclusion/exclusion.

The axes I am referring to are not the individual ascriptions of race, class, gender, nationality, sexuality, etc., that others have rightly highlighted as sources of exclusion and experiences of "intersectionality."[37] Instead, consistent with the notion that these characteristics and their meanings are always in the process of construction, my focus is on the multiple, interrelated *mechanisms* of that construction. Many citizens in these southern European nations – as in neighboring EU countries and the United States – may be excluded from full membership, and indeed the "exclusive" nature of late modern society may problematize the very concept of community.[38] But, the location of immigrant workers with respect to several, overlapping mechanisms of exclusion – law, economics, ideologies of race, etc. – defines their unique experience, and explains both the governments' calls for tolerance and the riots unleashed in El Ejido and Salandra.

My emphasis on these mechanisms that shore up immigrant marginality is not meant to imply that the immigrant population is uniformly poor and hopelessly and forever subordinated. For one thing, as we saw in the Introduction, the foreign populations in these countries are enormously diverse, with almost half coming from other affluent Western nations, and some wealthy individuals from the third world coming with substantial social and economic capital. Secondly, some upward mobility is likely to occur over time for a few of the currently marginalized, given the sheer force of human agency and what sometimes amounts to 70-hour workweeks. There are already signs of settlement – if not incorporation – as the rates of bi-national marriage, naturalization, family unification, and immigrant children in school, have all risen substantially over the last decade. But, the question is not, "Can this or that individual eventually integrate despite the obstacles?" Rather, the issue is whether these late modern societies and their counterparts elsewhere create and recreate cohorts of immigrants the virtue of which is their dis-integration. It is likely, given the barriers discussed here, that the marginal status of many long-time immigrants will persist for years – if not generations; but, the endurance of a *class* of marginalized immigrants is even more likely, with all its implications of backlash, violence, and exclusion.

NOTES

Chapter 1

1. Héctor Maravall Gómez-Allende (Director General of the Spanish Institute of Migration and Social Services, IMSERSO), "Indicadores de la Inmigración y el Asilo en España," *Observatorio Permanente de la Inmigración*, No. 1 (May), 1998: 1. In a subsequent issue of this government report on immigrant integration, Gómez-Allende's successor spoke of the importance of immigrants' "social integration" and the "rich contribution that these men and women make to our society, which is now the society of all of us" (Alberto Galerón de Miguel, "Indicadores de la Inmigración y el Asilo en España," *Observatorio Permanente de la Inmigración*, No. 10 (January), 2000: 1).

2. Enzo Bianco, Italian Minister of the Interior, introducing the annual report on the state of public safety in Italy. Enzo Bianco, "Considerazioni del Ministro dell'Interno," *Rapporto del Ministro dell'Interno sullo Stato della Sicurezza in Italia* (Bologna: Il Mulino), 2001: 21.

3. "Moro" is the disparaging Spanish term for "Moor/Arab." During the period of the El Ejido riot, a webpage urged people to go on a "caza del moro" – "Arab hunt" (SOS Racismo, *El Ejido: Racismo y Explotación Laboral* (Barcelona: Icaria), 2001: 49).

4. Excellent accounts of these events can be found in SOS Racismo, *El Ejido*, and Foro Civico Europeo, Comité Europeo de Defensa de los Refugiados e Inmigrantes, *El Ejido: Tierra Sin Ley* (Estella-Navarra: Gráficas Lizarra), 2001.

5. Marino Bisso, "Linciamo gli Albanesi," *La Repubblica*, January 14, 2000: 16.

6. Ghassan Hage, *White Nation: Fantasies of White Supremacy in a Multicultural Society* (New York: Routledge), 2000: 15.

7. The term "third-world countries" is awkward in this context, particularly as I have just referred to the presence of "third-world laborers in first-world economies," thereby calling attention to the interpenetration of

supposedly distinct worlds. As Hardt and Negri point out, "[T]he spatial divisions of the three Worlds (First, Second, and Third) have been scrambled so that we continually find the First World in the Third, the Third in the First, and the Second almost nowhere at all" (Michael Hardt and Antonio Negri, *Empire* (Cambridge: Harvard University Press), 2000: xiii). But, while the worlds' populations may have been "scrambled," the mixing is by no means complete, and in any case does not obliterate the broad-brush distinctions among the various economies of this now globalizing world.

8. Hage, *White Nation*: 20.

9. It is estimated that from 1946 to 1970, almost seven million Italians migrated to jobs in France, Switzerland, West Germany, Belgium, the Netherlands, and Luxembourg; over two million Spaniards made the same trip in the 1960s (OECD estimates, cited in Russell King and Krysia Rybaczuk, "Southern Europe and the International Division of Labour: From Emigration to Immigration," in Russell King (ed.), *The New Geography of European Migrations* (London: Belhaven Press), 1993: 176). Entire towns and villages in southern Italy are still known as "Paesi Fiat," places where virtually every family sent its young men to work in the legendary Fiat automobile factories in and around Turin in northwestern Italy (Donald Martin Carter, *States of Grace: Senegalese in Italy and the New European Immigration* (Minneapolis: University of Minnesota Press), 1997: 32).

10. In a 1991 study of 1,525 legal and illegal immigrants in Italy, approximately 40% said they chose Italy as a destination because of work opportunities there, and an equal number mentioned ease of entrance (Consiglio Nazionale dell'Economia e del Lavoro, *Immigrati e Societá Italiana* (Rome: Editalia), 1991: 43).

11. Caritas, *Immigrazione: Dossier Statistico 2003* (Rome: Edizioni Anterem), 2003.

12. Maria Immacolata Macioti and Enrico Pugliese, *Gli Immigrati in Italia* (Bari: Editori Laterza), 1991; Enrico Pugliese, "Gli Immigrati nel Mercato del Lavoro e nella Struttura dell'Occupazione," in Enrico Pugliese (ed.), *Rapporto Immigrazione: Lavoro, Sindacato, Societá* (Rome: Ediesse), 2000; Maurizio Ambrosini, *Utili Invasori: L'inserimento degli Immigrati nel Mercato del Lavoro* (Milan: FrancoAngeli), 1999; Giustina Orientale Caputo, "Salari di Fatto dei Lavoratori Immigrati in Italia," in Pugliese, *Rapporto Immigrazione*.

13. Kenneth Maxwell and Steven Spiegel, *The New Spain: From Isolation to Influence* (New York: Council on Foreign Relations Press), 1994: 89.

14. "El Empleo ha Crecido en Cataluña el 22.1% en Cinco Años, por debajo del 24.2% de la Media Española," *El País*, July 16, 2002: 7.

15. Ministerio del Interior, Delegación del Gobierno para la Extranjería y la Inmigración, Observatorio Permanente de la Inmigración, *Boletín Estadístico de Extranjería e Inmigración*, No. 1, March, 2004: 2.

16. Ministerio de Trabajo y Asuntos Sociales, *Boletín Estadísticas Laborales*, Vol. 167, March, 2002; Colectivo IOÉ, *Inmigración y Trabajo en España: Trabajadores Inmigrantes en el Sector de la Hostelería* (Madrid: Secretaría

General de Asuntos Sociales), 1999: 70; Manuel Altozano, "Quiero Ser Limpiador," *El País*, July 3, 2002: 23.

17. Quoted in "Miedo a lo Desconocido," *Mercado*, February 24, 1992: 27.

18. Franco Papitto, "Immigrati, Salta l'accordo UE; Lite tra Ministri, Francia e Svezia: Niente Tolleranza Zero," *La Repubblica*, June 18, 2002: 2; Sebastian Rotella, "EU Plans to Beef Up Borders," *Los Angeles Times*, June 23, 2002: A3; Anna Terrón I Cusí, "Lo que no se Ha Hecho en Sevilla," *El País*, July 3, 2002: 12.

19. Personal interviews, Spain and Italy, 1996–2002.

20. Macioti and Pugliese, *Gli Immigrati in Italia*; Pugliese, "Gli Immigrati nel Mercato del Lavoro"; Alegría Borrás, *Diez Años de la Ley de Extranjería: Balance y Perspectivas* (Barcelona: Fundación Paulino Torras Doménech), 1995; Antonio Izquierdo, *La Inmigración Inesperada* (Madrid: Editorial Trotta), 1996.

21. The tension between calls for immigrant assimilation and acclaim for cultural pluralism is longstanding in the United States, where it is not so much the logical inconsistency of the two propositions that offends, but the political implications of the concept of assimilation in this age of the politics of identity and difference. As Rubén Rumbaut tells it, "What had seemed like a bland and straightforward enough description – an observable outcome of adaptation to new environments, a familiar process of 'learning the ropes' and 'fitting in . . . – bec[a]me an explosive and contested prescription, value laden with arrogant presumptions of ethnic superiority and inferiority." Rubén G. Rumbaut, "Assimilation and its Discontents: Between Rhetoric and Reality," *International Migration Review*, Vol. 31, No. 4, 1997: 923–960.

22. Under the rubric "diversity work," I include such things as public relations campaigns highlighting the benefits of multiculturalism and calling for tolerance of diversity. A prime example of such "diversity work" is the website of the Immigration Bureau within the Spanish Department of Labor (Instituto de Migraciones y Servicios Sociales, Ministerio de Trabajo y Asuntos Sociales, www.imsersomigracion.upco.es), which at the time of this writing opened with its logo – a cartoon drawing of a white hand and a black hand giving a "high-five," with the words "Vive y Convive" (the equivalent of "Let's all get along"), and the caption "Campaign for multicultural coexistence and against racism and xenophobia."

23. Kitty Calavita, "Immigration, Law, and Marginalization in a Global Economy: Notes from Spain," *Law and Society Review*, Vol. 32, 1998: 529–566; and Kitty Calavita, "Italy and the New Immigration," in Wayne A. Cornelius, Philip L. Martin, and James F. Hollifield (eds.), *Controlling Immigration: A Global Perspective* (Stanford: Stanford University Press, 2nd edn), 2004.

24. Ben Agger, *Public Sociology: From Social Facts to Literary Acts* (New York: Rowman & Littlefield), 2000.

25. Kitty Calavita, "The Limits of Law: An Analysis of Immigration Law Implementation in Italy and Spain," National Science Foundation grant proposal, Law and Social Science Program, SES 0004218, 2000: 1.

26. Murray Edelman, *Political Language – Words that Succeed and Policies that Fail* (New York: Academic Press), 1977.

27. Sarat and Kearns critique the "instrumental" approach to law which "takes an external stance. It posits a relatively sharp distinction between legal standards, on one hand, and nonlegal human activities on the other. It then explores the effects of the former on the latter." Austin Sarat and Thomas R. Kearns (eds.), *Law in Everyday Life* (Ann Arbor: University of Michigan Press), 1993: 21. To the extent that the dichotomy between the law in the books and the law in action is portrayed as if it consisted of pure legal activity on the one hand and indeterminate human discretion on the other, it is susceptible to such critiques.

28. Joel B. Grossman, "The Supreme Court and Social Change," in Stuart Nagel (ed.), *Law and Social Change* (Beverly Hills: Sage Publications), 1970; James P. Levine and Theodore L. Becker, "Toward and Beyond a Theory of Supreme Court Impact," in Stuart Nagel (ed.), *Law and Social Change* (Beverly Hills: Sage Publications), 1970; Sheldon Eckland-Olson and Steve J. Martin, "Organizational Compliance with Court-Ordered Reform," *Law and Society Review*, Vol. 22, 1988: 359–383.

29. Julie Horney and Cassia Spohn, "Rape Law Reform and Instrumental Change in Six Urban Jurisdictions," *Law and Society Review*, Vol. 25, 1991: 117–153.

30. Horney and Spohn, "Rape Law Reform": 120, 150, and 148.

31. Michael Lipsky, *Street-Level Bureaucracy: Dilemmas of the Individual in Public Services* (New York: Russell Sage), 1980.

32. David Sudnow, "Normal Crimes: Sociological Features of the Penal Code in the Public Defender Office," *Social Problems*, Vol. 12, 1965: 255–276; Robert M. Emerson and Blair Paley, "Organizational Horizons and Complaint Filing," in Keith Hawkins (ed.), *The Uses of Discretion* (Oxford: Clarendon Press), 1992: 239.

33. Janet Gilboy, "Penetrability of Administrative Systems: Political 'Casework' and Immigration Inspection," *Law and Society Review*, Vol. 26, 1992: 273–314.

34. Kitty Calavita, "The Contradictions of Immigration Lawmaking: The Immigration Reform and Control Act of 1986," *Law and Policy*, Vol. 11, 1989: 17–47; Kitty Calavita, *Inside the State: The Bracero Program, Immigration, and the INS* (New York: Routledge), 1992.

35. Kitty Calavita, "The Paradoxes of Race, Class, Identity and 'Passing': Enforcing the Chinese Exclusion Acts, 1882–1910," *Law and Social Inquiry*, Vol. 25, 2000: 1–40.

36. Kitty Calavita, "Chinese Exclusion and the Open Door with China: Structural Contradictions and the 'Chaos' of Law, 1882–1910," *Social and Legal Studies*, Vol. 10, 2001: 221–222.

37. ISMU-Cariplo, *Sesto Rapporto sulle Migrazioni 2000* (Milan: Franco-Angeli), 2001: 6.

38. Aristide R. Zolberg, "Modes of Incorporation: Toward a Comparative Framework," in Veit Bader (ed.), *Citizenship and Exclusion* (London: Macmillan), 1997: 143.

39. Jorge Bustamante, "Commodity-Migrants: Structural Analysis of Mexican Immigration to the US," in Stanley Ross (ed.), *Views Across the Border* (Albuquerque: University of New Mexico Press), 1978; James D. Cockcroft, *Outlaws in the Promised Land: Mexican Immigrant Workers and America's Future* (New York: Grove Press), 1986; Cornelius, Martin, and Hollifield, *Controlling Immigration*; Calavita, "Immigration, Law, and Marginalization."

40. Zolberg, "Modes of Incorporation": 143.

41. See Richard Sennett, "Growth and Failure: The New Political Economy and its Culture," in Mike Featherstone and Scott Lash (eds.), *Spaces of Culture: City-Nation-World* (London: Sage), 1999; Eve Darian-Smith, *Bridging Divides: The Channel Tunnel and English Legal Identity in the New Europe* (Berkeley: University of California Press), 1999; Zygmunt Bauman, *Community: Seeking Safety in an Insecure World* (Cambridge: Polity Press), 2001; David Harvey, "The Spaces of Utopia," in David Theo Goldberg, Michael Musheno, and Lisa C. Bower (eds.), *Between Law and Culture: Relocating Legal Studies* (Minneapolis: University of Minnesota Press), 2001; Lisa E. Sanchez, "Enclosure Acts and Exclusionary Practices," in Goldberg, Musheno, and Bower, *Between Law and Culture*; and Peter Dreier, John Mollenkopf, and Todd Swanstrom, *Place Matters: Metropolitics for the Twenty-First Century* (Lawrence: University of Kansas Press), 2001.

42. Patricia Ewick and Susan S. Silbey, *The Common Place of Law: Stories from Everyday Life* (Chicago: University of Chicago Press), 1998.

43. Georg Simmel, *The Sociology of Georg Simmel*, translated and edited by Kurt H. Wolff (New York: Free Press), 1950.

44. Pierre Bourdieu, "Preface," in Sayad Abdelmalek, *L'Immigration: Ou les Paradoxes de l'Altérité* (Brussels: De Boeck-Wesmael), 1991: 9.

45. Rogers Brubaker, *Citizenship and Nationhood in France and Germany* (Cambridge: Harvard University Press), 1992: 47.

46. Ali Behdad, "Nationalism and Immigration to the United States," *Diaspora*, Vol. 6, 1997: 155–156.

47. Bonnie Honig, *Democracy and the Foreigner* (Princeton: Princeton University Press), 2001.

48. T. H. Marshall, *Citizenship and Social Class and Other Essays* (Cambridge: Cambridge University Press), 1950.

49. Marshall's conceptualization, while garnering ever more attention over the years, has also drawn substantial criticism for its Eurocentricity, its neglect of the dynamics of social exclusion in the twentieth century, and its now dated optimism regarding the success of the welfare state in reducing the social inequality associated with capitalism (see especially, Samuel Clark, "Amending the Whig Interpretation of Citizenship: A Review Essay on *Extending Citizenship, Reconfiguring States*," *Contemporary Sociology*, Vol. 31 (July), 2002: 382–385; and, Bryan S. Turner (ed.), *Citizenship and Social Theory* (London: Sage Publications), 1993).

50. Brubaker, *Citizenship and Nationhood*: 21.

51. Michael Walzer, *Spheres of Justice: A Defense of Pluralism and Equality* (New York: Basic Books), 1983: 42.

52. Joseph H. Carens, "Aliens and Citizens: The Case for Open Borders," in Ronald Beiner (ed.), *Theorizing Citizenship* (Albany: State University of New York Press), 1995.

53. Alessandro Dal Lago, *Non-Persone: L'Esclusione dei Migranti in una Società Globale* (Milan: Interzone), 1999.

54. Steven Castles and Godula Kozack, *Immigrant Workers and Class Structure in Western Europe* (New York: Oxford University Press), 1973; Wayne A. Cornelius, "The US Demand for Mexican Labor," in Wayne A. Cornelius and Jorge A. Bustamante (eds.), *Mexican Migration in the United States: Origins, Consequences, and Policy Options* (La Jolla, CA: Center for US – Mexican Studies, University of California, San Diego), 1989; Michael J. Piore, *Birds of Passage: Migrant Labor and Industrial Societies* (New York: Cambridge University Press), 1979.

55. Marianne Constable makes a different point in regard to the special marginality of illegal immigrants. She argues that the notion of sovereignty in a democratic society applies both to the state as an autonomous entity capable of imposing laws on people, and to citizens who must be autonomous legal agents with the free will and ability to obey. But, "the 'unlawfulness' or 'illegality' of the illegal alien is such that the alien individual seems not quite an autonomous legal subject, being neither legally recognized citizen nor legally recognized stranger." As such, "they come to resemble under law ... the regulatable resources of the territory more than its self-determining subjects." Marianne Constable, "Sovereignty and Governmentality in Modern American Immigration Law," *Studies in Law, Politics, and Society*, Vol. 13, 1993: 260.

56. James F. Hollifield, *Immigrants, Markets, and States: The Political Economy of Postwar Europe* (Cambridge: Harvard University Press), 1992; Yasemin Nuhoglu Soysal, *Limits of Citizenship: Migrants and Postnational Membership in Europe* (Chicago: University of Chicago Press), 1994. In this depiction, immigrants – with their extensive civil, political, and social rights – have become Marshallian "citizens."

57. Peter H. Schuck, *Citizens, Strangers, and In-Betweens: Essays on Immigration and Citizenship* (Boulder, CO: Westview Press), 1998: 163–164.

58. Robin Cohen, *Contested Domains: Debates in International Labour Studies* (London: Zed Books), 1991: 151–165; Rogers Brubaker, "Introduction," in Rogers Brubaker (ed.), *Immigration and the Politics of Citizenship in Europe and North America* (New York: University Press of America), 1989. See also Laura Balbo's discussion of the three categories of membership in Western Europe: full citizenship, denizenship, and non-citizenship (Laura Balbo, "Cittadini, Cittadini-dimezzati, Non-cittadini," *Inchiesta*, No. 90, 1990: 23–26).

59. Warren Magnusson, *The Search for Political Space: Globalization, Social Movements and the Urban Political Experience* (Toronto: University of Toronto Press), 1996: 9–10. See also Richard Falk, "The Making of Global Citizenship," in Jeremy Brecher, John Brown Childs, and Jill Cutler (eds.),

Global Visions: Beyond the New World Order (Montreal: Black Rose Press), 1993; and Linda Bosniak, "Citizenship Denationalized," *Indiana Journal of Global Legal Studies*, Vol. 7, 2000: 447–509.

60. Samuel Clark, "Amending the Whig Interpretation of Citizenship": 383.
61. Richard Falk, "The Decline of Citizenship in an Era of Globalization," *Citizenship Studies*, Vol. 4, 2000: 6.
62. Brubaker, *Citizenship and Nationhood*: 36.
63. Rainer Baubock, *Transnational Citizenship: Membership Rights in International Migration* (Aldershot: Edward Elgar), 1994. See also David Abraham, "Citizenship Solidarity and Rights Individualism: On the Decline of National Citizenship in the US, Germany, and Israel," seminar paper presented at Center for Comparative Immigration Studies, University of California, San Diego, May 7, 2002: 7.
64. Kenneth L. Karst, *Belonging to America: Equal Citizenship and the Constitution* (New Haven: Yale University Press), 1989; Ediberto Román, "Members and Outsiders: An Examination of the Models of United States Citizenship as Well as Questions Concerning European Union Citizenship," *University of Miami International and Comparative Law Review*, Vol. 9, 2000–2001: 81–113; Leti Volpp, " 'Obnoxious to their Very Nature': Asian Americans and Constitutional Citizenship," *Citizenship Studies*, Vol. 5, 2001: 57–71; Kevin Johnson, " 'Melting Pot' or 'Ring of Fire': Assimilation and the Mexican-American Experience," *California Law Review*, Vol. 85, 1997: 1259–1312; Roger Wilkins, *Jefferson's Pillow: The Founding Fathers and the Dilemma of Black Patriotism* (Boston: Beacon Press), 2001; Nira Yuval-Davis, *Gender and Nation* (Thousand Oaks, CA: Sage Publications), 1997; and Tom Bottomore "Citizenship and Social Class, Forty Years On," in T. H. Marshall and Tom Bottomore (eds.), *Citizenship and Social Class* (London: Pluto Press), 1992: 69.
65. Renato Rosaldo, "Cultural Citizenship in San Jose, California," *PoLAR*, Vol. 17, 1994: 57–63.
66. Ronald Beiner, "Introduction," in Ronald Beiner (ed.), *Theorizing Citizenship* (Albany: State University of New York Press), 1995: 3. An altogether different perspective on citizenship argues that it is precisely when it is most inclusive that it is most oppressive. Thus, "[t]he expansion of citizenship to previously excluded groups could be problematic or even oppressive, as opposed to laudable or liberatory" because it undermines particularity and difference. Stephanie A. Levin, "Reexamining Citizenship: Legal Fictions, Actual Identities," paper presented at the Law and Society Association Meeting, Vancouver, May 30, 2002: 8; see also Iris Marion Young, "Polity and Group Difference: A Critique of the Ideal of Universal Citizenship," in Beiner, *Theorizing Citizenship*.
67. Aihwa Ong, *Buddha Is Hiding: Refugees, Citizenship, the New America* (Berkeley: University of California Press), 2003.
68. Walzer, *Spheres of Justice*: 63.
69. Benedict Anderson, *Imagined Communities: Reflections on the Origin and Spread of Nationalism* (London: Verso), 1983: 15.
70. Bauman, *Community*: 50.

71. Quoted from the Cultural Globalization Project, in *ibid.*: 55. Of course, not all cosmopolitans "carry an American passport." In *Flexible Citizenship*, Aihwa Ong writes of Asian elites who make their home both in California and across the Pacific, shuttling back and forth, identifying with both their nationalities and, at the same time, neither (Aihwa Ong, *Flexible Citizenship: The Cultural Logics of Transnationality* (Durham, NC: Duke University Press), 1999).

72. "The World" is a product of the Norwegian firm ResidenSea USA (*sic*) (www.cruiseserver.net/travelpage/ships/rs_resid.asp).

73. Nikos Papastergiadis, *The Turbulence of Migration: Globalization, Deterritorialization and Hybridity* (Cambridge: Polity Press), 2000: 20.

74. Teresa P. R. Caldeira, *City of Walls: Crime, Segregation, and Citizenship in São Paulo* (Berkeley: University of California Press), 2000.

75. Falk, "The Decline of Citizenship": 10. Former Secretary of Labor Robert Reich links America's very economic and social survival to the question of whether "there is still enough concern about American society to elicit sacrifice from all of us – especially from the most advantaged and successful of us [those Bauman says have 'seceded'] – to help the majority regain the ground it has lost and fully participate in the new global economy." Robert Reich, *The Work of Nations* (New York: Knopf), 1991: 9.

76. Abraham, "Citizenship Solidarity and Rights Individualism": 49.

77. Baubock, *Transnational Citizenship*; Falk, "The Decline of Citizenship."

78. Anthony Giddens refers to this double-whammy broadsiding the community as the weakening of social relations through both "time-space distanciation" and "disembedding." Anthony Giddens, *The Consequences of Modernity* (Cambridge: Polity Press), 1990. See also Saskia Sassen, *Losing Control? Sovereignty in an Age of Globalization* (New York: Columbia University Press), 1996.

79. Schuck, *Citizens, Strangers, and In-Betweens.*

80. Tahar Ben Jelloun, *Le Pareti della Solitudine* (Turin: Giulio Einaudi Editore), 1997: xiv. Translated from *La Réclusion Solitaire* (Paris: Editions Denoel), 1976.

Chapter 2

1. It has been estimated that a million Arab and Berber immigrants settled on the Iberian peninsula in the eighth century alone: Lydia Esteve González and Richard MacBride, "Fortress Europe: Fear of Immigration? Present and Future of Immigration Law and Policy in Spain," *UC Davis Journal of International Law and Policy*, Vol. 6, No. 2, 2000: 153–191.

2. Mario Caciagli and David I. Kertzer, *Italian Politics: The Stalled Transition* (Boulder, CO Westview Press), 1996; David Nelken, "Stopping the Judges," in Caciagli and Kertzer, *Italian Politics*; Giulio Sapelli, "The Transformation of the Italian Party System," *Journal of Modern Italian Studies*, Vol. 2, No. 2, 1997: 167–187; Patrizia Pederzoli and Carlo Guarnieri, "The Judicialization of Politics, Italian Style," *Journal of Modern Italian Studies*,

Vol. 2, No. 3, 1997: 321–336; John A. Agnew, *Place and Politics in Modern Italy* (Chicago: University of Chicago Press), 2002.

3. *Ibid.*: 201. For an excellent discussion of the emergence of the Lega Nord and its "territorial constituency," see Anna Cento Bull and Mark Gilbert, *The Lega Nord and the Northern Question in Italian Politics* (London: Palgrave), 2001: 67.

4. The campaign's focus on the strategically packaged personal attributes of Berlusconi as an individual represented an Americanization of Italian politics. Not since Mussolini had a politician in Italy (where the primary emphasis is generally on party politics, not personal charisma) been so depicted as a national hero. For an excellent summary of Berlusconi's rise to power, personalistic appeal, and political trajectory, see Paul Ginsborg, "The Patrimonial Ambitions of Silvio B," *New Left Review*, May–June, 2003: 21–64.

5. Michael Braun, "The Confederated Trade Unions and the Dini Government: The Grand Return to Neo-Corporatism?" in Caciagli and Kertzer, *Italian Politics*: 205.

6. See Carlo Trigilia, "Italy: The Political Economy of a Regionalized Capitalism," *South European Society and Politics*, Vol. 2, No. 3, 1997: 52–79.

7. For a more detailed discussion of these regional political cultures, see Agnew, *Place and Politics in Modern Italy*: 111–121.

8. Richard Gunther, Giacomo Sani, and Goldie Shabad, *Spain after Franco: The Making of a Competitive Party System* (Berkeley: University of California Press), 1986; Andrew J. Richards, "Spain: From Isolation to Integration," in Ronald Tiersky (ed.), *Europe Today: National Politics, European Integration, and European Security* (Lanham: Rowman and Littlefield), 1999.

9. Robert M. Fishman, *Working-Class Organization and the Return to Democracy in Spain* (Ithaca: Cornell University Press), 1990.

10. "Spain Has Changed," interview with Prime Minister José María Aznar, *Newsweek*, April 10, 2000: 24.

11. Fishman, *Working-Class Organization*: 2. See also Richard Gunther, Giacomo Sani, and Goldie Shabad, *Spain after Franco*.

12. Kerstin Hamann, "The Pacted Transition to Democracy and Labour Politics in Spain," *South European Society and Politics*, Vol. 2, No. 2, 1997: 110–138.

13. Richards, "Spain: From Isolation to Integration."

14. Comisión Interministerial de Extranjería, *Anuario Estadístico de Extranjería* (Madrid: Imprenta Nacional del Boletín Oficial del Estado), 1995: 138.

15. John Casey, "La Admisión e Integración de los Inmigrantes Extranjeros," in Joan Subirats and Ricard Gomá (eds.), *Las Políticas Públicas en España* (Madrid: Ariel), 1997: 12.

16. Izquierdo, *La Inmigración Inesperada*: 71.

17. *Ibid.*: 142.

18. *Ibid.*: 141–142.

19. The next major step in European unification – the Maastricht Treaty which officially created European citizens – was signed by EC members in February, 1992, to be effective in November, 1993. Title VI of this agreement dealt with asylum, border controls, immigration, and drugs, and established a European policing system (Europol). It also formed a committee to advise the Council, comprised of the Ministers of Interior and Justice of the member countries. While Schengen and Maastricht attempted to move toward a coordinated European policy on immigration and asylum, as one high official put it, there remained "teething problems" (quoted in John Benyon, "The Politics of Police Cooperation in the European Union," *International Journal of the Sociology of Law*, Vol. 24, 1996: 365). The Treaty of Amsterdam, effective in 1999, which authorized the EU to enact immigration laws across member states, did little to solve these problems.

20. The Bill, which was introduced by the Socialist government in power at the time, was uncontroversial in both the House and Senate and elicited little public debate prior to its passage. Congreso de los Diputados, *Boletín Oficial del Estado*, No. 158, July 3, 1985: 20824–20829.

21. Congreso de los Diputados, *Boletín Oficial de las Cortes Generales*, No. 132, May 8, 1985.

22. Articles 7–10, in *Boletín Oficial del Estado*, No. 158, July 3, 1985: 20825.

23. There were only 44,000 applicants to this program, which was widely criticized for its lack of publicity and coordination, and which was launched at a time of widespread fear and confusion among immigrants who had become illegal overnight as a consequence of the new visa and permit requirements. Of these applicants, only 23,000 were able to fulfill the program requirements relating to ongoing, legitimate work contracts or other means of support in the formal economy. Colectivo IOÉ, *Los Trabajadores Extranjeros en España: Informe para el Instituto Sindical de Estudios* (Madrid: Colectivo IOÉ), 1992; Antonio Izquierdo, *La Inmigración en España: 1980–1990* (Madrid: Ministerio de Trabajo y de la Seguridad Social), 1992.

24. Article 26, in *Boletín Oficial del Estado*, No. 158, July 3, 1985: 20825. A provision that would have allowed administrative authorities to conduct deportations without judicial input was declared unconstitutional in 1987 (Tribunal Constitucional, Sentencia No. 115/1987).

25. Lidia Santos, "Elementos Jurídicos de la Integración de los Extranjeros," in Georges Tapinos (ed.), *Inmigración e Integración en Europa* (Barcelona: Itinera Libros), 1993: 113.

26. See Vicente Font Boix, *El Trabajador Extranjero y la Regularización de 1991* (Barcelona: Itinera Cuadernos), 1991.

27. Pedro Aresté, "Los Cupos de Trabajadores en 1993 y 1994," in Borrás, *Diez Años*.

28. Throughout this period, Spain's refugee and asylum procedures were increasingly restrictive, as with other EC countries at this time. By 1993, 96% of applicants for refugee status in Spain were denied, with only 1,287 admitted (Izquierdo, *La Inmigración Inesperada*: 104). By 1996, there were

only approximately 5,500 refugees living in Spain, mostly from the former Yugoslavia, China and central Africa. Casey, "La Admisión e Integración": 28; Comisión Interministerial de Extranjería, *Anuario Estadístico*, 1995.

29. The office of Director General of Immigration was located at this time in the Department of Labor and Social Security. The Aznar government has taken an increasingly restrictive stance on immigration, as we will see in a moment, and the office has been moved to the Department of the Interior, signaling its primary function as a police activity.

30. Noting the absence of legislative detail in developing immigration policy, one legislator told his colleagues in the House of Representatives that they should not "give a blank check" to the executive branch and to the regions. Cortes Generales, *Diario de Sesiones del Congreso de los Diputados*, No. 100, April 9, 1991: 4889.

31. Reproduced in Ministerio del Interior, *Normativa Básica de Extranjería* (Madrid: Secretaría General Técnica), 1996: 248–249.

32. Cortes Generales, *Diario de Sesiones del Congreso de los Diputados*, No. 580, December 9, 1992: 17465.

33. Ministerio de Asuntos Sociales, Dirección General de Migraciones, *Plán para la Integración Social de los Inmigrantes* (Madrid: Ministerio de Asuntos Sociales), 1995: 9–10.

34. *Boletín Oficial del Estado*, "Ley Organica sobre Derechos y Libertades de los Extranjeros en España y su Integracion Social," Disposiciones Generales, *Boletín Oficial del Estado*, No. 10, January 12, 2000: 1139–1150.

35. All Spaniards must register in their local city hall as residents. This requirement of immigrants is therefore technically no more than is required of citizens, except that in the case of the undocumented, such registration is often problematic, as we will see in Chapter 5.

36. In effect, this law reduced the period of time required to obtain a permanent residency card from the six years stipulated in 1996 to five years.

37. González and MacBride, "Fortress Europe": 171.

38. Quoted in Núria Vives i Ferrer, "Las Modificaciones de la Ley de Extranjería: Historia de una Odisea Parlamentaria," in SOS Racismo, *Informe Anual 2001 sobre el Racismo en el Estado Español* (Barcelona: Icaria Editorial), 2001: 48.

39. Legge 30 dicembre 1986, No. 943, *Gazzetta Ufficiale*, No. 8, January 12, 1987.

40. Legge 28 febbraio 1990, No. 39, *Gazzetta Ufficiale*, No. 49, February 28, 1990.

41. Legge 6 marzo 1998, No. 40, *Gazzetta Ufficiale*, No. 59, March 12, 1998.

42. Decreto Legislativo, 25 luglio 1998, No. 286, Article 46, *Gazzetta Ufficiale*, No. 191, August 18, 1998.

43. Quoted in SOS Racismo, *El Ejido*: 74.

44. Diego López Garrido, "La Batalla Legal," *El País*, June 16, 2002: 16; Vives i Ferrer, "Las Modificaciones de la Ley de Extranjería."

45. José María Ruiz de Huidobro, "El Regimén Legal de la Inmigración en España: El Continuo Cambio," *Migraciones*, Vol. 9 (June), 2001: 78.

46. Francisco Javier Durán Ruiz, "Immigration Policy in Spain: The Relationship between Legal Status, Rights, and the Social Integration of Immigrants in Spain," paper presented at the Center for Comparative Immigration Studies, University of California, San Diego, La Jolla, CA, October 19, 2002: 3. The term "counter-reformation" refers to the fact that the law constitutes a reform of the 4/2000 reform, and brings Spanish immigration policy closer to the policy in effect after passage of the first law in 1985.

47. Boletín Oficial del Estado, "Derechos y Libertades de los Extranjeros en España y su Integración Social," *Texto Integrado de las Leyes Orgánicas 4/2000, de 11 de enero, y 8/2000, de 22 de Diciembre.* Madrid: Boletín Oficial del Estado.

48. This, together with several other provisions, has been contested as unconstitutional by several local regions and by the opposition Socialist Party in what is likely to be a lengthy legal wrangle.

49. Consistent with this approach, the regulatory plan drawn up subsequent to the enactment of 8/2000 (Plan Greco, to be discussed below) established a paramilitary, high-tech system of border control complete with sensors, radars, night-vision cameras, and sophisticated communication devices. This technological complex of controls, referred to as SIVE after the Spanish acronym for Integrated Service of Exterior Vigilance, began as a pilot project in the Canary Islands, has since been installed on the Cadiz coast near Morocco, and is slated for use throughout the Andalusian coast.

50. The special legalization program for Ecuadorians was prompted by events following a highly publicized accident in southern Spain, in which twelve Ecuadorian workers were killed in a collision between the van that was taking them to work and a train. When protests erupted over the conditions in which illegal Ecuadorians lived and worked in Spain, the government conjured up a program in which Ecuadorians were told to return to Ecuador to apply for the quota system and come back to Spain at government expense. It was forced to cancel this expensive "circular regularization" program when over 25,000 Ecuadorians applied, replacing it with the much cheaper "Operación Ecuador" which legalized Ecuadorians within Spain. Wayne A. Cornelius, "Spain: The Uneasy Transition from Labor Exporter to Labor Importer," in Cornelius, Martin, and Hollifield, *Controlling Immigration*.

51. Durán Ruiz, "Immigration Policy in Spain": 6.

52. Personal interview, Madrid, July, 2002.

53. Berlusconi's coalition threatened to unravel in the face of some of the punitive measures proposed by Umberto Bossi, leader of the Northern League and Minister of Reform in Berlusconi's cabinet. The Prime Minister reportedly urged Bossi to back off from his most radical demands, warning, "Be careful, the coalition's survival is really at risk" (quoted in Giorgio Battistini, "Da Ciampi Stop alla Lega: Umanitá con i Clandestini," *La Repubblica*, March 20, 2002: 1). One commentator remarked that Berlusconi was in an "arm-wrestling match" with Bossi who was alienating centrist members of the coalition ("Immigrati, L'Italia ha Capacitá Limitate," *Corriere della Sera*, May 17, 2002: 1).

54. Giuseppe D'Avanzo, "Clandestini, Stato d'Emergenza," *La Repubblica*, March 19, 2002: 1.
55. Legge 30 luglio 2002, No. 189, *Gazzetta Ufficiale*, No. 199, August 26, 2002.
56. Umberto Bossi, quoted in Giovanna Casadio, "Immigrati, la Legge Fantasma," *La Repubblica*, January 22, 2003: 12; Roberto Calderoli, quoted in Giancarlo Mola, "Sanatoria Immigrati 600 Mila le Richieste," *La Repubblica.it*, www.repubblica.it, November 13, 2002: 2.
57. Roberto Zuccolini, "Immigrati, Espulsioni Piú Facili," *Corriere della Sera*, July 27, 2001: 1.
58. Quoted in Piero Colaprico, "Immigrati, Patto Bossi-Fini, 'Resta Solo chi ha un Lavoro,'" *La Repubblica*, August 7, 2001: 8.
59. Quoted in "Costerá 800 Euro Regolarizzare un Lavoratore Extracomunitario," *Nuovo Quotidiano di Puglia*, August 4, 2002: 5. Presumably, the Italian word "sanatoria" (equivalent to "amnesty") implies forgiveness or even a full-fledged "forgetting" ("amnesia"), exceeding the intent of this law which was to "regularize" without the implication of a pardon.
60. Quoted in Colaprico, "Immigrati, Riforma in Arrivo": 19.
61. "Impronte e Contratti: Ecco le Nuove Regole," *Corriere della Sera*, July 12, 2002: 2.
62. Sandro Magister, "Lasciate che Vengano a Noi," *L'Espresso*, August 7, 2002: 58.
63. "Quella Legge é Razzista," *Il Tirreno*, July 26, 2002: 1.
64. "Immigrati, Impronte per Legge," *La Repubblica*, July 12, 2002: 1.
65. Quoted in Casadio, "Immigrati, Via alla Nuova Legge": 2.
66. Quoted in Andrea Gagliardi, "Immigrati, Bufera sulla Legge," *La Repubblica*, July 13, 2002: 21.
67. Quoted in Giorgio Lonardi, "Qui in Veneto Servono, Sanno Lavorare Bene," *La Repubblica*, July 13, 2002: 21.
68. SOS Racismo, *Informe Anual 2002 sobre el Racismo en el Estado Español* (Barcelona: Icaria Editorial), 2002: 75. Yasemin Nuhoglu Soysal has suggested that "[m]ajor political parties [in Europe] more often than not exhibit a propensity for alignment rather than dissention in their immigration politics and platforms" (Soysal, *Limits of Citizenship*: 35). Whatever the truth of this statement in other Europoean countries, it is not the case in Spain and Italy, at least at the level of public discourse.
69. Ministerio del Interior, Delegación del Gobierno para la Extranjería y la Inmigración, *Programa GRECO* (Madrid: Ministerio del Interior), 2001: 18.
70. Luciano Fasano and Francesco Zucchini, "L'implementazione Locale del Testo Unico sull'immigrazione," in ISMU-Cariplo, *Sesto Rapporto sulle Migrazioni in Italia* (Milan: FrancoAngeli), 2001: 39–50 at 39.
71. Monica McBritton and Mario Giovanni Garofalo, "La Legge sull'immigrazione e il Lavoro," in E. Pugliese (ed.), *Rapporto Immigrazione*: 102.
72. Author interview, Rome, July, 1992.
73. Author interviews, Rome, July, 1992.
74. Author interview, Rome, July, 1992.

75. Pierluigi Onorato, "Per uno Statuto dello Straniero," *Democrazia e Diritto*, Vol. 6 (1989): 307.

76. Caritas/Migrantes, "Anticipazioni del 'Dossier Statistico Immigrazione 2003,'" Preliminary Report from Press Conference, Rome, March 10, 2003: 1 and 11. Immigration experts and NGO personnel explain that these numbers refer to applications and not distinct people. Since domestic helpers and others who had two or more part-time jobs with different employers were required to submit separate applications for each job, the number of actual people who applied is estimated to be about 15% lower than the number of applications. In addition, experts point out that 200,000 applications were submitted in the last two weeks, subsequent to the government circular allowing workers to obtain legalization for six months by denouncing their employers, and that some of the latter may turn out to be fictitious (but in the meantime, the immigrant applicant has secured a brief legal respite). Finally, front agencies were reportedly set up that for a substantial fee posed as an immigrant's employer; in other cases employers temporarily "hired" a worker and then legalized them, again for a substantial fee (Personal communication, November, 2002). In the end, it is unclear how many actual underground employers really "emerged."

77. Northern League Senator Roberto Calderoli, quoted in *Notizie ANSA*, "Calderoli: Cacceremo chi é senza Requisiti," November 13, 2002, www.stranieriinitalia.com.

78. Casadio, "Immigrati, la Legge Fantasma": 12. Ironically, those who await notification are "prisoners in Italy," unable to return to their home countries without jeopardizing their application (*ibid.*: 12).

79. Asher Colombo and Giuseppe Sciortino, *Stranieri in Italia: Assimilati ed Esclusi* (Bologna: Il Mulino), 2002.

80. Izquierdo, *La Inmigración Inesperada*: 150–151.

81. *Ibid.*: 125 and 73.

82. Cohen, *Contested Domains*.

83. McBritton and Garofalo, "La Legge sull'immigrazione": 104.

84. Durán Ruiz, "Immigration Policy in Spain": 45.

85. Tano Gullo, "Se é Questo il Modo di Accoglierli," *Supplemento, La Repubblica*, July 20, 2001: 59.

86. Durán Ruiz, "Immigration Policy in Spain": 26.

87. Personal interview, Barcelona, June, 2002.

88. Ewick and Silbey, *The Common Place of Law*: 102.

89. Javier de Lucas, *Europa: Convivir con la Diferencia? Racismo, Nacionalismo y Derechos de las Minorias* (Madrid: Editorial Tecnos), 1994: 92.

90. Cortes Generales, *Diario de Sesiones del Congreso de los Diputados*, No. 100, April 9, 1991: 4889.

91. Quoted in Andreu Domingo Valls, Jaume Clapés Estrada, and Maria Prats Ferret, *Condicions de Vida de la Població d'origen Africà i Llatinoamericà a la Regió Metropolitana de Barcelona: Una Aproximació Qualitativa* (Barcelona: Diputació de Barcelona), 1995: 39.

92. *Ibid.*: 40.

93. Quoted in *ibid.*: 40.
94. Fasano and Zucchini, "L'implementazione Locale del Testo Unico": 50.
95. Author interview, Venice, July, 2001. Another example of the disparate effects of regional discretion can be found in the implementation of a recent legalization program in Spain. Núria Vives i Ferrer points out that in Barcelona, the applicant rejection rate in 2000 was 71%, while in Madrid only 17% were rejected. This discrepancy may be explained in part by the fact that overall Moroccan applicants were far more likely to be denied (50%) than Latin Americans or Eastern Europeans (30–35%), and Barcelona had a disproportionate number of Moroccan applicants; however, the magnitude of the discrepancy exceeds even this apparent discrimination based on nationality. Vives i Ferrer, "Las Modificaciones": 54. Even more dramatic is the difference between the 8.7% acceptance rate in Melilla and what amounted to a 100% acceptance rate in the cities of Huelva and Zaragoza. Indicative of the fact that this is not just about the ethnicity of applicants or the varying quality of the applications, some applicants were apparently rejected in one jurisdiction and accepted in another. Durán Ruiz, "Immigration Policy in Spain": 28.
96. SOS Racismo, *Informe Anual 2001*: 74.
97. Diego López Garrido, "La Batalla Legal," *El País*, June 16, 2002: 16. In this editorial, Garrido talks of "perverse laws with perverse consequences," in reference to the difficulty of achieving and maintaining legality under Aznar's law, Law 8/2000.
98. Mercedes Jabardo, "Etnicidad y Mercado de Trabajo: Inmigración Africana en la Agricultura Catalana," *Perspectiva Social*, Vol. 36, 1995: 81–95.
99. There were immigrants who were working illegally in the underground economy, but they were under no threat of deportation, and were reportedly better integrated in the community than later cohorts. Izquierdo, *La Inmigración Inesperada*.
100. Personal interview, Barcelona, June, 2002.
101. These studies included, respectively, interviews with seventy-five Latin American and African immigrants in the Barcelona region, and fifty Moroccan families in Madrid. Domingo Valls, Clapés Estrada, and Prats Ferret, *Condicions de Vida*; Pablo Pumares, *La Integración de los Inmigrantes Marroquíes: Familias Marroquíes en la Comunidad de Madrid* (Barcelona: Fundación "La Caixa"), 1996.
102. Quoted in Domingo Valls, Clapés Estrada, and Prats Ferret, *Condicions de Vida*: 125 and 127.
103. Enrico Bonerandi, "Brució Rumeno, 30 Anni di Carcere," *La Repubblica*, March 20, 2001: 24.
104. "Così Colf e Lavoratori Potranno 'Emergere,'" *Corriere della Sera*, July 12, 2002: 2; "Immigrazione: Mantovano, Denunciare Illegalitá Imprenditori 'Chiedere a Immigrati Pagamento Contributi Equivale a Ricatto,'" *Notizie ANSA*, www.stranieriinitalia.com/notiziario2/, September 28, 2002. Such extortion is reminiscent of reports in the late 1980s that

employers in the United States were requiring their undocumented workers to pay a bond up front to cover the cost of any future fine imposed
under the 1986 employer sanctions law.

105. Caritas/Migrantes, "Anticipazioni": 1.
106. "Colf Straniere Cacciate per Evitare L'assunzione," *La Gazzetta del
Mezzogiorno*, June 11, 2002: 15. The problem is not always with employers, who sometimes petition the government for legalization for their
workers to no avail. When employers of 5,000 Moroccan strawberry
workers in Andalusia applied for their legalization, the Aznar government turned them down, and instead imported 7,000 Polish women on
temporary quotas to replace them in the strawberry fields. Liliana Suárez-
Navaz, who conducted her dissertation fieldwork in rural Andalusia, spec-
ulates: "Women were seen [by the government] as being more committed
to going back home to their families after the work contracts were termi-
nated" (Personal interview, Madrid, July, 2002).
107. "Immigrazione: Buttiglione, Sanatoria un'Operazione di Pulizia," *Notizie
ANSA*, www.stranieriinitalia.com/notiziario2/, November 12, 2002,
emphasis added.
108. Susan Bibler Coutin, *Legalizing Moves: Salvadoran Immigrants' Struggle
for US Residency* (Ann Arbor: University of Michigan Press), 2003:
29.
109. Quoted in "Immigrazione, é Scontro tra An e la Lega," *La Repubblica.it*,
http://www.repubblica.it, November 7, 2002: 2. The National Alliance
and the Northern League are both pro-business and do not look favorably on workers taking their employers to court in any circumstance,
and so it is not surprising that they balked at the idea of *undocumented
immigrant workers* playing this role. More interesting here is the twisted
logic required to argue that employers in the underground economy
have the option ("allows for, but does not require") of *not* making their
workers legal, or that such a forced legalization would negatively impact
immigrants' integration (relative to remaining undocumented, one must
assume).
110. Pumares, *La Integración de los Inmigrantes Marroquíes*: 87–89; Izquierda,
La Inmigración Inesperada: 73.
111. Santos, "Elementos Jurídicos": 111.
112. F. Ray Marshall, "Economic Factors Influencing the International Migration of Workers," in S. Ross (ed.), *Views Across the Border*: 169.
113. Quoted in Gianluigi De Vito, "Non Piace la Bossi-Fini," *La Gazzetta del
Mezzogiorno*, July 13, 2002: 4.
114. Claude Meillassoux, *Maidens, Meal and Money: Capitalism and the
Domestic Community* (Cambridge: Cambridge University Press), 1981:
122.
115. Soysal, *Limits of Citizenship*: 33.
116. Volpp, "'Obnoxious to their Very Nature'": 62. Volpp is quoting Lisa
Lowe, *Immigrant Acts: On Asian American Cultural Politics* (Durham, NC:
Duke University Press), 1996: 4.
117. Vives i Ferrer, "Las Modificaciones": 52.

Chapter 3.
1. The term "Useful Invaders" is the literal translation of Maurizio Ambrosini's book on immigrants in the Italian economy, *Utili Invasori.*
2. Quoted in "Fazio: 'Saranno gli Immigrati a Salvare le Pensioni Italiane,'" *La Repubblica,* July 31, 1999: 23.
3. Ministerio del Interior, *Programa Greco*: 17.
4. Thomas Fuller, "Low Birthrates Pose Challenge for Europe," *International Herald Tribune,* December 12, 2002: 6 (IHT Online, www.iht.com/articles/).
5. Jeffrey Fleishman, "Low Birthrate in Italy Could Be Death Knell of Many Small Towns," *San Diego Union-Tribune,* February 10, 2000: A21.
6. "Fazio," *La Repubblica,* 23. Fleishman, "Low Birthrate": A26. The United Nations Population Division predicts that Italy would have to admit over 2.2 million immigrants annually over the next thirty years to stave off demographically induced economic and fiscal crises (United Nations Population Division, *Replacement Migration: Is It a Solution to Declining and Ageing Populations?* (New York: United Nations Secretariat), 2000.
7. "Comuni: Milano; Popolazione Stabile, Ma per Arrivo Immigrati," *Notizie ANSA,* December 27, 2002, www.stranieriinitalia.com.
8. Sebastián Tobarra, "Una Fuente de Riqueza," *El País,* June 16, 2002: 10; Charo Nogueira, "La Natalidad Crece en España por Tercer Año Consecutivo Gracias a la Inmigración," *El País,* June 27, 2002: 27.
9. Caritas/Migrantes, "Anticipazioni": 7; Maria Novella de Luca, "Gli Immigrati Sono Molti di Piú Ma Non Sappiamo Conviverci," *La Repubblica,* March 28, 2002: 13; Tito Boeri, Gordon Hanson, and Barry McCormick (eds.), *Immigration Policy and the Welfare System: A Report for the Fondazione Rodolfo Debenedetti in Association with the William Davidson Institute* (Oxford: Oxford University Press), 2002: 8; Center for Immigration Studies (http://www.cis.org).
10. For an excellent case study of the bureaucratic politics and practices of government data collection, interpretation, and dissemination, see Kevin D. Haggerty, *Making Crime Count* (Toronto: University of Toronto Press), 2001.
11. Istituto Nazionale di Statistica, *Annuario Statistico Italiano,* "La Popolazione Straniera Residente in Italia al 1 Gennaio 2001," http://www.istat.it; Gruppo Abele, *Annuario Sociale 2001*: 571. Caritas deals extensively with immigrants in the provision of services, and is widely regarded as the most authoritative source on information about immigrants. They argue that the Interior Ministry data often exclude minors who do not always have separate residence permits.
12. Caritas, *Immigrazione: Dossier Statistico 2003* (Rome: Edizioni Anterem), 2003.
13. Paraphrased in Gian Antonio Stella, "Altivole, Un Abitante su Sette é Immigrato," *Corriere della Sera,* March 19, 2001: 17. One small Tuscan town, San Donnino, in the periphery of Florence, was "rebaptized" "San Pechino" by journalists in the early 1990s when thousands of Chinese immigrants arrived to work in the leather-tanning industry. Fabio Berti,

Esclusione e Integrazione: Uno Studio su due Comunitá di Immigrati (Milan: FrancoAngeli), 2000: 77.

14. CNNItalia Online, "Bianco sull'Immigrazione: Ecco i Veri Numeri," www.CNNItalia.it/Italia/, December 18, 2000; Gruppo Abele, *Annuario Sociale 2001* (Milan: Feltrinelli Editore), 2001: 553; "Southern Europe," *Migration News*, Vol. 9, No. 1, January, 2002: 27.

15. Floya Anthias and Gabriella Lazaridis, "Introduction," in Floya Anthias and Gabriella Lazaridis (eds.), *Gender and Migration in Southern Europe: Women on the Move* (New York: Berg), 2000: 7.

16. Gruppo Abele, *Annuario Sociale 2001*: 573; Ministro dell'Interno, *Rapporto del Ministro dell'Interno sullo Stato della Sicurezza in Italia* (Bologna: Il Mulino), 2001: 278.

17. Victoria Chell-Robinson, "Female Migrants in Italy: Coping in a Country of New Immigration," in Anthias and Lazaridis, *Gender and Migration in Southern Europe*.

18. Juan Díez Nicolás and María José Ramírez Lafita, *La Inmigración en España: Una Década de Investigaciones* (Madrid: Ministerio de Trabajo y Asuntos Sociales, Secretaría General de Asuntos Sociales), 2001: 22; Ministerio del Interior, cited in Delegación del Gobierno, *Boletín Estadístico*, 2004: 4. "España Acoge a Más de un Millón de Inmigrantes Legales," *ABC*, April 17, 2002.

19. "Southern Europe," *Migration News*, Vol. 10, No. 3, July, 2003: 37.

20. Ministerio del Interior, *Anuario Estadístico de Extranjería* (Madrid: Imprenta Nacional del Boletín Oficial del Estado), 2000: 94–95.

21. Durán Ruiz, "Immigration Policy in Spain": 7.

22. These estimates are collected from Spain's NGOs and are cited in Amnesty International, "Spain: Crisis of Identity, Race-Related Torture, and Ill-Treatment by State Agents," April 16, 2002: 3, www.amnesty.org.

23. Ministerio del Interior, *Anuario Estadístico*: 102.

24. Natalia Ribas-Mateos, "Female Birds of Passage: Leaving and Settling in Spain," in Anthias and Lazaridis, *Gender and Migration in Southern Europe*: 181.

25. Entering Spain through its airports as a tourist is the most common form of entry for unauthorized immigrants. While sea entry is the second most common method, it ranks an undisputed first in media coverage and law enforcement (see Chapter 6). In 2001, over three-quarters of those apprehended trying to enter the country illegally were detained in the Strait of Gibraltar (Wayne Cornelius, "Spain: The Uneasy Transition from Labor Exporter to Labor Importer," in *Controlling Migration*).

26. Dominique Grisoni and Hughes Portelli, *Le Lotte Operaie in Italia dal 1960 al 1976* (Milan: Rizzoli), 1977: 161.

27. For an excellent discussion of these dualities, see Agnew, *Place and Politics in Modern Italy*.

28. The literal meaning of "mezzogiorno" is "midday" or "noon." The identification of the south with midday presumably derives from its association with bright sunlight and a warm climate.

29. Since the rise to power of Berlusconi and his allies in the Northern League, whose complaints about the alleged corruption and inefficiency of the Mezzogiorno constitute a central ingredient of their political platform (Bossi early in his career advocated the outright secession of the north), the south is unlikely to benefit under their watch from any infusion of new government resources.

30. Francesco Forte, *Industria, Governo, Sottogoverno* (Turin: Societá Editrice Internazionale), 1976: 17.

31. The GDP in Italy increased by just 2.5% in 2001 and an anemic one-tenth of one per cent in 2002, with small and medium-sized firms offsetting losses in the monopoly sector (Luisa Grion, "Italia Vicina alla Crescita Zero," *La Repubblica*, May 16, 2002: 2).

32. Paolo Griseri, "L'indotto Fiat Travolto dalla Crisi Cancellati 24 Mila Posti," *La Repubblica*, December 30, 2002: 1, www.repubblica.it. "Istat, nelle Piccole Imprese Piú Lavoro e Meno Salario," *CNNitalia*, July 21, 2000: 1, www.cnnitalia.it.

33. Marco Patucchi, "Export Italiano in Ripresa ma il Nord-est 'Emigra,'" *La Repubblica*, July 18, 2001: 26.

34. Maurizio Ambrosini, *La Fatica di Integrarsi: Immigrati e Lavoro in Italia* (Bologna: Il Mulino), 2001: 49.

35. Griseri, "L'indotto Fiat": 1.

36. Eurispes, *Rapporto Italia 2001* (Rome: Ufficio Stampa Eurispes), 2001: 752–762; Gruppo Abele, *Annuario Sociale 2001*: 688; Institute of Economic and Social Research, CGIL, cited in "Tre Milioni di Lavoratori in Nero, Due su Tre al Sud," *Rassegna On Line*, www.rassegna.it.

37. Eurispes, *Rapporto Italia 2001*: 752–762.

38. "Piú di una Azienda su Due Impiega Lavoratori in Nero," *City Roma*, January 15, 2003: 1–2.

39. This practice was particularly common among the southern Italian workers in the Fiat factories in and around Turin in the 1950s, 1960s, and 1970s, but it persists today and is now a critical ingredient of this post-Fordist economy. Luciano Gallino, *Il Lavoro e il Suo Doppio: Seconda Occupazione e Politiche del Lavoro in Italia* (Bologna: Il Mulino), 1985; Carter, *States of Grace*.

40. Clemente Tartaglione, "Riallineamento e Sommerso nel Mezzogiorno," Presentazione dell'Osservatorio per l'Emersione nel Mezzogiorno, IRES CGIL, Rome, February 16, 2001.

41. Eurispes, *Rapporto Italia 2001*: 752–762.

42. Salvatore Avitabile, "Salento, Irregolaritá in un'azienda su Due," *Corriere del Mezzogiorno*, August 6, 2002: 7.

43. Caritas/Migrantes, "Anticipazioni": 2.

44. "Lavoro: In Lombardia Sono 500,000 i Lavoratori in Nero Denuncia della CGIL," *Notizie ANSA*, December 5, 2002: 1, www.stranieriinitalia.com.

45. US Department of State, Bureau of European Affairs, "Background Notes: Italy," October, 1999: 9, www.state.gov. According to some estimates, the three unions represent 12 million people, or over 50% of the official

workforce of 23 million ("Big 3 Labor Unions Call for 1-Day Strike," *Los Angeles Times*, March 27, 2002: A11).

46. "Leftists Decry Italy's Labor Proposals," *Los Angeles Times*, March 24, 2002: A12; Associated Press, "Nationwide Strike Hobbles Italy," *Los Angeles Times*, April 17, 2002: A4; "L'Italia si é Fermata: Tredici Milioni in Sciopero, Centinaia di Migliaia nelle Piazze," *La Repubblica*, April 17, 2002: 1.

47. Slobodan Djajic, "Illegal Immigration and Resource Allocation," *International Economic Review*, Vol. 38, No. 1, 1997: 98.

48. Tito Boeri, Gordon Hanson, and Barry McCormick (eds.), *Immigration Policy and the Welfare System: A Report for the Fondazione Rodolfo Debenedetti in Association with the William Davidson Institute* (Oxford: Oxford University Press), 2002: 56. On an index where 100 represents average gross labor costs for the EU, the figure for Italy is 130.7. The Netherlands is highest, at 148.3.

49. "L'economia Italiana é Meno Competitiva," *Corriere della Sera*, November 12, 2002: 1, www.corriere.it. Other studies come to similar, but less dire, conclusions: Luisa Grion, "Italia, Troppe Tasse e Caro-Tariffe," *La Repubblica*, July 29, 2002: 11.

50. Elena Polidori, " 'L'Italia Frena ma Puó Ripartire con Meno Tasse e Salari Flessibili,' " *La Repubblica*, March 15, 2001: 3.

51. Roberto Rizza, "Trasformazioni del Lavoro, Nuove Forme di Precarizzazione Lavorativa e Politiche di Welfare: Alcune Riflessioni Preliminari," *Sociología del Lavoro*, Vols. 78–79, 2000: 13–27; Gruppo Abele, *Annuario Sociale 2001*: 686.

52. Mario Centorrino, "Il Lavoro Interinale? Avvantaggia Solo il Nord Italia," *L'unitá*, July 22, 2001: 11. So scarce is formal, part-time work in the south that temporary employment agencies are discouraged from opening local branches there.

53. Roberto Rizza, "Trasformazioni": 13.

54. Some analysts of the post-Fordist model have cited the Emilia-Romagna region of Italy, with its proliferation of small shops and just-in-time production, as the prototype for successful production in the new global economy: Werner Sengenberger and Frank Pyke (eds.), *Industrial Districts and Local Economic Regeneration* (Geneva: International Institute of Labour Studies), 1992.

55. The counterpart of this relatively high unemployment rate is the labor market participation rate. According to a European Union study, Italy has the lowest *employment* rate in Europe, at 54.5% (compared to the EU average of 64%, and 76% in the top-ranked Denmark): "UE, in Crescita l'Occupazione," *La Gazzetta del Mezzogiorno*, August 30, 2002: 2.

56. Roberto Petrini, "Lavoro, Boom del Posto Fisso," *La Repubblica*, March 28, 2002: 6; Istituto Centrale di Statistica (ISTAT), *Annuario Statistico Italiano* (Rome: Istituto Poligrafico dello Stato), 2001; "Occupazione Record, Mai Cosí Alta dal '93," *Corriere della Sera*, March 28, 2002: 10; Caritas, *Immigrazione: Dossier Statistico 2000* (Rome: Edizioni Anterem), 2000; Eurispes,

Rapporto Italia 2001: 134–135; Gruppo Abele, *Annuario Sociale 2001*: 685.

57. "Disoccupati: Il Sud Peggio della Bulgaria," *La Repubblica*, August 6, 2002: 25.
58. Gruppo Abele, *Annuario Sociale 2001*: 712–724; Luisa Grion, "I Poveri Crescono al Nord; Sono Otto Milioni in Tutta Italia," *La Repubblica*, August 1, 2001: 33; Giovanna Casadio, "Roma, di Miseria si Muore; Ecco l'esercito dei Poveri," *La Repubblica*, March 15, 2001: 12.
59. Grisoni and Portelli, *Le Lotte Operaie*: 161.
60. "Un Nuovo Assunto su Quattro Sará Extracomunitario," *La Gazzetta del Mezzogiorno*, July 14, 2002: 14.
61. Cited in "Lavoro: CGIL, Nelle PMI 60% Immigrati, 23% nel Manifatturiero," *Notizie ANSA*, December 18, 2002, www.stranieriinitalia.com.
62. Eurispes, *Rapporto Italia 2001*: 361.
63. Quoted in Tom Hundley, "Cultural Attitudes Blamed for Italy's Labor Crisis," *Chicago Tribune Online*, www.chicagotribune.com, February 23, 2001: 1.
64. Maria Luisa Colledani, "Transfrontalieri, la Nuova Risorsa," *Il Sole 24 Ore*, April 30, 2001: 1.
65. Giustina Orientale Caputo, "Salari di Fatto dei Lavoratori Immigrati in Italia," in E. Pugliese (ed.), *Rapporto Immigrazione*: 88.
66. *Ibid.*
67. *Ibid.*: 92.
68. Gian Antonio Stella, "Altivole, Un Abitante su Sette é Immigrato," *Corriere della Sera*, March 19, 2001: 17.
69. Caputo, "Salari di Fatto": 90.
70. *Ibid.*
71. Osservatorio Ares, "I Dati dell'Osservatorio Ares 2000," report presented at a conference on *Flussi Migratori e Politiche per la Salute*, Sicily, March 26, 2001; "Immigrazione: +15% Annuo Presenza Stagionali Agricultura," *Notizie ANSA*, February 4, 2002, www.stranieriinitalia.com.
72. Clemente Tartaglione, "Riallineamento e Sommerso nel Mezzogiorno," *Presentazione dell'Osservatorio per l'Emersione del Lavoro Sommerso nel Mezzogiorno, IRES CGIL*. Rome, February 16, 2001.
73. "Immigrazione: +15%," *Notizie ANSA*.
74. Alioune Gueye, "Il Rafforzamento della Presenza degli Immigrati nelle Aziende e la Contrattazione Sindacale," in Pugliese, *Rapporto Immigrazione*; Caputo, "Salari di Fatto."
75. Caputo, "Salari di Fatto": 89.
76. Luca Fazzo, "Immigrati, Sará un 2001 Record: Il Governo ne Fará Entrare 83 Mila," *La Repubblica*, March 15, 2001: 29.
77. Anthias and Lazaridis, "Introduction": 7.
78. Caputo, "Salari di Fatto": 92; Maurizio Ambrosini, "Il Lavoro," in ISMU-Cariplo, *Sesto Rapporto*: 92.
79. See Jacqueline Andall, "Cape Verdean Women on the Move: 'Immigration Shopping' in Italy and Europe," *Modern Italy*, Vol. 4, No. 2, 1999: 241–257.

80. I once overheard an Italian friend who was doing much of the housework while his wife was suffering a difficult pregnancy, say glibly, "Faccio il filippino" ("I'm the filipino," i.e. the domestic help).

81. Rhacel Salazar Parreñas, *Servants of Globalization: Women, Migration, and Domestic Work* (Stanford: Stanford University Press), 2001: 199.

82. Victoria Chell-Robinson, "Female Migrants in Italy: Coping in a Country of New Immigration," in Anthias and Lazaridis, *Gender and Migration in Southern Europe*: 119.

83. Enrico Pugliese, "Gli Immigrati nel Mercato del Lavoro e nella Struttura dell'Occupazione," in E. Pugliese (ed.), *Rapporto Immigrazione*: 18.

84. Gianluigi De Vito, "Lavoro Dunque Non Sono," *La Gazzetta del Mezzogiorno*, February 13, 2002: 15.

85. Ambrosini, "Il Lavoro": 92.

86. Caputo, "Salari di Fatto": 92. An ethnographic study corroborates the wage differential, reporting that Filipinas "experience a 'top of the pile' situation . . . and are able to command the highest wages" (Chell-Robinson, "Female Migrants in Italy": 110–111).

87. Francesca Decimo, "Reti di Solidarietá e Strategie Economiche di Donne Somale Immigrate a Napoli," *Studi Emigrazione*, Vol. 33, 1996: 474–475.

88. Jacqueline Andall, "Organizing Domestic Workers in Italy: The Challenge of Gender, Class, and Ethnicity," in Anthias and Lazaridis (eds.), *Gender and Migration in Southern Europe*: 165.

89. Gueye, "Il Rafforzamento": 136.

90. Laura Zanfrini, "Il Lavoro degli 'Altri': Gli Immigrati nel Sistema Produttivo Bergamasco," *Quaderni ISMU*, No. 1, 1996; Berti, *Esclusione e Integrazione*: 134.

91. *Ibid.*

92. Pugliese, "Gli Immigrati nel Mercato del Lavoro": 65.

93. Giovanni Mottura, "Immigrati e Sindacato," in E. Pugliese (ed.), *Rapporto Immigrazione*: 123–124.

94. "Lavoro: Extracomunitari, Poco Sindacato al Nord, Piú al Sud; in Campania 'Sindacalizzazione' Superiore alla Media Regionale," *Notizie ANSA*, January 12, 2002, www.stranieriinitalia.com.

95. Eurispes, *Rapporto Italia 2001*: 359; annual reports of Fondazione Cariplo-ISMU and Caritas, cited in "Marocchino, Lavora a Tempo Pieno e Manda a Casa 613 Euro Ogni Anno," *La Gazzetta del Mezzogiorno*, June 5, 2002: 5.

96. Ires, cited in "Lavoro: CGIL, Nelle PMI 60% Immigrati, 23% nel Manifatturiero," *Notizie ANSA*, December 18, 2002, www. stranieriinitalia .com.

97. Osservatorio Ares, "I Dati dell'Osservatorio Ares 2000," presented at a conference on *Flussi Migratori e Politiche per la Salute*, Sicily, March 26, 2001.

98. Annual reports of Fondazione Cariplo-ISMU and Caritas, cited in *La Gazzetta del Mezzogiorno*, "Marocchino": 5.

99. Ambrosini, *Utili Invasori*; Ambrosini, *La Fatica di Integrarsi*.

100. Quoted in De Vito, "Non Piace la Bossi-Fini": 4.
101. Boeri, Hanson, and McCormick, *Immigration Policy and the Welfare System*: 27.
102. Andrea Gavosto, Alessandra Venturini, and Claudia Villosio, "Do Immigrants Compete with Natives?," *Labour*, Vol. 13, No. 3, 1999: 603–622; Alessandra Venturini and Claudia Villosio, "Are Immigrants Competing with Natives in the Italian Labour Market? The Employment Effect," discussion paper for the Institute for the Study of Labor, No. 467, April, 2002: 1–27.
103. Ambrosini, *La Fatica di Integrarsi*: 61–62.
104. *Ibid.*: 174.
105. Ambrosini, *Utili Invasori*.
106. Investment in the public sector in Spain in 1972 reached just 21% of its GDP, while the comparable figure for the UK was 50%, and between 34% and 38% in the United States, Germany, and Italy (J. Segura Sánchez, "Spain: Shaping Factors," in Alexis Jacquemin and David Wright (eds.), *The European Challenges Post 1992: Shaping Factors, Shaping Actors* (Brookfield, VT: Edward Elgar), 1993: 401).
107. "A Survey of Spain," *Economist*, December 14, 1996: 3–18.
108. Jorge J. Maté García, *Demanda, Oferta y Ajustes Salariales en el Mercado de Trabajo Español* (Valladolid: Secretariado de Publicaciones, Universidad de Valladolid), 1994: 18 and 27.
109. "La Renta 'Per Capita' en España Crece un 5.9% Hasta 16,148 Euros," *El País*, July 17, 2002: 51; see also Centro de Estudios del Cambio Social, *Informe España 2002* (Madrid: Fundación Encuentro), 2002.
110. Juan Jimeno and Luís Toharia, *Unemployment and Labor Market Flexibility: Spain* (Geneva: International Labour Office), 1994: 7.
111. Kathryn A. Woolard, "The 'Crisis in the Concept of Identity' in Contemporary Catalonia, 1976–1982," in Gary McDonogh (ed.), *Conflict in Catalonia: Images of an Urban Society* (Gainesville, FL: University of Florida Press), 1986: 57.
112. A number of Spanish social scientists have addressed this internal movement, which at the time was conceptualized as "immigration." Thus, when sociologist Carlota Solé wrote in 1982 of the importance of "immigrants" in Catalan society, it was these internal migrants who were her focus: Carlota Solé, *Los Inmigrantes en la Sociedad y en la Cultura Catalanas* (Barcelona: Ediciones Península), 1982; see also Antonio Jutglar (ed.), *La Inmigración en Cataluña* (Barcelona: Edima), 1977.
113. Richards, "Spain: From Isolation to Integration"; Centro de Estudios del Cambio Social, *Informe España 2002*: 366; Kenneth Maxwell and Steven Spiegel, *The New Spain: From Isolation to Influence* (New York: Council on Foreign Relations Press), 1994: 78–79.
114. Faustino Miguélez Lobo, "El Trabajo Sumergido en España en la Perspectiva del Acta Única Europea," *Papers: Revista de Sociologia, Universitat Autonoma de Barcelona*, Vol. 32, 1989: 118.
115. Eurispes, *Rapporto Italia*.

116. Cited in Almudena Mazuelos, "Tres de Cada Cuatro Contratos Firmados en el 96 Duraron Menos de Tres Meses," *Ya*, January 24, 1997: 17.

117. OECD study, cited in "Más del 80% de los Jóvenes en España Tiene un Contrato Temporal," *El País*, July 22, 2002: 51.

118. Labor advocates in Spain and Italy call such temporary and contingent employment "precarious" work, in that it is uncertain and insecure. A recent spate of industrial accidents in Spain reveals the literal meaning of "precarious" work, as union officials have documented the link between contingent work and a high accident rate ("Pujol Admite que la Siniestralidad Laboral es 'Más Elevada de lo Normal,'" *El País*, July 20, 2002: 4).

119. *Boletín Mensual de Estadística*, Vol. 64, April, 1997 (Madrid: Instituto Nacional de Estadística); OECD, *Main Economic Indicators*, May, 2002: 26. The 13% figure is from labor market surveys conducted by the OECD. The rate of *registered* unemployment recorded by the Spanish Department of Labor – comprised of only those who have registered with the unemployment office – is just over 9% (Ministerio de Trabajo y Asuntos Sociales, Instituto Nacional del Empleo, Estadística de Empleo, January, 2002, Table 13.6, www.inem.es).

120. Centro de Estudios del Cambio Social, *Informe España 2002*: 524.

121. Maxwell and Spiegel, *The New Spain*; Segura Sánchez, "Spain: Shaping Factors."

122. "A Survey of Spain," *Economist*, December 14, 1996: 7. Interestingly, a national survey reports that over half of respondents said they would move for a good job ("Las Familias Necessitan . . .," *El País*, June 28, 2002: 27), suggesting perhaps that Spaniards perceive the current job offerings an insufficient incentive to move.

123. Ministerio de Asuntos Sociales, Dirección General de Migraciones, *Anuario de Migraciones* (Madrid: Secretaría General Técnica), 1995: 197–198.

124. Maté García, *Demanda, Oferta y Ajustes Salariales*: 26.

125. A labor–management accord struck in the spring of 1997 between the largest employer associations and the union confederations was one response to this perception of labor market rigidity. This controversial pact makes it easier and cheaper for employers to lay off workers, and provides for a certain percentage of sub-contract wages for entry-level apprentices (Idoya Noanin, "La Crítica de la Mayoría de IU al Papel Sindical en el Pacto Laboral Hace Aflorar Contradicciones Internas," *El País*, April 20, 1997: 17).

126. Vicenc Navarro, "Un Nuevo Dogma en España," *El País*, May 5, 1997: 13. This analyst counters the dogma with the observation that Spanish employers themselves are intransigent in their labor relations: "As much talk as there is about labor rigidity, there is little discussion of the great rigidity of employers" (*ibid.*: 14).

127. Consejo Economico y Social, *Economia, Trabajo y Seguridad* (Madrid: Consejo Economico y Social), 1995: 491.

128. Carlos García Serrano, Miguel Ángel Malo, and Luís Toharia, *La Pobreza en España* (Madrid: Ministerio de Trabajo y Asuntos Sociales), 2000; see also "España Ocupa el Tercer Peor Lugar de la UE en el índice de la ONU de Desarrollo Humano," *El País*, July 24, 2002: 25.
129. Tobarra, "Una Fuente de Riqueza": 10.
130. Ministerio del Interior, *Balance 2000: Extranjería e Inmigración* (Madrid: Oficina de Relaciones Informativas y Sociales), 2001: 34.
131. *El Mundo*, December 22, 2001, cited in SOS Racismo, *Informe Anual 2002*: 296.
132. Ministerio del Interior, *Balance 2000*: 35.
133. "La Prostitució és un Estigma per a les Dones," *La Veu del Carrier*, March–April, 2002: 23.
134. Cited in Díez Nicolás and José Ramírez Lafita, *La Voz de los Inmigrantes*: 75.
135. SOS Racismo, *Informe Anual 2002*: 89–90.
136. Colectivo IOÉ, *Inmigración y Trabajo en España* (Madrid: Secretaría General de Asuntos Sociales), 1999.
137. Domingo Valls, Clapés Estrada, and Prats Ferret, *Condicions de Vida*: 136; Pumares, *La Integración de los Inmigrantes Marroquíes*: 86.
138. *Ibid.*
139. Quoted in Domingo Valls, Clapés Estrada, and Prats Ferret, *Condicions de Vida*: 131.
140. Quoted in *ibid.*: 137.
141. Lluís Visa, "Más de 3000 Inmigrantes Vagan Sin Trabajo en Lleida por la Disminución de la Cosecha de Fruta," *El País*, July 8, 2002: 25. Lluís Visa, "Temporeros Sin Trabajo," *El País*, July 24, 2002, Cataluña: 1.
142. The following discussion of hothouse agriculture and the role of immigrants in it comes from the report of SOS Racismo following the riots (SOS Racismo, *El Ejido*), from the European Union study of the same events (Foro Civico Europeo, *El Ejido*), and from Zoubir Chattou, "Los Trabajadores Agrícolas Marroquíes de el Ejido: De la Invisibilidad a la Toma de Conciencia de Sí Mismos," *Migraciones*, Vol. 8, 2000: 203–229.
143. SOS Racismo, *El Ejido*: 16 and 19.
144. *Ibid.*: 19.
145. Chattou, "Los Trabajadores Agrícolas": 216.
146. SOS Racismo, *El Ejido*: 22.
147. SOS Racismo, *Informe Anual 2002*: 89.
148. Jabardo, "Etnicidad y Mercado de Trabajo": 81 and 84.
149. Nigel Harris, *The New Untouchables: Immigration and the New World Worker* (London: St. Martin's Press), 1995.
150. Ambrosini, *La Fatica di Integrarsi*: 174, emphasis added.
151. *Ibid.*: 58–59.
152. F. Ray Marshall, "Economic Factors": 169.
153. Aristide Zolberg, "Wanted But Not Welcome: Alien Labor in Western Development," in William Alonso (ed.), *Population in an Interacting World* (Cambridge: Harvard University Press), 1987.

Chapter 4

1. Masao Yamaguchi, "Kinship, Theatricality, and Marginal Reality in Japan," in Ravindra K. Jain (ed.), *Text and Context: The Social Anthropology of Tradition* (Philadelphia: Institute for the Study of Human Issues), 1977: 154, quoted in David Engel, "The Oven Bird's Song: Insiders, Outsiders, and Personal Injuries in an American Community," *Law and Society Review*, Vol. 18, 1984: 573.

2. William Isaac Thomas and Florian Znaniecki, *The Polish Peasant in Europe and America* (New York: Knopf), 1927; Robert E. Park and Ernest W. Burgess, *Introduction to the Science of Sociology* (Chicago: University of Chicago Press), 1921; W. Lloyd Warner and Leo Srole, *The Social Systems of American Ethnic Groups* (New Haven: Yale University Press), 1945; Milton M. Gordon, *Assimilation in American Life: The Role of Race, Religion, and National Origins* (New York: Oxford University Press), 1964.

3. Nathan Glazer and Daniel Patrick Moynihan, *Beyond the Melting Pot: The Negroes, Puerto Ricans, Jews, Italians, and Irish of New York City* (Cambridge: MIT Press), 1963; Nathan Glazer, "Is Assimilation Dead?," *Annals of the American Academy of Political and Social Sciences*, Vol. 530, 1993: 122–136; Russell A. Kazal, "Revisiting Assimilation: The Rise, Fall, and Reappraisal of a Concept in American Ethnic History," *American History Review*, Vol. 100, No. 2, 1995: 437–471. Later, it was argued that the concept of assimilation had "fallen into undeserved disrepute": Richard D. Alba and Victor Nee, "Rethinking Assimilation Theory for a New Era of Immigration," *International Migration Review*, Vol. 31, No. 4, 1996: 825–873.

4. Nathan Glazer, *We Are All Multiculturalists Now* (Cambridge: Harvard University Press), 1998: 96–97.

5. Rubén G. Rumbaut, "Assimilation and Its Discontents: Between Rhetoric and Reality," *International Migration Review*, Vol. 31, No. 4, 1997: 923–960.

6. Carlota Solé and her colleagues provide an excellent overview of the concept both historically and in the contemporary European immigration context: Carlota Solé, Rosa Alcalde, Josep Pont, Kátia Lurbe, and Sónia Parella, "El Concepto de Integración desde la Sociología de las Migraciones," *Migraciones*, Vol. 12, 2002: 9–41.

7. Zincone, *Primo Rapporto*: 30 and 32.

8. For a good discussion of NGO activity on behalf of immigrants in Spain, and Granada in particular, see Gunther Dietz, *El Desafío de la Interculturalidad: El Voluntariado y las ONG ante el Reto de la Inmigración. El Caso de la Ciudad de Granada* (Granada: Proyecto sur de Ediciones), 2000.

9. Gloria Indennitate, "Gli Sbarchi degli Immigrati in uno Spot di Trenta Secondi," *La Gazzetta del Mezzogiorno*, July 13, 2001: 24.

10. This and all following references to the 1998 Turco-Napolitano law can be found in Luigi Di Maio, Maria Proto, and Maria Cristina Longarzia, *Manuale di Legislazione sugli Stranieri: Integrato dalle Norme del Regolamento di Attuazione* (Rome: Edizioni Laurus Robuffo), 2000, Appendix: Decreto Legislativo, 25 July 1998, No. 286, "Testo Unico delle Disposizioni

Concernenti la Disciplina dell'immigrazione e Norme sulla Condizione dello Straniero."

11. The Berlusconi government, under some pressure from EU protocols, passed Law No. 39 on March 1, 2002, reaffirming its commitment to barring discrimination on the basis of race, ethnicity, country of origin, or religion. Discrimination was understood to be either "direct or indirect" and included any activity or attitude that limited access to health care, housing, public education, social services, and employment (reproduced in "Leggi, Decreti e Circolari," *Gli Stranieri*, Vol. 9, No. 2, 2002: 142–143).

12. Veneto official, personal interview, Venice, July, 2001.

13. Consiglio Nazionale dell'Economia e del Lavoro, Organismo Nazionale di Coordinamento per le Politiche di Integrazione Sociale degli Stranieri, *Per Politiche Locali di Integrazione Sociali dei Cittadini Stranieri*, mimeo, Vicenza, January 12, 2001: 1.

14. The province is the level of government between cities and regions, and is constituted of a major city and its surrounding territory.

15. President of the Council of Ministers Decree (DPCM), "Establishment in Every Province of Territorial Councils for Immigration," December 18, 1999; Decree of the Minister for Social Solidarity, "Guide for the Preparation of Regional Programs," December 6, 1999. Reproduced in Giovanna Zincone, *Secondo Rapporto sull'integrazione degli Immigrati in Italia* (Bologna: Il Mulino), 2001: 820–821.

16. The term "multietnicitá" (multi-ethnicity) is often used instead of "multiculturalismo," which suggests a greater commitment to cultural diversity than is acceptable in some quarters.

17. Law cited in Ennio Codini, "Gli Aspetti Normativi," in ISMU-Cariplo (eds.), *Sesto Rapporto sulle Migrazioni 2000* (Milan: FrancoAngeli), 2001: 25–30 at 29.

18. Quoted in Barbara Faedda, "Le Politiche dell'Integrazione: Le Norme e le Esperienze," *Gli Stranieri*, Vol. 8, No. 2, 2001: 94, emphasis added.

19. Cultural issues dominate the public discourse on immigration. Indeed, the "immigration problem" often appears to be synonymous with "multiculturalism." Asked to give a talk before a group of students at an Italian university, I was chagrined when the host – who knew only that I was to speak about immigration – told the audience that I would be addressing the "problem of the mosque in Italy."

20. See, for example, Piedmont's Regional Law No. 64, passed on November 8, 1989, "Interventi Regionali a Favore degli Immigrati Extracomunitari in Piemonte"; Emilia-Romagna's Law No. 14, passed on February 21, 1990, "Iniziative Regionale in Favore dell'emigrazione e Immigrazione"; and Tuscany's Law No. 22, passed on March 22, 1990, "Interventi a Sostegno dei Diritti Extracomunitari in Toscana."

21. For details on these criteria and the breakdown of regional disbursements, see Giovanna Zincone, *Primo Rapporto sull'integrazione degli Immigrati in Italia* (Bologna: Il Mulino), 2000: 452–465; Giovanna Zincone, *Secondo Rapporto sull'integrazione degli Immigrati in Italia* (Bologna: Il Mulino), 2001: 773–790.

22. Luciano Fasano and Francesco Zucchini, "L'implementazione Locale del Testo Unico sull'immigrazione," in ISMU-Cariplo (eds.), *Sesto Rapporto sulle Migrazioni 2000* (Milan: FrancoAngeli), 2001: 49.

23. Barbara Faedda, "Le Politiche dell'Integrazione: Le Norme e le Esperienze," *Gli Stranieri*, Vol. 8, No. 2, 2001: 96.

24. Personal interview, Bologna, July, 2001.

25. Magdi Allam, "Tunisi, alle Porte del Deserto 'La Scuola dell'immigrato,' " *La Repubblica*, March 18, 2001: 18.

26. See, for example, Rome's, at www.comune.roma.it/ info_cittadino_schede_index6_htm.

27. Luciano Fasano and Francesco Zucchini, "L'implementazione Locale del Testo Unico sull'immigrazione," in ISMU-Cariplo (eds.), *Sesto Rapporto sulle Migrazioni 2000* (Milan: Francoangeli), 2001: 39–50.

28. Barbara Faedda, "Le Politiche dell'Integrazione: Le Norme e le Esperienze," *Gli Stranieri*, Vol. 8, No. 2, 2001: 92–101 at 96.

29. John A. Agnew, *Place and Politics in Modern Italy*: 115–116.

30. Marco Cantalupi and Maurizio Marengon, "Il Mercato del Lavoro," *Emilia-Romagna Lavoro* (Bologna: Regione Emilia-Romagna), November, 2002: 14; Angela Soverini, "Il Profilo dell'Economia Regionale," *Emilia-Romagna Lavoro* (Bologna: Agenzia Emilia-Romagna), November, 2002: 9–13; Regione Emilia-Romagna, *Economia e Lavoro in Emilia-Romagna: Rapporto Congiunturale 2000* (Bologna: Regione Emilia-Romagna), 2000.

31. Regione Emilia-Romagna "Statistiche," in *Emilia-Romagna Lavoro* (Bologna: Regione Emilia-Romagna), November, 2002: 100.

32. Regione Emilia-Romagna, Giunta Regionale, "Linee Regionali d'intervento per la Promozione della Sicurezza, della Regolaritá e della Qualitá Sociale delle Condizioni di Lavoro in Emilia-Romagna," unpublished mimeo, 2001: 11.

33. Caritas, *Immigrazione: Dossier Statistico 2000* (Rome: Edizioni Anterem), 2000: 293.

34. Pino Abella, Maurizio Marengon, and Angela Soverini, "Il Mercato del Lavoro in Emilia-Romagna," in Maura Franchi (ed.), *Istruzione Formazione Lavoro in Emilia-Romagna: Rapporto 2000* (Bologna: Graffiti), 2001: 442 and 444.

35. Regione Emilia-Romagna, Giunta Regionale, *Con Questa Faccia da Straniero: Rapporto sull'immigrazione in Emilia-Romagna* (Bologna: Regione Emilia-Romagna), 2001: 1.

36. Provincia di Bologna, "Immigrati a Bologna: I Numeri, Le Tendenze," *Osservatorio delle Immigrazioni*, No. 1, February 2001: 7.

37. Fernanda Minuz, "L'Esperienza dei Corsi di Formazione Linguistica per Persone Adulte Straniere dell'ISI di Bologna," in Osservatorio Metropolitano delle Immigrazioni (ed.), *La Societá Multietnica*, No. 3, December 1998: 189.

38. Marina Orsini-Jones and Francesca Gattullo, "Migrant Women in Italy: National Trends and Local Perspectives," in Floya Anthias and Gabriella Lazaridis (eds.), *Gender and Migration in Southern Europe*: 130.

39. Regione Emilia-Romagna, "Iniziative Regionali in Favore dell'emigrazione e dell'immigrazione," Legge Regionale No. 14, 21 February 1990.

40. Regional Law 2/85, Article 5; Regional Law 14/90; Regional Law 5/91. See María Adriana Bernardotti and Giovanni Mottura, *Il Gioco delle Tre Case: Immigrazione e Politiche Abitative a Bologna dal 1990 al 1999* (Turin: L'Harmattan Italia), 1999: 17.

41. Marina Orsini-Jones and Francesca Gattullo, "Migrant Women in Italy": 131.

42. Regione Emilia-Romagna, Assessorato Politiche Sociali, Immigrazione, "III Programma per l'attuazione del D.Lgs. 25 Luglio 1998, N. 286," unpublished mimeo, June 20, 2001: 9–10; Emilia-Romagna official, personal interview, June, 2001.

43. Regione Emilia-Romagna, Assessorato Politiche Sociali, Immigrazione, "III Programma per l'attuazione del D.Lgs. 25 Luglio 1998, N. 286": 11–12 and 21.

44. María Adriana Bernardotti and Giovanni Mottura, *Il Gioco delle Tre Case*: 23.

45. Document requesting funds for fifty emergency beds, quoted in María Adriana Bernardotti and Giovanni Mottura, *Il Gioco delle Tre Case*: 25.

46. *Ibid.*: 29.

47. Quoted in *Ibid.*: 29 and 31.

48. *Ibid.*: 28.

49. Istituzione dei Servizi per l'immigrazione, Comune di Bologna, *Newsletter*, June, 1999: 1.

50. Osservatorio Metropolitano delle Immigrazioni (ed.), *La Societá Multietnica*, No. 3, December, 1998: 189–253.

51. Istituzione dei Servizi per l'immigrazione, Comune di Bologna, *Newsletter*, June, 1999; ISI representative, personal interview, Bologna, July, 2001.

52. María Adriana Bernardotti and Giovanni Mottura, *Il Gioco delle Tre Case*: 17.

53. Personal interviews, Bologna, July, 2001.

54. www.comune.it/iperbole/immigra/servimm.htm.

55. Personal interview, Bologna, July, 2001.

56. Giunta Regionale dell'Emilia-Romagna, "Erogazione di Interventi Sanitari nell'ambito del Programma Assistenziale a Favore di Cittadini Stranieri," February 8, 2002, http://centrostudi.gruppoabele.org.

57. Adriano Ebner, *Radici Venete* (Venice: Regione del Veneto, Giunta Regionale), 2000: 55.

58. Aris Accornero, Bruno Anastasia, Maurizio Gambuzza, Elisabetta Gualmini, and Maurizio Rasera, *Solo una Grande Giostra: La Diffusione del Lavoro a Tempo Determinato* (Milan: FrancoAngeli), 2000.

59. Alessandra Carini, "Il Nordest non é Piú Ribelle Ora Vuol Contare a Roma," *La Repubblica*, July 14, 2001: 18.

60. Bruno Anastasia, Anna de Angelini, Maurizio Gambuzza, and Maurizio Rasera (eds.), *Il Mercato del Lavoro nel Veneto* (Milan: FrancoAngeli), 2001: 42.

61. Sergio Rosato, "Preface," in Bruno Anastasia, Anna de Angelini, Maurizio Gambuzza, and Maurizio Rasera (eds.), *Il Mercato del Lavoro nel Veneto*: 9; Sandro Gattei, "L'andamento del Mercato del Lavoro nelle Province Italiane tra il 1999 e il 2001," *Informazioni SVIMEZ*, Vol. 9, Nos. 1–2, 2002: 14.

62. Luisa Grion, "Vicenza e Livorno Sono le 'Superstar,'" *La Repubblica*, July 29, 2002: 11.

63. Sergio Rosato, "Preface": 9.

64. "Un Nuovo Assunto su Quattro Sará Extracomunitario," *La Gazzetta del Mezzogiorno*, July 14, 2002: 14.

65. Migration News, "Southern Europe," Vol. 9, No. 10, October 2002: 26.

66. Sergio Rosato, "Preface": 339–340.

67. Barbara Faedda, "L'integrazione Attraverso il Lavoro: Il 'Caso Veneto,'" *Gli Stranieri*, Vol. 9, No. 2, March–April 2002: 164.

68. See, for example, "Immigrazione: Da Regione Veneto Emendamento su Ruolo Regioni Assessore Veneto Zanon Chiede Accordi Programma Stato-Regioni," *Notizie ANSA*, March 4, 2002, www.stranieriinitalia.it.

69. "Incentivi di Mobilitá e Piú Immigrati la Ricetta degli Industriali," January 12, 2001, www.CNNitalia.it.

70. Legge Regionale No. 9, January 30, 1990; Legge Regionale No. 42, August 30, 1993.

71. Veneto official, personal interview, Venice, July, 2001.

72. Ministero del Lavoro e delle Politiche Sociali e Regione Veneto, "Accordo di Programma," June 15, 2001: 2.

73. Veneto official, personal interview, Vicenza, July, 2001.

74. Raffaele Zanon, quoted in "Veneto Approva Piano Triennale Immigrazione," *Veneto Globale*, Vol. 4, No. 6, June, 2001: 1, www.regione.veneto.it.

75. Consiglio Regionale del Veneto, "Piano Triennale di Massima 2001–2003 di Iniziative ed Interventi nel Settore dell'immigrazione," Deliberazione No. 20, June 26, 2001: Preamble, 3.

76. *Ibid.*: Preamble, 4.

77. *Ibid.*: 2–4.

78. Regione del Veneto, Segretaria Generale della Programmazione, "Programma di Iniziative di Interventi in Materia di Immigrazione Anno 2001," July 13, 2001.

79. Barbara Faedda, "L'integrazione Attraverso il Lavoro: Il 'Caso Veneto,'" *Gli Stranieri*, Vol. 9, No. 2, March–April 2002: 165.

80. Veneto official, personal interview, Venice, July, 2001.

81. Quoted in Manuela Fato, "Politiche Migratorie in un Paese di Vecchia Immigrazione e in uno di Nuova Immigrazione: Francia e Italia a Confronto," Masters Thesis, University of Naples, Federico II, Sociology, 1999–2000.

82. Barbara Faedda, "L'integrazione Attraverso il Lavoro": 163–164.

83. "Ma Quale Razza Padana, Quella Gente Ci Serve," *Il Manifesto*, August 27, 2002:10.

84. Giancarlo Mola, "Ottanta Sindaci del Nordest a Lezione di Immigrazione," October 22, 2002: 1, www.repubblica.it.
85. "Immigrazione: 'Glocal', Datori di Lavoro e Sindacati Assieme," *Notizie ANSA*, October 4, 2002, www.stranieriinitalia.com.
86. Quoted in Tom Hundley, "Cultural Attitudes Blamed for Italy's Labor Crisis," February 23, 2001: 3, www.chicagotribune.com.
87. Quoted in "Ma Quale Razza Padana, Quella Gente Ci Serve,":10.
88. Quoted in Giancarlo Mola, "Ottanta Sindaci del Nordest a Lezione di Immigrazione," October 22, 2002: 1, www.repubblica.it.
89. Veneto official, personal interview, Venice, July, 2001.
90. Veneto official, personal interview, Venice, July, 2001.
91. Caritas official, personal interview, Veneto, July, 2001.
92. David Montgomery, "Empire, Race and Working-Class Mobilizations," in Peter Alexander and Rick Halpern (eds.), *Racializing Class, Classifying Race: Labour and Difference in Britain, the USA and Africa* (New York: St. Martin's Press), 2000: 12.
93. Council of Ministers, announcing the 1991 legalization program, quoted in Pedro Aresté, "Regularizaciones," in Alegría Borrás (ed.), *Diez A os de la Ley de Extranjería*: 184; Cortes Generales, *Diario de Sesiones del Congreso de los Diputados*, No. 580, December 9, 1992: 17465.
94. Consejo de Ministros, *Plan para la Integración Social de los Inmigrantes* (Madrid: Ministerio de Asuntos Sociales), 1995: 9.
95. Ministerio del Interior, Delegación del Gobierno para la Extranjería y la Inmigración, *Programa GRECO (Programa Global de Regulación y Coordinación de la Extranjería y la Inmigración en Espa a)* (Madrid: Ministerio del Interior), 2001: 18, 34, and 47.
96. "Atención a Inmigrantes y Refugiados," unpublished IMSERSO report, July, 2002: 1.
97. Government Press Release, "El Gobierno Trabaja para la Plena Integración de los Inmigrantes," Ministerio del Interior, Delegación del Gobierno para la Extranjería y la Inmigración, July 1, 2002.
98. Government Press Release, "El Gobierno Trabaja para la Plena Integración de los Inmigrantes": 2.
99. Quoted in Amnesty International, "Spain: Crisis of Identity, Race-Related Torture and Ill-Treatment by State Agents," April 16, 2002: 6, www.amnesty.org.
100. Personal interview, Madrid, June, 2002.
101. Catalan government official, personal interview, Barcelona, July, 2002.
102. In Madrid, more than 50% of recently arrived immigrants come from Spanish-speaking countries, while in Barcelona they account for under 20%. In contrast, Moroccans represent 30% of Catalonia's immigrants, and just 10% of immigrants in Madrid. Miguel Noguer, "El Problema (Además) de Aprender Catalán," *El País*, June 16, 2002: 16.
103. Personal interviews, Barcelona, July, 2002. In another indication of the importance placed on immigrants learning Catalan, the "Generalitat" (the central Catalan government) recently signed an agreement with the Islamic Council in Barcelona, to teach the Catalan language and culture

to local imams. Miguel Noguer, "El Problema (Además) de Aprender Catalán": 16.

104. Generalitat de Catalunya, *Connecta amb Catalunya: Guia d'acollida* (Barcelona: Generalitat de Catalunya), undated: 9.

105. Generalitat de Catalunya, *Pla Interdepartamental d'Immigració 2001–2004* (Barcelona: Generalitat de Catalunya), 2002: 121–122.

106. Personal interview, Barcelona, July, 2002.

107. Hinting at the possibility that the cultural interpretation might be over-emphasized, the Plan notes: "It is important to avoid a 'culturalist' reading of social and economic conflicts." Generalitat de Catalunya, *Pla Interdepartamental d'Immigració 2001–2004*: 135.

108. Generalitat de Catalunya, *Pla Interdepartamental d'Immigració 2001–2004*: 134–135.

109. For an excellent description of these issues and the limitations of the Plan, both on paper and in action, see Katia Lurbe i Puerto, "Incursión Sociológica sobre la Enajenación de l@s Otr@s: Estudio sobre el Tratamiento de la Diferencia Etnica en la Salud Mental," PhD Dissertation, Department of Sociology, Universitat Autonoma de Barcelona, directed by Professor Carlota Solé Puig, 2002. The @ symbol is used by Lurbe i Puerto in Spanish articles to eliminate the sexist implications of using the masculine "o" as a default.

110. Generalitat de Catalunya, *Pla Interdepartamental d'Immigració 2001–2004*: 283–288.

111. Catalan Department of Health official, personal interview, Barcelona, July, 2002.

112. Physician with Barcelona clinic, personal interview, Barcelona, July, 2002.

113. Ricard Zapata-Barrero, *L'hora dels Immigrants: Esferes de Justícia i Polítiques d'acomodació* (Barcelona: Laia Tresserra), 2002: 96–103.

Chapter 5

1. Quoted in Carter, *States of Grace*: 38.

2. SOS Racismo, *Informe Anual*: 164.

3. Giovanna Zincone, "A Model of 'Reasonable Integration': Summary of the First Report on the Integration of Immigrants in Italy," *International Migration Review*, Vol. 34, No. 3, 2000: 956. Zincone writes that immigrants are not in last place with regard to salary: "An unexpected, though not particularly comforting, piece of information regards the question of wage equality: it now appears to be more of a disadvantage being a woman in Italy than being an immigrant" (the intersectionality of female and immigrant is left for us to imagine). For a more complete report, see Giovanna Zincone, "Immigrati: Quali Politiche per l'integrazione," *Il Mulino*, Vol. 49, January–February 2000: 80–91.

4. Comune di Vicenza, Assessorato Servizi Sociali, *Progetto Vicenza Globale*, unpublished report, 2001: 8.

5. ISMU-Cariplo, *Quinto Rapporto sulle Migrazioni* (Milan: FrancoAngeli), 1999; Zincone, *Secondo Rapporto*: 206.

6. Rosa Aparicio and Andrés Tornos, *Estrategias y Dificultades Características en la Integración Social de los Distintos Colectivos de Inmigrantes Llegados a Espa a* (Madrid: Instituto de Migraciones y Servicios Sociales), 2001: 67.

7. SOS Racismo, *Informe Anual 2002*: 96–98. See also Carles Valls, "Es Busca Pis per Immigrant," *La Veu del Carrer*, March–April, 2001: 5.

8. SOS Racismo, *Informe Anual 2001*: 163–165.

9. Zincone, *Secondo Rapporto*: 215.

10. Quoted in Keith B. Richburg, "Widely Scorned, Illegal Workers Do Europe's Heavy Lifting," *Washington Post*, August 3, 2002: A16.

11. Personal interview, Madrid, June, 2002.

12. Quoted in Marco Galluzzo, " 'Chi Vuole Entrare Farebbe Bene a Imparare Prima l'italiano,' " *Corriere della Sera*, July 12, 2002: 3.

13. Gianluca Luzi, " 'Piano Europeo Anticlandestini' Accordo tra Berlusconi e Aznar," *La Repubblica*, June 6, 2002: 9. The use of the term "clandestini," which technically means those who surreptitiously cross the border and remain underground, to refer generically to undocumented immigrants – most of whom enter legally and alternate between legal and illegal status – serves the rhetorical purpose of demonizing them and setting them apart as "outlaws," a theme we will pursue in the next chapter.

14. Pumares, *La Integración de los Inmigrantes Marroquíes*: 81.

15. Bianca Di Giovanni, "Costa Caro Fare L'immigrato in Regola," *L'unitá*, July 26, 2001: 1.

16. Quoted in Domingo Valls, Clapés Estrada, and Prats Ferret, *Condicions de Vida*: 137.

17. Pierluigi Francesco Chiesa, "Sindacato e Lavoratori Immigrati: Il Caso Italiano," in Osservatorio Comunale delle Immigrazioni di Bologna (eds.), *Dal Lavoro alla Famiglia: Percorsi Migratori a Confronto* (Turin: L'Harmattan Italia), 1999.

18. Gruppo Abele, *Annuario Sociale 2001*: 525.

19. Lluís Visa, "Temporeros sin Trabajo," *El País*, July 24, 2002: Catalu a 1.

20. Berti, *Esclusione e Integrazione*: 137; Zincone, *Secondo Rapporto*: 217–219.

21. Manuel Altozano, " 'Quiero Ser Limpiador,' " *El País*, July 3, 2002: 23.

22. Herbert Brucker, Gil S. Epstein, Barry McCormick, Gilles Saint-Paul, Alessandra Venturini, and Klaus Zimmermann, "Welfare State Provision," in Boeri, Hanson, and McCormick (eds.), *Immigration Policy and the Welfare System*: 75.

23. Maurizio Ambrosini (ed.), *Accogliere Attivamente: La Risorsa della Formazione Professionale per la Promozione Sociale degli Immigrati* (Turin: Casa di Carità, Arti e Mestieri), 2000; Ambrosini, *La Fatica di Integrarsi*: 174.

24. Words of an immigration official in Vicenza, Italy, speaking about their integration program, personal interview, Vicenza, July, 2001. While pleased with the principles formally set down, he was skeptical of their implementation, saying, "It sounds good in principle, but we will have to see . . ."

25. T. H. Marshall, *Class, Citizenship, and Social Development: Essays by T. H. Marshall* (Garden City, NY: Doubleday), 1964.
26. Zincone, *Secondo Rapporto*: 215.
27. Consiglio Nazionale dell'Economia e del Lavoro, Organismo Nazionale di Coordinamento per le Politiche di Integrazione Sociale degli Stranieri, *Per Politiche Locali di Integrazione Sociale dei Cittadini Stranieri* (Vicenza: Consiglio Nazionale dell'Economia e del Lavoro), mimeo, 1999: 15. The notion that health is "capital" to be invested is a peculiar one, carrying with it the implication that this is essentially an exchange. Whether or not this is a good "investment," given the apparently meager returns, is an open question.
28. Fondazione ISMU-Cariplo, *Quarto Rapporto sulle Migrazioni 1998* (Milan: FrancoAngeli), 1999: 125–131; Fondazione ISMU-Cariplo, *Sesto Rapporto*: 115–126; Gruppo Abele, *Annuario Sociale 2001*: 559.
29. Reported in Gruppo Abele, *Annuario Sociale 2001*: 540.
30. Zincone, *Secondo Rapporto*: 215.
31. Consiglio Nazionale dell'Economia e del Lavoro, *Per Politiche Locali*: 15. In an effort to address cultural and linguistic difficulties, the Association of Foreign Doctors in Italy provides several clinics in Rome with foreign doctors for immigrant patients. The practice has been proclaimed a success, with these clinics in their first year attracting 3,500 visits by immigrants, but these separate facilities appear to violate the announced principle of "normalization," or mainstreaming immigrants through "normal" social channels ("Sanitá: Medici Stranieri per Stranieri, in 1 Anno 3500 Visite il Bilancio dell'AMSI negli Ambulatori di Roma," *Notizie ANSA*, November 30, 2002, www.stranieriinitalia.com).
32. Quoted in Paolo Conti, "Io, Clandestino per Due Anni, Vivo Ancora nel Terrore," *Corriere della Sera*, January 20, 2002: 5.
33. Ley General de Sanidad 14/86; Real Decreto 1088/1989, *Boletín Oficial del Estado*, No. 219, September 9, 1989.
34. *Boletín Oficial del Estado*, "Derechos y Libertades de los Extranjeros en Espa a y su Integración Social," *Texto Integrado de las Leyes Orgánicas 4/2000, de 11 enero, y 8/2000, de 22 de diciembre* (Madrid: Boletín Oficial del Estado), 2000.
35. Quoted in SOS Racismo, *Informe Anual 2001*: 164. The similarity between this description of the incidence of tuberculosis among immigrants and its relationship to their living conditions bears an uncanny resemblance to Castles and Kosack's description of the illness among immigrant workers in France, Germany, Switzerland, and Britain in the 1950s and 1960s, many of whom were Spanish and Italian (Castles and Kosack, *Immigrant Workers and Class Structure*: 325–330).
36. Lurbe i Puerto, *Incursión Sociológico*.
37. Quoted in SOS Racismo, *Informe Anual 2000*: 94. Similarly offensive advice has been given to immigrants in the context of housekeeping. A Peruvian woman interviewed for a national study told the interviewer that sometimes employers think they have to explain everything to their Peruvian housekeepers. "They treat us as ignorant," she said, " . . . as if we

didn't know what a vacuum cleaner or a kitchen is" (Aparicio and Tornos, *Estrategias y Dificultades*: 108).

38. Ministra de Sanidad, quoted in SOS Racismo, *Informe Anual 2001*: 164.

39. SOS Racismo, *Informe Anual 2000*: 95; Barcelona physician, personal interview, Barcelona, July, 2002; see also José Luis Solana Ruiz, "Análisis y Reflexiones en Torno a una Década (1990–1999) de Intervención y Trabajo Social con la Población Inmigrante," in Francisco Checa (ed.), *Las Migraciones a Debate: De las Teorias a las Prácticas Sociales* (Barcelona: Icaria Editorial), 2002.

40. Reported and quoted in SOS Racismo, *Informe Anual 2001*: 164–165.

41. Cornelius and Bustamante, *Mexican Migration to the United States*; Todd A. Eisenstadt and Cathryn L. Thorup, *Caring Capacity Versus Carrying Capacity* (La Jolla: Center for US – Mexican Studies, University of California, San Diego), 1994; Cockcroft, *Outlaws in the Promised Land*.

42. Aparicio and Tornos, *Estrategias y Dificultades*: 73 and 85.

43. Alegría Borrás and Cristina González, "Aspectos Concretos de la Integración Social," in A. Bórras (ed.), *Diéz A os*: 214–230.

44. SOS Racismo, *Informe Anual 2001*: 165.

45. José Luis Solana Ruiz, "Análisis y Reflexiones": 2002; Barcelona physician, personal interview, Barcelona, July, 2002; Medicos del Mundo, cited in SOS Racismo, *Informe Anual 2001*: 163.

46. Unless otherwise specified, the information cited here was gleaned from discussions with the medical staff and administrators at this Barcelona clinic, July, 2002.

47. City of Barcelona study, cited in Lurbe i Puerto, *Incursión Sociológico*: 142.

48. Health clinic official, personal interview, Barcelona, July, 2002.

49. The reference to immigrants' "displacement" in this context brings to mind once again Coutin's description of undocumented Salvadoran immigrants in the United States and their "spaces of non-existence" (Coutin, *Legalizing Moves*: 29).

50. In both Spain and Italy, the default health care for immigrants who are excluded from the national health system is provided by a vast network of NGOs, such as Medicos sin Fronteras, Caritas, etc. These groups fill an important vacuum and provide a critical social service, but they are not a substitute for the national health service, membership in which signifies social belonging and guarantees care.

51. Aparicio and Tornos, *Estrategias y Dificultades*: 67.

52. SOS Racismo, *Informe Anual 2002*: 96–98. See also Carles Valls, "Es Busca Pis per Immigrant": 5.

53. "Las Viviendas de Tetuán Necesitan 10,000 Millones para Mantenerse en Pie," *El Mundo*, May 17, 2000: 2.

54. Francisco Beltrán Campillo and Jesús Mi ano Martínez, *Censo y Caracterización de las Infraviviendas Usadas por Inmigrantes en la Región de Murcia: 1996* (Madrid: Instituto de Migraciones y Servicios Sociales), 1997: 14.

55. Luís Zaurín, "La Inmigración Marca el Futuro de Santa Coloma," *La Veu del Carrer*, January–February, 2002: 7.

56. Ajuntament de Barcelona, Departament d'Estadística, *Guia Estadística: Ciutat Vella en Xifres* (Barcelona: Ajuntament de Barcelona), 2002: 4.

57. Comune di Bologna, "La Casa: Primo Problema per Tutti," *Osservatorio delle Immigrazioni*, No. 1, February, 2001: 11.

58. *Ibid.*: 11.

59. Zincone, *Primo Rapporto*: 324 and 319.

60. Zincone, *Secondo Rapporto*: 193.

61. ISMU-Cariplo, *Quinto Rapporto*; Zincone, *Secondo Rapporto*: 206.

62. ISMU-Cariplo, *Quinto Rapporto*. Looking at the "bright spot," the director of the commission to review integration in Italy observes: "For most, 50 to 70%, the housing arrangments are 'decent' according to Italian standards" (Zincone, "A Model of 'Reasonable Integration'": 957).

63. Ares, "Il Coloro delle Case: Primo Rapporto sulla Condizione Abitativa degli Immigrati in Italia," Ares Report, 2000: 3, www.sunia.it. The Domus Aurea is the lavish home of the Roman Emperor Nero, replete with gold ornamentation (hence the "Golden Home" nomenclature), the ruins of which have recently been opened to the public.

64. "Southern Europe," *Migration News*, Vol. 11, No. 1, 2004: 39.

65. Ares, "Il Coloro delle Case": 3.

66. Zincone, *Secondo Rapporto*: 209.

67. Berti, *Esclusione e Integrazione*: 89.

68. Comune di Bologna, "La Casa": 11; Bernardotti and Mottura, *Il Gioco delle Tre Case*: 12.

69. *Ibid.*: 12.

70. Antonio Sciotto, "Dopo il Lavoro, una Casa," *Il Manifesto*, July 19, 2001: 12.

71. Cestim (Centro Studi Immigrazione di Verona), "Indagine Esplorativa sulle Condizioni e Prospettive di Alloggio della Populazione Immigrata," undated report.

72. Ares, "Il Coloro delle Case": 2–3.

73. Sara Menafra, "Immigrati in Fuga da Villa Magistratini," *Il Manifesto*, August 30, 2001: 10; Ares, "Il Coloro delle Case": 3; Luca Fazio, "Milano, 59 Bengalesi in Tre Monolocali," *Il Manifesto*, January 5, 2002: 15; Diletta Desio, "L'inferno Apoff," *Il Manifesto*, April 1, 2001: 5.

74. Ares, "Il Coloro delle Case": 2.

75. Riccardo Chiari, "Uccisi dal Freddo," *Il Manifesto*, January 5, 2002: 8; Ares, "Il Coloro delle Case": 3.

76. Quoted in Concita de Gregorio, "Storia di Irma, Colf Peruviana, 'Ora Saró Clandestina a Vita,'" *La Repubblica*, July 13, 2002: 21.

77. ISMU-Cariplo, *Quinto Rapporto*.

78. Zincone, *Secondo Rapporto*: 209 and 208.

79. Laura Caffagnini, "Una Casa in Comune," *Il Manifesto*, June 3, 2001: 4; "Case per Immigrati," *Il Manifesto*, January 19, 2001: 5.

80. Zincone, "A Model of 'Reasonable Integration'": 958.

81. Quoted in Riccardo Chiari, "Uccisi dal Freddo," *Il Manifesto*, January 5, 2002: 8.

82. Fazio, "Milano, 59 Bengalesi": 15.

83. "Case per Immigrati," *Il Manifesto*, January 19, 2001: 5.
84. Ares, "Il Coloro delle Case": 4.
85. Comune di Vicenza, "Progetto Vicenza Globale," unpublished report, 2001: 9.
86. Ares, "Il Coloro delle Case": 5.
87. By law, legal immigrants are eligible for regular public housing. How-ever, the fierce competition for relatively few units depends on a points system and, since a large number of points accrues to those who have been evicted from their previous housing, immigrants who are without housing are at a distinct disadvantage. Ironically, many locals apparently think that immigrants are favored in the public housing system, creating a resentment that officials must contend with (Zincone, *Secondo Rapporto*: 204).
88. Ares, "Il Coloro delle Case": 4.
89. Quoted in *ibid*.: 2.
90. Quoted in Cinzia Gubbini, "Con Tantissimo Affitto," *Il Manifesto*, Jan-uary 19, 2001: 4.
91. Quoted in *La Repubblica*, "Non Affitto agli Immigrati," May 30, 2001: 10.
92. Istituto per gli Studi sulla Pubblica Opinione, "L'atteggiamento degli Ital-iani nei Confronti degli Immigrati," unpublished research report, 2002: 112.
93. Comune di Bologna, "La Casa": 12.
94. Davide Peró, "Immigrants and Politics in Left-Wing Bologna: Results from Participatory Action Research," in Russell King and Richard Black (eds.), *Southern Europe and the New Immigrations* (Brighton, England: Academic Press), 1997: 167.
95. Quoted in Peró, "Immigrants and Politics": 172–173.
96. Comune di Vicenza, "Progetto Vicenza Globale": 9.
97. Caldeira, *City of Walls*: 1–2.
98. The spatial segregation of housing is accompanied by children's segrega-tion in school. In Italy, where there is a strong tradition of public educa-tion, school segregation is primarily the result of the kind of segregated housing discussed above. But, in Spain, where large numbers of local stu-dents attend private schools, immigrants are concentrated in the public education system. In a finding that city officials call "very disconcerting," it has recently been revealed that in Barcelona only one out of three pupils attends a public school, with the percentage increasing only in neighborhoods disproportionately inhabited by immigrants ("Sólo uno de Cada Tres Alumnos Va a la Escuela Pública en Barcelona," *El País*, July 19, 2002: 7).
99. Berti, *Esclusione e Integrazione*: 89.
100. Robert Castel, "Le Insidie dell'esclusione," *Assistenza Sociale*, Vol. 2, 1996, quoted in Berti, *Esclusione e Integrazione*: 30.
101. Coutin, *Legalizing Moves*.
102. Julie R. Watts, *An Unconventional Brotherhood: Union Support for Liberal-ized Immigration in Europe*, Monograph Series, No. 1, Center for Compar-ative Immigration Studies (La Jolla, CA: University of California, San

Diego), 2000; Giovanni Mottura, "Immigrati e Sindacato," in E. Pugliese (ed.), *Rapporto Immigrazione*; Pierluigi Francesco Chiesa, "Sindacato e Lavoratori Immigrati: Il Caso Italiano nel Contesto Europeo," in Osservatorio Comunale delle Immigrazioni di Bologna (ed.), *Dal Lavoro alla Famiglia: Percorsi Migratori a Confronto* (Turin: L'Harmattan Italia), 1999.

103. *Ibid.*: 85–89.
104. "Immigrants in Spain Protest New Law," *Los Angeles Times*, February 5, 2001: A4.
105. Carles Valls, "La Revolta dels 'Sense Papers,'" *La Vue del Carrer*, January–February, 2001: 3.
106. SOS Racismo, *Informe Anual 2001*: 73.
107. "Casi un Centenar de Inmigrantes Dejan el Encierro de la Universidad de Sevilla," *El País*, July 18, 2002: 30; "Inmigrantes Encerrados en Sevilla Inician una Huelga de Hambre," *El País*, July 20, 2002: 25.
108. Gruppo Abele, *Annuario Sociale 2001*: 518.
109. Fabrizio Roncone, "Immigrati, Decine di Migliaia contro le Espulsioni," *Corriere della Sera*, January 20, 2002: 5; "Rome March Supports Immigration", *Los Angeles Times*, January 20, 2002: A4; Giovanna Casadio, "Immigrati, 100 Mila a Roma, 'No alla Legge Fini-Bossi,'" *La Repubblica*, January 20, 2002: 10.
110. Claudia Fusani, "Caritas e Arci Pronte a Disubbidire: 'Ospiteremo Noi gli Irregolari,'" *La Repubblica*, July 12, 2002: 3; "Protesta: Impronte per il Premier," *La Repubblica*, June 6, 2002: 8.
111. Cipputo is a legendary comic-strip character who migrates from the rural south of Italy and becomes a labor organizer and hero in the factories of the north.
112. "Immigrati, a Vicenza il Primo Sciopero," *Corriere della Sera*, May 16, 2002: 13.
113. "Extracomunitari in Sciopero," *La Repubblica*, May 16, 2002: 11.
114. "Lavoro: Extracomunitari; Poco Sindacato al Nord, Piú al Sud. In Campania 'Sindacalizzazione' Superiore alla Media Regionale," *Notizie ANSA*, January 12, 2002, www.stranieriinitalia.com.
115. "Lavoro: Nella 'Fabbrichetta' Scioperano Solo Extracomunitari: Un Immigrato Denuncia il Caso al Congresso CGIL Lombardia," *Notizie ANSA*, January 15, 2002, www.stranieriinitalia.com.
116. Chiesa, "Sindacato e Lavoratori": 111–114.
117. Personal interview, Madrid, June, 2002; "North Africans in Spain's South Stage a Sit-In," *New York Times*, International Edition, June 11, 2002: A3.
118. Carter, *States of Grace*: xi.
119. Bernardotti and Mottura, *Il Gioco delle Tre Case*: 28–29.
120. Francesca Decimo, "Gli Elementi di un Conflitto Urbano: Questione Abitativa e Immigrazione Marocchina a Bologna," in Giuseppe Sciortino and Asher Colombo (eds.), *Stranieri in Italia: Un Immigrazione Normale* (Bologna: Il Mulino), 2003.
121. Ares, "Il Coloro delle Case": 3
122. Forum official, personal interview, Bologna, June, 2001.
123. Orsini-Jones and Gattullo, "Migrant Women in Italy": 133.

124. *Ibid.*: 132.
125. Decimo, "Gli Elementi di un Conflitto Urbano".
126. *Ibid.*: 78.
127. Francesca Decimo, "Reti di Solidarietá e Strategie Economiche di Donne Immigrate a Napoli," *Studi Emigrazione*, Vol. 23, 1996: 493–494.
128. Leo R. Chavez, "Settlers and Sojourners: The Case of Mexicans in the United States," *Human Organization*, Vol. 47, 1988: 95–108.
129. Andall, "Cape Verdean Women on the Move": 246.
130. Carter, *States of Grace*: x.

Chapter 6

1. Ben Jelloun, *Le Pareti della Solitudine*: xiv.
2. I use the French word "alterité" because of its more common use than the rather awkward English equivalent, "alterity." I prefer this term to the more straightforward "difference," because of its implication of process, its suggestion of "alteration."
3. Ilvo Diamanti and Fabio Bordignon, "Immigrazione e Cittadinanza in Europa," *Quaderni FNE, Collana Osservatori*, No. 5, 2002: 12–13; Fabio Bordignon, "Gli Immigrati Fanno Meno Paura," *La Repubblica*, March 20, 2002: 10–11.
4. Diamanti and Bordignon, "Immigrazione e Cittadinanza": 12–13.
5. Díez Nicolás and José Ramírez Lafita, *La Inmigración en Espa a.* The index was constructed by asking respondents for their degree of agreement with such statements as "The economic situation of Spaniards is hard enough without having to subsidize immigrants," and "I would prohibit my daughter from going out with a man who is Roma, North African, black African, South American, or eastern European."
6. *Ibid.*: 121.
7. *Ibid.*: 81. The reference here to the "verbalization" of attitudes suggests that the authors are sensitive to the fact that polls do not necessarily tap attitudes, but rather the willingness to express them. Interesting in this regard, far fewer Spaniards themselves express negative attitudes toward immigrants than ascribe them to others. In this study, *half* of all respondents said "Spaniards in general" hold "negative" attitudes toward immigrants, with another 4% calling Spaniards' attitudes "very negative" (*ibid.*: 115).
8. Diamanti and Bordignon, "Immigrazione e Cittadinanza": 13. In a different survey, conducted by the prestigious research foundation, Centro de Investigaciones Sociológicas (CIS), respondents ranked immigration fifth among the social problems plaguing the country, after unemployment, public safety, economic problems, and terrorism ("Las Familias Necesitan el Seguro de Paro para Sobrevivir, Según el CIS," *El País*, June 28, 2002: 27).
9. Quoted in Belén Agrela, "La Política de Inmigración en España: Reflexiones sobre la Emergencia del Discurso Cultural," *Migraciones Internacionales*, Vol. 1, No. 2, 2002: 116.

10. *Osservatorio Europeo sul Razzismo e la Xenofobia*, cited in "Europa (In)tollerante," *Il Manifesto*, March 21, 2001: 6. Recent controversy over an Italian judge's decision to order the removal of a crucifix in an Italian school at the behest of a Muslim resident of Italy almost certainly has increased the percentage of Italians who perceive immigrants to be a "cultural threat." The order set off a firestorm of official and popular reactions against the "Islamic invasion" ("Furor Over Cross Reflects Italy's Changing Reality," *Los Angeles Times*, November 2, 2003: A3).
11. Diamanti and Bordignon, "Immigrazione e Cittadinanza": 13–15; Fabio Bordignon, "Gli Immigrati Fanno Meno Paura," *La Repubblica*, March 20, 2002: 10–11.
12. Diamanti and Bordignon, "Immigrazione e Cittadinanza": 13.
13. "Censis: Immigrazione, un Problema per 18.7% degli Italiani," *Notizie ANSA*, December 6, 2002; Istituto per gli Studi sulla Pubblica Opinione, "L'atteggiamento degli Italiani nei Confronti degli Immigrati", unpublished report, 2002: 5; see also "Crimini, Alto Rischio nelle Grandi Città," *La Repubblica*, March 16, 2001: 25.
14. Dario Melossi, "The Other in the New Europe: Migrations, Deviance, Social Control," in Penny Green and Andrew Rutherford (eds.), *Criminal Policy in Transition* (Oxford: Hart Publishing), 2000: 160; see also Dario Melossi, "Multiculturalismo e Sicurezza in Emilia–Romagna: Prima Parte," *Quaderni di Città Sicure*, Vol. 5, No. 15, January, 1999: 17–135.
15. Cited in "Southern Europe," *Migration News*, Vol. 9, No. 3, 2002: 30.
16. Istituto per gli Studi sulla Pubblica Opinione, "L'atteggiamento": 17, 23, and 106.
17. *Ibid.*: 131.
18. Authors of a Caritas report cite a study that shows that in Italy and Germany the greatest hostility is reserved for immigrants from Eastern European countries, while in France and Spain hostility is more likely to be reserved for those from the third world. They conclude: "It seems the closer you are to a country of origin, the greater your fear of those immigrants." Caritas, *Immigrazione*: 205–206.
19. Diamanti and Bordignon, "Immigrazione e Cittadinanza": 13.
20. Cited in "Southern Europe," *Migration News*, Vol. 9, No. 6, 2002: 22.
21. Cited in "Tres de Cada Cuatro Espa oles Relacionan la Inmigración con la Inseguridad Ciudadana," *ABC*, May 15, 2002: 20.
22. Díez Nicolás and José Ramírez Lafita, *La Inmigración en Espa a*: 182.
23. Istituto per gli Studi sulla Pubblica Opinione, "L'atteggiamento": 106; Censis, "Le Paure degli Italiani," unpublished report, Rome, July 20, 2000, Table 10.
24. Marzio Barbagli, *Immigrazione e Criminalitá in Italia* (Bologna: Il Mulino), 1998.
25. Gruppo Abele, *Annuario Sociale 2001*: 327–329; "Crimini, Alto Rischio nelle Grandi Città," *La Repubblica*, March 16, 2001: 25; Ministro dell'Interno, *Rapporto del Ministro*; Centro de Estudios del Cambio Social, *Informe Espa a 2002*: 551. The crime rate in Spain has since increased

("La Delincuencia en Espa a Aumentó un 5% en los Primeros Meses del A o," *El País*, July 22, 2002: 1 and 18).

26. Giuseppe D'avanzo, "Perché Bossi Cavalca la Politica della Paura," *La Repubblica*, March 19, 2002: 15; Alessandra Stanley, "Immigration is Emerging as Early Issue in Italy's Vote," *New York Times*, August 8, 2000: A7; Barry Renfrew, "Europe Giving the Boot to Left-Leaning Governments," *San Diego Union-Tribune*, June 17, 2002: A3.

27. Quoted in R. Jeffrey Smith, "Europe Bids Immigrants Unwelcome," *Washington Post*, July 23, 2000: A18. In her extensive discourse analysis of the National Alliance party, Jessika Ter Wal points out that the ideology of the AN is complex and, on the issue of immigration, fairly diverse. Much of the AN discourse she analyzed suggests an attempt to disassociate itself from the neo-fascist party, the Movimento Sociale Italiano (MSI), from which it emerged in 1995. Nonetheless, she concludes that "[t]he discourse of the AN still clearly has a strong nationalist core based on the need to preserve values of national and ethnic belonging." Jessika Ter Wal, "The Discourse of the Extreme Right and Its Ideological Implications: The Case of the Alleanza Nazionale on Immigration," *Patterns of Prejudice*, Vol. 34, No. 4, 2000: 49. See also Jessika Ter Wal, "Comparing Argumentation and Counter-Argumentation in Italian Parliamentary Debate on Immigration," in Martin Reisigl and Ruth Wodak (eds.), *The Semiotics of Racism* (Vienna: Passagen Verlag), 2000.

28. Loic Wacquant, *Parola d'Ordine: Tolleranza Zero* (Milan: Feltrinelli Editore), 2000: 22.

29. D'avanzo, "Perché Bossi": 15.

30. Quoted in John Tagliabue, "Italy Issues Decree to Destroy Ships Used in Refugee Transport," *San Diego Union-Tribune*, March 29, 2002: A18.

31. "Ciampi: Meno Immigrati," *La Repubblica*, May 17, 2002: 1; " 'Immigrati, L'Italia ha Capacitá Limitate,' " *Corriere della Sera*, May 17, 2002: 1.

32. Giuseppe D'Avanzo, "Clandestini, Stato d'emergenza," *La Repubblica*, March 19, 2002: 1; for more discussion on Bossi's political uses of fear, see Margarita Cachafeiro Gómez-Reino, *Ethnicity and Nationalism in Italian Politics: Inventing the Padania: Lega Nord and the Northern Question* (Burlington, VT: Ashgate), 2002; and Bull and Gilbert, *The Lega Nord*.

33. Reproduced in Dal Lago, *Non-Persone*: 127.

34. Quoted in Guido Passalacqua, "Bossi, Ultimatum al Governo 'Basta Immigrati o Salta Tutto,' " *La Repubblica*, March 19, 2002: 4.

35. Quoted in "Southern Europe," *Migration News*, Vol. 9, No. 4, 2002: 27.

36. Quoted in "Southern Europe," *Migration News*, Vol. 8, No. 5, 2001: 22, emphasis added.

37. Quoted in "Southern Europe," *Migration News*, Vol. 8, No. 3, 2001: 5.

38. Quoted in Guido Passalacqua, "Bossi, Ultimatum al Governo": 4; quoted in Roberto Zuccolini, "La Loggia: La Lega Ha Ragione, Rigore Necessario," *Corriere della Sera*, March 20, 2002: 8.

39. Quoted in *ibid.*: 8.

40. Alberto Morandi, Editorial, *La Padania*, January 21, 1998: 1.

41. Quoted in Claudia Fusani, "Criminalitá, la Sfida del Governo," *La Repubblica*, May 17, 2002: 4; see also Flavio Haver, "Operazione Alto Impatto: Espulsi 351 Clandestini," *Corriere della Sera*, May 17, 2002: 5.

42. Daniel Williams, "Berlusconi, Too, Puts Crime and Immigration in Spotlight," *International Herald Tribune*, IHT Online, May 20, 2002: 2, www.iht.com.

43. Cartoon by Ellekappa, *La Repubblica*, May 17, 2002: 4.

44. Governor of Region of Piedmont, quoted in Simone Boiocchi, "Sostenere le Nascite, Non gli Extracomunitari," Lapadania.com, April 3, 2001.

45. Roberto Maroni, Minister of Welfare, quoted in "Immigrazione: Maroni, Apertura su Voto alle Amministrative ma in un Percorso di Integrazione e con Garanzie," *Notizie ANSA*, www.stranieriinitalia.com, June 21, 2002.

46. Quoted in Roberto Zuccolini, "'Sí Solo agli Immigrati con un Lavoro,'" *La Repubblica*, July 13, 2001: 6.

47. Quoted in Luke Baker, "'Wildfire Influz' Blamed for Spike in Robberies," *National Post Online*, Reuters News Service, April 25, 2002: 2–3. In a counterpoint to the "defenseless citizen" imagery, the current center-left mayor points out that the previous year in a nearby town, Albanians were blamed for the gruesome murder of a mother and her young son, sparking an angry anti-immigrant rally; later it was discovered that the culprits were the woman's teenage daughter and her boyfriend.

48. Quoted in "Southern Europe," *Migration News*, Vol. 9, No. 4, 2002: 27.

49. Quoted in "Rightists Protest in Milan, Seeking Curbs on Muslims in Italy," *Reuters News Service*, October 19, 2001, http://web.lexis-nexis.com.

50. Quoted in Claudio Holzner, "Re-Birth of Islam in Italy: Between Indifference and Intolerance," *Journal of the International Institute*, Vol. 3, No. 2, 2003, www.umich.edu.

51. Ranan R. Lurie, "Siege Mentality in Fortress Europe," *Los Angeles Times*, May 12, 2002: M5.

52. Quoted in "Immigrazione: Diliberto, Si Svela Anima Fascista del Governo," *Notizie ANSA*, January 15, 2002, www.stranieriinitalia.it.

53. Quoted in Fabrizio Roncone, "Immigrati, Decine di Migliaia contro le Espulsioni," *Corriere della Sera*, January 20, 2002: 5.

54. Massimiliano di Massa, "Immagini d'immigrati," *Rivista Elettronica di Scienze Umane e Sociali*, Vol. 1, No. 2, 2003: 2.

55. "Southern Europe," *Migration News*, Vol. 9, No. 9, 2002: 25; Alessandra Stanley, "Immigration is Emerging as Early Issue in Italy's Vote", *New York Times*, August 8, 2000: A7.

56. "Southern Europe," *Migration News*, Vol. 7, No. 9, 2000: 19; see also "Italy: 463 Illegal Immigrants Taken Off Fishing Boat," *Los Angeles Times*, September 30, 2001: A32; Marjorie Miller, "In Europe, Wave of Illegal Migration Has Deadly Cost," *Los Angeles Times*, July 15, 2000: A1 and A6.

57. "Southern Europe," *Migration News*, Vol. 10, No. 3, 2003: 39.

58. "21 Illegal Albanian Migrants Die Trying to Sail to Italy," *Los Angeles Times*, January 11, 2004: A3.

59. Ben Jelloun, *Le Pareti della Solitudine*: xiv.

60. See, for example, "In Calabria Peschereccio Carico di Clandestini: Non Mangiavano da Giorni," *Corriere della Sera*, July 13, 2001: 6; Pier Francesco Fedrizzi, "Clandestini Marchiati dai Boss," *La Repubblica*, July 19, 2001: 22.

61. Zincone, *Secondo Rapporto*: 281–282.

62. The search was done using Google. Although I expected to find a discrepancy when I initiated the Internet search, these numbers vastly exceeded my expectations, even allowing for the fact that a few of the Internet entries of "clandestini" have other references, for example, "clandestine abortions."

63. Alberto D'Elia, "La Devianza dell'Immigrato Straniero nei Media: I Risultati di una Ricerca nel Salento," *Dei Delitti e delle Pene*, Vol. 6, No. 3, 1999: 77–113.

64. Elisa Manna and Carla Scaramella, "Tuning into Diversity: Immigrati e Minoranze Etniche nei Media," Censis Research Report No. 18-04-2002, Rome, April, 2002.

65. Antonio Polito, "Immigrazione: La UE si Divide; Parla Aznar: Lotta Dura contro i Clandestini," *La Repubblica*, June 18, 2002: 1 and 14.

66. Mikel Azurmendi, *Estampas de El Ejido: Un Reportaje sobre la Integración del Inmigrante* (Madrid: Taurus), 2001.

67. Guido Caldiron, *La Destra Plurale: Dalla Preferenza Nazionale alla Toleranza Zero* (Rome: Manifestolibri), 2000: 212.

68. Quoted in Jorge A. Rodríguez, " 'La Solución es que el Gobierno no Nos Envíe ni un Inmigrante Más'," *El País*, July 5, 2002: 24.

69. Quoted in J. Casqueiro and A. Diez, "Aznar Defiende la Reforma de la Ley de Extranjería para Combatir a las Mafias," *El País*, May 25, 2000: 28.

70. Personal interview, Madrid, June, 2002.

71. Quoted in José Antonio Zarzalejos, " 'Ma l'Europa non Tornerá Indietro: Sará Lotta Dura Contro i Clandestini,'" *La Repubblica*, June 18, 2002: 3.

72. Quoted in Fabrizio Finzi, "Immigrazione: Aznar–Berlusconi, Insieme per Norme Severe," *Notizie ANSA*, June 5, 2002: 2.

73. Quoted in José Antonio Zarzalejos, "'Ma l'Europa non Tornerá Indietro": 3.

74. Luís R. Aizpeolea, "Zapatero Exhibe su Discurso Más Duro Contra la Política 'Autoritaria y Antisocial' de Aznar," *El País*, July 16, 2002: 13; Mercedes Jansa, "Aznar Anuncia má Dura amb els Reincidents i 'Sesne Papers,' " *El Periódico*, July 16, 2002: 3.

75. "Concluye el Vallado Exterior de la Frontera de Ceuta tras Casi Siete A os de Obras," *El País*, February 4, 2000: 4; Dante Matelli, "Melilla, Baluardo d'Europa," *L'Espresso*, January 9, 1997: 12; Caldiron, *La Destra Plurale*: 210–212.

76. "Southern Europe," *Migration News*, Vol. 9, No. 9, 2002: 26.

77. Cornelius, "Spain: The Uneasy Transition".

78. More than 18 million Africans and Latin Americans came through Spain's airports on tourist visas in 2002, approximately one million of whom did not depart ("Southern Europe," *Migration News*, Vol. 10, No. 10, 2003: 40).

79. Ignacio Cembrero, "Nadie Quiere Vivir en Marruecos," *El País*, June 16, 2002: 11–13.

80. "Detenidos 71 Inmigrantes y Siete Patrones de Pateras en Canarias," *El País*, June 30, 2002: 30; "Casi un Centenar de Inmigrantes Detenidos tras Llegar en Patera a las Costas de Cadíz," *ABC*, May 13, 2002: 7; "15 More Bodies Found After Sinking of Boat," *Los Angeles Times*, November 1, 2003: A4.

81. *El País*, August 8, 1999, quoted in Caldiron, *La Destra Plurale*: 211.

82. Agrela, "La Política de Inmigración": 104; Enrique Santamaría, *La Incógnita del Extra o: Una Aproximación a la Significación Sociológica de la 'Inmigración no Comunitaria'* (Barcelona: Anthropos), 2002.

83. Bernat Gasulla, "El Suculento Negocio de los Clandestinos," *El Periódico de la Semana*, March 17–23, 1997: 3.

84. "Caravans of Slaves," *El Periódico de la Semana*, March 17–23, 1997: 1.

85. "Un Argellino Hiere a Seis Guardias Civiles en Calahorra," *ABC*, May 14, 2002: 12; Luis Gómez, "Culpables y Víctimas de la Violencia," *El País*, June 16, 2002: 9.

86. "Aznar Propone Leyes Más Duras Contra la Delincuencia y la Inmigración Ilegal," *El País*, July 16, 2002: 1.

87. Luís Gómez, "Culpables y Víctimas de la Violencia": 9.

88. Dario Melossi, "Alla Ricerca di una 'Vita Tranquilla': Immigrazione, Criminalitá e *Italian Way of Life*," *Quaderni di Città Sicure*, Vol. 1, 2000: 21.

89. Manuel Altozano, "Los Inmigrantes Irregulares Detenidos en 4 Meses se Duplican en Relación con 2001," *El País*, July 12, 2002: 26.

90. *Ibid.*: 26.

91. Manuel Delgado, "Criminalization of Immigrants?", in Conference Proceedings of the Graduate Program in Criminology, University of Barcelona, *Actas de las Jornadas del Graduat en Criminologia i Política Criminal, 2000 y 2001* (Barcelona: University of Barcelona), 2003: 221.

92. Domingo Marchena, "'Aquí Sólo Lloramos,'" *La Vanguardia*, June 4, 1997: 27.

93. "Magrebíes Bajo Sospecho," *La Vanguardia*, June 4, 1997: 20.

94. Sebastian Rotella, "Spain Arrests 16 in Terror Crackdown," *Los Angeles Times*, January 25, 2003: A3.

95. Ministro dell'Interno, *Rapporto del Ministro*; Dino Martirano, "'Carceri Affollate, Rimpatriamo gli Immigrati,'" *Corriere della Sera*, July 25, 2001: 15.

96. Zincone, *Secondo Rapporto*: 289.

97. Ministro dell'Interno, *Rapporto del Ministro*: 322.

98. *Ibid.*: 345.

99. Zincone, *Secondo Rapporto*: 289 and 281.

100. Ministro dell'Interno, *Rapporto del Ministro*: 324–325.

101. Zincone, *Secondo Rapporto*: 300.

102. *Ibid.*: 281.

103. Dal Lago, *Non-Persone*: 30.

104. Melossi, "Alla Ricerca di una 'Vita Tranquilla'": 40.

105. Marco Lagazzi, Daniela Malfatti, E. Pallestrini, and N. Rossoni, "Immigrazione, Comportamento Criminale e Sanzione Penale," *Rassegna Italiana di Criminologia*, Vol. 1, 1996: 161.

106. Quoted in Melossi, "The Other in the New Europe": 165.

107. Cited in Dal Lago, *Non-Persone*: 31.

108. Quoted in *ibid.*: 33.

109. *Ibid.*: 34 and 32, emphasis in original.

110. Zincone, *Secondo Rapporto*: 293–299.

111. Melossi, "The Other in the New Europe": 166.

112. Zincone, *Secondo Rapporto*: 280.

113. *Ibid.*: 295.

114. *Ibid.*: 300.

115. Roberto Bergalli, "Presentación de las Jornadas": 15.

116. Quoted in Melossi, "Alla Ricerca di una 'Vita Tranquilla'": 33.

117. Quoted in Asher Colombo, "Hope and Despair: 'Deviant' Immigrants in Italy," *Journal of Modern Italian Studies*, Vol. 2, No. 1, 1997: 17.

118. Ewick and Silbey, *The Common Place of Law*: 103–104.

119. Melossi, "The Other in the New Europe": 152. Melossi provides a detailed analysis of the factors involved in the disproportionate incarceration of immigrants in Italy and other European countries in Dario Melossi, "La 'Sovrarappresentazione' degli Stranieri nei Sistemi di Giustizia Penale Europei e Italiano," *Diritto Immigrazione e Cittadinanza*, Vol. 4, 2003: 11–27.

120. Alison Young, *Imagining Crime: Textual Outlaws and Criminal Conversations* (London: Sage Publications), 1996; Jonathan Simon, *Poor Discipline: Parole and the Social Control of the Underclass, 1890–1990* (Chicago: University of Chicago Press), 1993.

121. Chia-Wen Lee, "Making America Through Crime and Justice: The Politics of National Identity in America's War on Terrorism," paper presented at the joint annual meetings of the Law and Society Association and the Canadian Law and Society Association, Vancouver, Canada, May 30–June 1, 2002.

122. See, for example, Ian Haney Lopez, *White by Law: The Legal Construction of Race* (New York: New York University Press), 1996; Ian Haney Lopez, *Racism on Trial: The Chicano Fight for Justice* (Cambridge, MA: Belknap Press of Harvard University Press), 2003; Mari J. Matsuda, *Where Is My Body? And Other Essays on Race, Gender, and the Law* (Boston: Beacon Press), 1996; Richard Delgado and Jean Stefancic (eds.), *Critical Race Theory: The Cutting Edge* (Philadelphia: Temple University Press), 2nd edn, 2000.

123. Francisco Valdes, Jerome McCristal Culp, and Angela Harris, "Battles Waged, Won, and Lost: Critical Race Theory at the Turn of the Millennium," in Francisco Valdes, Jerome McCristal Culp, and Angela Harris (eds.), *Crossroads, Directions, and a New Critical Race Theory* (Philadelphia: Temple University Press), 2002: 2.

124. Haney Lopez, *Racism on Trial*: 119.

125. Michael Omi and Howard Winant, *Racial Formation in the United States: From the 1960s to the 1980s* (New York: Routledge and Kegan Paul), 1986: x.

126. Noel Ignatiev, *How the Irish Became White* (New York: Routledge), 1995:1.

127. Manuel Delgado, "Criminalization of Immigrants?": 218.
128. *Ibid.* In this context, the "disjuncture between physical and legal presence" described by Coutin (Coutin, *Legalizing Moves*: 29) takes an ironic turn, as it is immigrants' hyper-visibility, or their intense physical presence, that leads to their criminalization.
129. Ferruccio Sansa, "E Per Salvare le Prostitute Corsi da Sarte e Cameriere," *La Repubblica*, July 29, 2002: 3.
130. Omi and Winant, *Racial Formation*: 62–63.
131. Amnesty International, "Spain: Crisis of Identity": 5 and 13.
132. "Una Impresa Rechaza a 250 Peticionarios de Empleo por su Raza o su Aparienzia," *El País*, July 4, 2002: 4.
133. Quoted in Agrela, "La Política de Inmigración": 111, emphasis added.
134. Quoted in Andrea Selva, " 'Vagoni Separati per gli Immigrati,' " *La Repubblica*, January 18, 2003: 27; see also Paolo Rumiz, "Viaggio sul 'Treno degli Africani,' " *La Repubblica*, January 19, 2003: 21.
135. Quoted in Jacqueline Andall, "Second-Generation Attitude?": 400.
136. Quoted in *ibid.*: 399.
137. Quoted in *ibid.*: 400.
138. Mary C. Waters, *Black Identities: West Indian Immigrant Dreams and American Realities* (Cambridge: Harvard University Press): 5.
139. Claire Jean Kim, "The Racial Triangulation of Asian Americans," *Politics and Society*, Vol. 27, 1999: 105–138.
140. Lluís Visa, "Miles de Temporeros Vagan por Lleida sin Trabajo tras las Últimas Tormentas de Granizo," *El País, Catalu a*, July 22, 2002: 1.
141. Etienne Balibar, "Is There a 'Neo-Racism'?," in Etienne Balibar and Immanuel Wallerstein (eds.), *Race, Nation, Class: Ambiguous Identities* (New York: Verso Press), 1991.
142. Quoted in Agrela, "La Política de Inmigración": 114.
143. Quoted in Amnesty International, "Spain: Crisis of Identity": 6.
144. Quoted in Ter Wal, "The Discourse of the Extreme Right": 45.
145. Quoted in Marzban Cooper, "Integración Rígida o Tolerancia Humana?", Letter to the Editor, *El País*, July 14, 2002: 13–14.
146. Verena Stolcke, "El 'Problema' de la Inmigración en Europa: El Fundamentalismo Cultural Como Nueva Retórica de Exclusión," *Mientras Tanto*, Vol. 55, 1993: 84.
147. Edward W. Said, *Orientalism* (New York: Vintage Books), 1979: 7.
148. Balibar, "Is There a 'Neo-Racism'?": 25.
149. Peter Fitzpatrick, " 'We Know What It Is When You Do Not Ask Us': Nationalism as Racism," in Peter Fitzpatrick (ed.), *Nationalism, Racism and the Rule of Law* (Brookfield, VT: Dartmouth Publishing), 1995: 18.
150. Quoted in Chiara Unguendoli, "Biffi Insiste: Fermiamo gli Islamici," *Corriere della Sera*, October 1, 2000: 5.
151. Reproduced in Dal Lago, *Non-Persone*: 47.
152. Quoted in Agrela, "La Política de Inmigración": 107.
153. Personal interview, July, 2001.

154. Quoted in Agrela, "La Política de Inmigración": 107.
155. Hage, *White Nation*: 16–17.
156. *Ibid.*: 17.
157. Aihwa Ong, "Cultural Citizenship as Subject-Making: Immigrants Negotiate Racial and Cultural Boundaries in the United States," *Current Anthropology*, Vol. 37, No. 5, 1996: 739.
158. Etienne Balibar, *Politics and the Other Scene* (New York: Verso), 2002: 44, emphasis in the original.
159. See Kitty Calavita and Liliana Suárez Navaz, "Spanish Immigration Law and the Construction of Difference: Citizens and 'Illegals' on Europe's Southern Border," in Richard Warren Perry and Bill Maurer (eds.), *Globalization under Construction: Governmentality, Law, and Identity* (Minneapolis: Minnesota University Press), 2003.
160. Herbert Gans, "Second Generation Decline: Scenarios for the Economic and Ethnic Futures of the Post 1965 American Immigrants," *Ethnic and Racial Studies*, Vol. 15, 1992: 173–192; Alejandro Portes and Min Zhou, "The New Second Generation: Segmented Assimilation and Its Variants (Interminority Affairs in the US: Pluralism at the Crossroads)," *Annals of the American Academy of Political and Social Science*, Vol. 530, 1993: 74–97; Marcelo M. Suarez-Orozco, "Becoming Somebody: Central American Immigrants in US Inner-City Schools," *Anthropology and Education Quarterly*, Vol. 18, No. 4, 1987: 287–299.
161. Waters, *Black Identities*.
162. Ben Jelloun, *Le Pareti della Solitudine*: xiv–xv.
163. In Italy too, the terminology used in the immigration debate is revealing. As Fabio Berti points out, "Until the early 1990s, a 'straniero' ['foreigner'] was a German, English, Dutch, or Swiss person who had chosen [to live in Italy] for at least part of the year . . . So, the designation 'straniero' never assumed pejorative or negative connotations but, if anything, called attention only to perhaps eccentric behavior. To have friends among these foreigners was a sign of distinction among locals . . . This positive conception of the term foreigner changed in the early 1990s, with the arrival of the first 'extracomunitari.'" Berti, *Esclusione e Integrazione*: 75.
164. Abdelmalek Sayad, "La Doppia Pena del Migrante: Riflessioni sul 'Pensiero di Stato,'" *Aut Aut*, Vol. 275, 1996: 10.
165. Personal interview, Madrid, June, 2002.
166. Quoted in SOS Racismo, *El Ejido*: 13.
167. D'Avanzo, "Perché Bossi Cavalca": 15.

Chapter 7

1. Francesca Decimo, personal interview, Bologna, July, 2001. Decimo's dissertation is entitled "Percorsi Femminili in Emigrazione: Donne Marocchine e Somale a Bologna" (1998).
2. Zolberg, "Wanted But Not Welcome".

3. Saskia Sassen-Koob, "Recomposition and Peripheralization at the Core," *Contemporary Marxism*, Vol. 5, 1982: 88–100; Saskia Sassen, *The Global City* (Princeton: Princeton University Press), 2001; Renato Rosaldo, "Ideology, Place, and People without Culture," *Cultural Anthropology*, Vol. 3, No. 1, 1988: 77–87.

4. Marshall, *Citizenship and Social Class*.

5. Eurispes, "Il Rapporto Eurispes 2003: Il Paese delle Diseguaglianze," www.rassegna.it/2003/.

6. Carlos Dáguer, " 'No Tenemos el Billete de Vuelta,' " *El País*, July 15, 2002: 31.

7. The reference is to Richard Sennett and Jonathan Cobb, *The Hidden Injuries of Class* (New York: Norton), 1993.

8. Ter Wal, "Comparing Argumentation and Counter-Argumentation": 147.

9. Quoted in *ibid.*: 144.

10. Others have made the point that immigration exposes an essential contradiction at the heart of the liberal theory of citizenship. As Turner puts it, there exists a "tension between the normative principles of liberal democracy and the exclusionary practices of nation-states." Bryan S. Turner, "Review Essay: Citizenship and Political Globalization," *Citizenship Studies*, Vol. 4, 2000: 84. Similarly, Cole argues: "With its universalist commitment to the moral equality of humanity, liberal theory cannot coherently justify these practices of exclusion, which constitute [non-citizen] 'outsiders' on grounds any recognisable liberal theory would condemn as arbitrary." Phillip Cole, *Philosophies of Exclusion: Liberal Political Theory and Immigration* (Edinburgh: Edinburgh University Press), 2000: 2. Samuel Clark also challenges the "Whig interpretation of citizenship," stressing its inherently exclusionary nature by arguing – citing Brubaker – that "citizenship was . . . established to control the movement of the migrant poor." "Today," he posits, "citizenship is the primary method of social closure employed to keep the victims of global poverty out of the wealthier countries." Clark, "Amending the Whig Interpretation of Citizenship: 383.

11. Marshall, *Class, Citizenship, and Social Development*.

12. See, most notably, Kenneth Karst, "Citizenship, Race, and Marginality," *William and Mary Law Review*, Vol. 30, 1989: 1–49; and Kenneth L. Karst, "The Bonds of American Nationhood," *Cardozo Law Review*, Vol. 21, 2000: 1141–1182; William Forbath, "Caste, Class, and Equal Citizenship," *Michigan Law Review*, Vol. 98, 1999: 1–75.

13. Ben Jelloun, *Le Pareti della Solitudine*: ix and xiv.

14. Sassen, *Losing Control*.

15. For an excellent discussion of various "globalization narratives," see Susan Silbey, " 'Let Them Eat Cake': Globalization, Postmodern Colonialism, and the Possibilities of Justice," Presidential Address, *Law and Society Review*, Vol. 31, 1997: 207–235.

16. Henk Overbeck, "Globalization, Sovereignty, and Transnational

Regulation: Reshaping the Governance of International Migration," in Bimal Ghosh (ed.), *Managing Migration: Time for a New International Regime?* (Oxford: Oxford University Press), 2000: 50.

17. United Nations, *The World's Women, 2000: Trends and Statistics* (New York: United Nations), 2000. Of course, not all of this migration is labor-related; much of it is triggered by war, civil strife, and other forms of political conflict.

18. Maurizio Ambrosini, "Le Sfide della Cittadinanza, Ripensare le Politiche Sociali nell'Epoca della Globalizzazione Economica," *Politiche Sociali e Servizi*, Vol. 1, 1996: 10 and 17.

19. Jock Young, *The Exclusive Society: Social Exclusion, Crime and Difference in Late Modernity* (London: Sage Publications), 1999: 1.

20. Jock Young, "Merton with Energy, Katz with Structure: The Sociology of Vindictiveness and the Criminology of Transgression," *Theoretical Criminology*, Vol. 7, No. 3, 2003: 399.

21. In this regard, it might be pointed out that the Americanization of Western culture – epitomized, for example, in the McDonaldization phenomenon – is probably a far greater threat to Italian and Spanish cultural traditions than is the much more highly debated "multiculturalism" accompanying immigration.

22. Zolberg, "Modes of Incorporation": 142.

23. Robert D. Putnam, *Bowling Alone: The Collapse and Revival of American Community* (New York: Simon and Schuster), 2000.

24. Indeed, Putnam's contention in *Bowling Alone* that Americans are less likely to join associations and clubs than they once were and are more prone to individualistic pursuits, opened up a vigorous debate about Americans' civic behavior, with some suggesting he exaggerated the trend, others arguing that the picture is more complicated than his portrayal implies, and still others contending that he was wrong altogether. See Garry Wills, "Putnam's America," *American Prospect*, Vol. 11, July 17, 2000; Paul Starr, "The Public Vanishes," *New Republic*, August 14, 2000: 35–37; Theda Skocpol and Morris Fiorina (eds.), *Civic Engagement in American Democracy* (Washington, DC: Brookings Institution Press), 1999; Everett Carl Ladd, *The Ladd Report* (New York: Free Press), 1999.

25. Anderson, *Imagined Communities*.

26. Roger Rouse, "Mexican Migration and the Social Space of Postmodernism," *Diaspora*, Vol. 1, No. 1, 1991: 12.

27. Walzer, *Spheres of Justice*: 38.

28. Anderson, *Imagined Communities*: 139.

29. Zolberg, "Modes of Incorporation": 153; *Webster's Ninth New Collegiate Dictionary* (Springfield, MA: Merriam-Webster), 1985: 486.

30. See Chapter 6, note 136.

31. Ong, "Cultural Citizenship": 737–762.

32. Andall, "Second-Generation Attitude?": 398.

33. Joseph R. Gusfield, *Symbolic Crusade: Status Politics and the American Temperance Movement* (Urbana: University of Illinois Press), 1963.

34. See Calavita and Suárez-Navaz, "Spanish Immigration Law."
35. Sarat and Kearns, *Law in Everyday Life*: 21–22.
36. Cohen, *Contested Domains*: 151.
37. Kimberle Crenshaw, "A Black Feminist Critique of Antidiscrimination Law and Politics," in David Kairys (ed.), *The Politics of Law: A Progressive Critique* (New York: Pantheon Books), 2nd edn, 1990.
38. Young, *The Exclusive Society*.

BIBLIOGRAPHY

Books and articles

ABC, "Tres de Cada Cuatro Españoles Relacionan la Inmigración con la Inseguridad Ciudadana." May 15, 2002: 20.

Abella, Pino, Maurizio Marengon, and Angela Soverini. 2001. "Il Mercato del Lavoro in Emilia-Romagna." Pp. 439–466 in *Istruzione Formazione Lavoro in Emilia-Romagna, Rapporto 2000*, edited by Maura Franchi. Bologna: Graffiti.

Accornero, Aria, Bruno Anastasia, Maurizio Gambuzza, Elisabetta Gualmini, and Maurizio Rasera. 2000. *Solo una Grande Giostra: La Diffusione del Lavoro a Tempo Determinato.* Milan: FrancoAngeli.

Agger, Ben. 2000. *Public Sociology: From Social Facts to Literary Acts.* New York: Rowland & Littlefield.

Agnew, John A. 2002. *Place and Politics in Modern Italy.* Chicago: University of Chicago Press.

Agrela, Belén. 2002. "La Política de Inmigración en España: Reflexiones sobre la Emergencia del Discurso Cultural." *Migraciones Internacionales.* January–February 2002, Vol. 1, No. 2: 93–121.

Aizpeolea, Luis R. 2002. "Zapatero Exhibe su Discurso Más Duro Contra la Política 'Autoritaria y Antisocial' de Aznar." *El País.* July 16, 2002: 13.

Ajuntament de Barcelona, Departament d'Estadística. 2002. *Guia Estadística: Ciutat Vella en Xifres.* Barcelona: Ajuntament de Barcelona.

Alba, Richard D. and Victor Nee. 1996. "Rethinking Assimilation Theory for a New Era of Immigration." *International Migration Review.* Vol. 31, No. 4: 825–873.

Allam, Magdi. 2001. "Tunisi, alle Porte del Deserto 'La Scuola dell'immigrato.'" *La Repubblica.* March 18, 2001: 18.

Altozano, Manuel. 2002. "Los Inmigrantes Irregulares Detenidos en 4 Meses se Duplican en Relación con 2001." *El País*. July 12, 2002: 26.

2002. "Quiero Ser Limpiador." *El País*. July 3, 2002: 23.

Aman, Alfred C. Jr. 1994. "Introduction: Migration and Globalization." *Indiana Journal of Global Studies*. Vol. 2: 1–4.

Ambrosini, Maurizio. 1996. "Le Sfide della Cittadinanza, Ripensare le Politiche Sociali nell'Epoca della Globalizzazione Economica." *Politiche Sociali e Servizi*. Vol. 1: 7–24.

1999. *Utili Invasori: L'inserimento degli Immigrati nel Mercato del Lavoro*. Milan: FrancoAngeli.

2000. *Accogliere Attivamente. La Risorsa della Formazione Professionale per la Promozione Sociale degli Immigrati*. Turin: Casa di Caritá, Arti e Mestieri.

2001. "Il Lavoro." Pp. 91–101 in *Sesto Rapporto sulle Migrazioni 2000*, edited by ISMU-Cariplo. Milan: FrancoAngeli.

2001. *La Fatica di Integrarsi: Immigrati e Lavoro in Italia*. Bologna: Il Mulino.

Anastasia, Bruno, Anna de Angelini, Maurizio Gambuzza, and Maurizio Rasera. 2001. *Il Mercato del Lavoro nel Veneto*. Milan: FrancoAngeli.

Andall, Jacqueline. 1999. "Cape Verdean Women on the Move: 'Immigration Shopping' in Italy and Europe." *Modern Italy*. Vol. 4, No. 2: 241–257.

2000. "Organizing Domestic Workers in Italy: The Challenge of Gender, Class, and Ethnicity." Pp. 145–171 in *Gender and Migration in Southern Europe: Women on the Move*, edited by Floya Anthias and Gabriella Lazaridis. New York: Berg.

2002. "Second-Generation Attitude? African-Italians in Milan." *Journal of Ethnic and Migration Studies*. Vol. 28, No. 3: 389–407.

Anderson, Benedict. 1983. *Imagined Communities: Reflections on the Origin and Spread of Nationalism*. London: Verso.

Anthias, Floya and Gabriella Lazaridis. 2000. "Introduction: Women on the Move in Southern Europe." Pp. 1–13 in *Gender and Migration in Southern Europe: Women on the Move*, edited by Floya Anthias and Gabriella Lazaridis. New York: Berg.

Anuario El País. 1997. Madrid: Ediciones El País.

Aparicio, Rosa and Andrés Tornos. 2001. *Estrategias y Dificultades Características en la Integración Social de los Distintos Colectivos de Inmigrantes Llegados a España*. Madrid: Instituto de Migraciones y Servicios Sociales.

Aresté, Pedro. 1995. "Los Cupos de Trabajadores en 1993 y 1994." Pp. 190–195 in *Diez Años de la Ley de Extranjería: Balance y Perspectivas*, edited by Alegría Borrás. Barcelona: Fundación Paulino Torras Domenech.

1995. "Regularizaciones." Pp. 182–190 in *Diez Años de la Ley de Extranjería: Balance y Perspectivas*, edited by Alegría Borrás. Barcelona: Fundación Paulino Torras Domenech.

Avitabile, Salvatore. 2002. "Salento, Irregolaritá in un'azienda su Due." *Corriere del Mezzogiorno*. August 6, 2002: 7.

Azurmendi, Mikel. 2001. *Estampas de El Ejido: Un Reportaje sobre la Integración del Inmigrante*. Madrid: Taurus.

Balbo, Laura. 1990. "Cittadini, Cittadini-dimezzati, Non-cittadini." *Inchiesta*. No. 90: 23–26.

Balibar, Etienne. 1991. "Is There a 'Neo-Racism'?" Pp. 17–28 in *Race, Nation, Class: Ambiguous Identities*, edited by Etienne Balibar and Immanuel Wallerstein. New York: Verso Press.

2002. *Politics and the Other Scene*. New York: Verso Press.

Barbagli, Marzio. 1998. *Immigrazione e Criminalitá in Italia*. Bologna: Il Mulino.

Battistini, Giorgio. 2002. "Da Ciampi Stop alla Lega: Umanitá con i Clandestini." *La Repubblica*. March 20, 2002: 1.

Baubock, Rainer. 1994. *Transnational Citizenship: Membership and Rights in International Migration*. Aldershot: Edward Elgar.

Bauman, Zygmunt. 2001. *Community: Seeking Safety in an Insecure World*. Cambridge: Polity Press.

Behdad, Ali. 1997. "Nationalism and Immigration to the United States." *Diaspora*. Vol. 6, No. 2: 155–178.

Beiner, Ronald. 1995. "Introduction." Pp. 1–28 in *Theorizing Citizenship*, edited by Ronald Beiner. Albany: State University of New York Press.

Benyon, John. 1996. "The Politics of Police Cooperation in the European Union." *International Journal of the Sociology of Law*. Vol. 24: 353–379.

Bergalli, Roberto. 2000. "Actas de las Jornadas del Graduat en Criminologia i Política Criminal, 2000 y 2001." Pp. 15–17 in *Presentación de las Jornadas*. University of Barcelona.

Bernardotti, María Adriana and Giovanni Mottura. 1999. *Il Gioco delle Tre Case: Immigrazione e Politiche Abitative a Bologna dal 1990 al 1999*. Turin: L'Harmattan Italia.

Berti, Fabio. 2000. *Esclusione e Integrazione: Uno Studio su Due Comunitá di Immigrati*. Milan: FrancoAngeli.

Bianco, Enzo. 2001. "Considerazioni del Ministro dell'Interno." Pp. 15–33 in *Rapporto del Ministro dell'Interno sullo Stato della Sicurezza in Italia*. Bologna: Il Mulino.

Bisso, Marino. 2000. "Linciamo gli Albanesi." *La Repubblica*. January 14, 2000: 16.

Boer, Monica den. 1995. "Moving between Bogus and Bona Fide: The Policing of Inclusion and Exclusion in Europe." Pp. 92–111 in *Migration and European Integration: The Dynamics of Inclusion and Exclusion*, edited by Robert Miles and Dietrich Thranhardt. London: Pinter Publishers.

Boeri, Tito, Gordon Hanson, and Barry McCormick. 2002. *Immigration Policy and the Welfare System: A Report for the Fondazione Rodolfo Debenedetti in Association with the William Davidson Institute*. Oxford: Oxford University Press.

Boix, Vicente Font. 1991. *El Trabajador Extranjero y la Regularización de 1991*. Barcelona: Itinera Cuadernos.

Bonerandi, Enrico. 2001. "Brució Rumeno, 30 Anni di Carcere." *La Repubblica*. March 20, 2001: 24.

Bordignon, Fabio. 2002. "Gli Immigrati Fanno Meno Paura." *La Repubblica*. March 20, 2002: 10–11.

Borrás, Alegría. 1995. *Diez Años de la Ley de Extranjería: Balance y Perspectivas*. Barcelona: Fundación Paulino Torras Domenech.

———. 1995. "La Influencia de la Evolución en el Medio Internacional sobre el Derecho Español de Extranjería en el Periodo 1985–1995." Pp. 21–48 in *Diez Años de la Ley de Extranjería: Balance y Perspectivas*, edited by Alegría Borrás. Barcelona: Itinera Libros.

Borrás, Alegría and Cristina González. 1995. "Aspectos Concretos de la Integración Social." Pp. 214–230 in *Diéz Años de la Ley de Extanjería: Balance y Perspectivas*, edited by Alegría Borrás. Barcelona: Itinera Libros.

Bosniak, Linda. 2000. "Citizenship Denationalized." *Indiana Journal of Global Studies*. Vol. 7: 447–509.

Bottomore, Tom. 1992. "Citizenship and Social Class, Forty Years On." Pp. 55–93 in *Citizenship and Social Class*, edited by T. H. Marshall and Tom Bottomore. London: Pluto Press.

Bourdieu, Pierre. 1991. "Preface." Pp. 1–9 in *L'Immigration: Ou les Paradoxes de l'Altérité*, edited by Sayad Abdelmalek. Brussels: De Boeck-Wesmael.

Braun, Michael. 1996. "The Confederated Trade Unions and the Dini Government: The Grand Return to Neo-Corporatism." Pp. 205–221 in *Italian Politics: The Stalled Transition*, edited by Mario Caciagli and David I. Kertzer. Boulder, CO: Westview Press.

Brubaker, Rogers. 1989. "Introduction." Pp. 1–27 in *Immigration and the Politics of Citizenship in Europe and North America*, edited by Rogers Brubaker. New York: University Press of America.

———. 1992. *Citizenship and Nationhood in France and Germany*. Cambridge: Harvard University Press.

Brucker, Herbert, Gil S. Epstein, Barry McCormick, Gilles Saint-Paul, Alessandra Venturini, and Klaus Zimmermann. 2002. "Welfare State Provision." Pp. 66–90 in *Immigration Policy and the Welfare System*, edited by Tito Boeri, Gordon Hanson, and Barry McCormick. New York: Oxford University Press.

Buisef, Dris. 1994. "Medios de Comunicación y Visiones del Magreb." *Voces y Culturas*. Vol. 6: 11–21.

Bull, Anna Cento, and Mark Gilbert. 2001. *The Lega Nord and the Northern Question in Italian Politics*. London: Palgrave.

Bustamante, Jorge. 1978. "Commodity-Migrants: Structural Analysis of Mexican Immigration to the US." Pp. 183–203 in *Views Across the Border*, edited by Stanley Ross. Albuquerque: University of New Mexico Press.

Caciagli, Mario and David I. Kertzer. 1996. *Italian Politics: The Stalled Transition*. Boulder, CO: Westview Press.

Caffagnini, Laura. 2001. "Una Casa in Comune." *Il Manifesto*. June 3, 2001: 4.

Calavita, Kitty. 1984. *US Immigration Law and the Control of Labor: 1820–1924*. London: Academic Press.

1989. "The Contradictions of Immigration Lawmaking: The Immigration Reform and Control Act of 1986." *Law and Policy*. Vol. 11: 17–47.

1992. *Inside the State: The Bracero Program, Immigration, and the INS*. New York: Routledge.

1994. "Italy and the New Immigration." Pp. 303–326 in *Controlling Immigration: A Global Perspective*, edited by Wayne A. Cornelius, Philip L. Martin, and James F. Hollifield. Stanford: Stanford University Press.

1996. "The New Politics of Immigration: 'Balanced-Budget Conservatism' and the Symbolism of Proposition 187." *Social Problems*. Vol. 43: 284–305.

1998. "Immigration, Law, and Marginalization in a Global Economy: Notes from Spain." *Law and Society Review*. Vol. 32: 529–566.

2000. "The Paradoxes of Race, Class, Identity and 'Passing': Enforcing the Chinese Exclusion Acts, 1882–1910." *Law and Social Inquiry*. Vol. 25: 1–40.

2001. "Chinese Exclusion and the Open Door with China: Structural Contradictions and the 'Chaos' of Law, 1882–1910." *Social and Legal Studies*. Vol. 10: 203–226.

Calavita, Kitty and Liliana Suárez-Navaz. 2003. "Spanish Immigration Law and the Construction of Difference: Citizens and 'Illegals' on Europe's Southern Border." Pp. 99–127 in *Globalization under Construction: Governmentality, Law, and Identity*, edited by Richard W. Perry and Bill Maurer. Minneapolis: Minnesota University Press.

Caldeira, Teresa P. R. 2000. *City of Walls: Crime, Segregation, and Citizenship in São Paulo*. Berkeley: University of California Press.

Caldiron, Guido. 2000. *La Destra Plurale: Dalla Preferenza Nazionale alla Toleranza Zero*. Rome: Manifestolibri.

Campillo, Francisco Beltrán, and Jesús Miñano Martínez. 1997. *Censo y Caracterización de las Infraviviendas Usadas por Inmigrantes en la Región de Murcia: 1996*. Madrid: Instituto de Migraciones y Servicios Sociales.

Del Campo, Salustiano. 1992. "Sobre el Racismo y la Xenofobia." *Cuenta y Razon del Pensamiento Actual*. Vol. 15: 73–74.

Cantalupi, Marco and Maurizio Marengon. 2002. "Il Mercato del Lavoro." Pp. 14–22 in *Emilia-Romagna Lavoro*. Bologna: Agenzia Emilia-Romagna.

Cantero, Josép María Navarro. 1994. "Requisitos para el Desarrollo de una Cultura de Respeto a la Diversidad." Pp. 267–272 in *Extranjeros en el Paraíso*, edited by el Colectivo Virico. Barcelona: Edicions La Lletra SCCL.

Caputo, Giustina Orientale. 2000. "Salari di Fatto dei Lavoratori Immigrati in Italia." Pp. 88–93 in *Rapporto Immigrazione: Lavoro, Sindacato, Societá*, edited by Enrico Pugliese. Rome: Ediesse.

Carens, Joseph H. 1995. *Aliens and Citizens: The Case for Open Borders*. Albany: State University of New York Press.

Carini, Alessandra. 2001. "Il Nordest non é Piú Ribelle Ora Vuol Contare a Roma." *La Repubblica*. July 14, 2001: 18.

Caritas. 2000. *Immigrazione: Dossier Statistico 2000*. Rome: Edizioni Anterem.
     2003. *Immigrazione: Dossier. Statistico 2003*. Rome: Edizione Anterem.

Carter, Donald Martin. 1997. *States of Grace: Senegalese in Italy and the New European Immigration*. Minneapolis: University of Minnesota Press.

Casadio, Giovanna. 2001. "Roma, di Miseria si Muore; Ecco l'esercito dei Poveri." *La Repubblica*. March 15, 2001: 12.
     2002. "Immigrati, 100 Mila a Roma, 'No alla Legge Fini-Bossi.'" *La Repubblica*. January 20, 2002: 10.
     2002. "Immigrati, Via alla Nuova Legge." *La Repubblica*. July 12, 2002: 2.
     2003. "Immigrati, la Legge Fantasma." *La Repubblica*. January 22, 2003: 12.

Casey, John. 1997. "La Admisión e Integración de los Inmigrantes Extranjeros." in *Las Políticas Públicas en España*, edited by Joan Subirats and Ricard Gomá. Madrid: Ariel.

Casqueiro, J., and A. Diez. 2000. "Aznar Defiende la Reforma de la Ley de Extranjería para Combatir a las Mafias." *El País*. May 25, 2000: 28.

Castel, Robert. 1996. "Le Insidie dell'esclusione." *Assistenza Sociale*, Vol. 2.

Castles, Stephen and Godula Kosack. 1973. *Immigrant Workers and Class Structure in Western Europe*. London: Oxford University Press.

Cembrero, Ignacio. 2002. "Nadie Quiere Vivir en Marruecos." *El País*. July 16, 2002: 11–13.

Centorrino, Mario. 2001. "Il Lavoro Interinale? Avvantaggia Solo il Nord Italia." *L'unitá*. July 22, 2001: 11.

Centro de Estudios del Cambio Social. 2002. *Informe España 2002*. Madrid: Fundación Encuentro.

Cesarani, David and Mary Fullbrook (eds.). 1996. *Citizenship, Nationality and Migration in Europe*. London: Routledge.

Chattou, Zoubir. 2000. "Los Trabajadores Agrícolas Marroquíes de el Ejido. De la Invisibilidad a la Toma de Conciencia de Sí Mismos." *Migraciones*. Vol. 8: 203–229.

Chavez, Leo R. 1988. "Settlers and Sojourners: The Case of Mexicans in the United States." *Human Organization*. Vol. 47: 95–108.

Chell-Robinson, Victoria. 2000. "Female Migrants in Italy: Coping in a Country of New Immigration." Pp. 103–123 in *Gender and Migration in Southern Europe: Women on the Move*, edited by Floya Anthias and Gabriella Lazaridis. New York: Berg.

Chiari, Riccardo. 2002. "Uccisi dal Freddo." *Il Manifesto*. January 5, 2002: 8.

Chiesa, Pierluigi Francesco. 1999. "Sindacato e Lavoratori Immigrati: Il Caso Italiano." Pp. 41–128 in *Dal Lavoro alla Famiglia: Percorsi Migratori a Confronto*, edited by Osservatorio Comunale delle Immigrazioni di Bologna. Turin: L'Harmattan Italia.

CIRES. 1995. "Informe CIRES: Actitudes hacia los Inmigrantes." Madrid: BBK.

CIS. 1996. "Actitudes ante la Inmigracíon." Madrid: CIS.

Clark, Samuel. 2002. "Amending the Whig Interpretation of Citizenship: A Review Essay on *Extending Citizenship, Reconfiguring States*." *Contemporary Sociology*. July 2002, Vol. 31: 382–385.

Cockcroft, James D. 1986. *Outlaws in the Promised Land: Mexican Immigrant Workers and America's Future*. New York: Grove Press.

Codini, Ennio. 2001. "Gli Aspetti Normativi." Pp. 25–30 in *Sesto Rapporto sulle Migrazioni 2000*, edited by ISMU-Cariplo. Milan: FrancoAngeli.

Cohen, Robin. 1991. *Contested Domains: Debates in International Labour Studies*. London: Zed Books.

Colaprico, Piero. 2001. "Immigrati, Patto Bossi-Fini, 'Resta Solo Chi Ha un Lavoro.'" *La Repubblica*. August 7, 2001: 8.

——— 2002. "Immigrati, Riforma in Arrivo." *La Repubblica*. August 9, 2002: 19.

Cole, Phillip. 2000. *Philosophies of Exclusion: Liberal Political Theory and Immigration*. Edinburgh: Edinburgh University Press.

Colectivo IOÉ. 1992. *Los Trabajadores Extranjeros en España: Informe para el Instituto Sindical de Estudios*. Madrid: Colectivo IOÉ.

——— 1999. *Inmigración y Trabajo en España: Trabajadores Inmigrantes en el Sector de la Hostelería*. Madrid: Secretaría General de Asuntos Sociales.

Colledani, Maria Luisa. 2001. "Transfrontalieri, la Nuova Risorsa." *Il Sole 24 Ore*. April 30, 2001: 1.

Colombo, Asher. 1997. "Hope and Despair: 'Deviant' Immigrants in Italy." *Journal of Modern Italian Studies*. Vol. 2, No. 1: 1–20.

Colombo, Asher and Giuseppe Sciortino. 2002. *Stranieri in Italia: Assimilati ed Esclusi*. Bologna: Il Mulino.

Comisión Interministerial de Extranjería. 1995. *Anuario Estadístico de Extranjería*. Madrid: Secretaría General Técnica, Ministerio de Justicia e Interior.

——— 2000. *Anuario Estadístico de Extranjería*. Madrid: Secretaría General Técnica, Ministerio de Justicia e Interior.

Comune di Bologna. 2001. "La Casa: Primo Problema per Tutti." Osservatorio delle Immigrazioni. February 2001, No. 1: 11.

Consejo Economico y Social. 1995. *Economia, Trabajo y Seguridad: Memorias sobre la Situación Socioeconomica y Laboral, España*. Madrid: Consejo Economico y Social.

Consiglio Nazionale dell'economia e del Lavoro. 1991. *Immigrati e Societá Italiana*. Rome: Editalia.

Constable, Marianne. 1993. "Sovereignty and Governmentality in Modern American Immigration Law." *Studies in Law, Politics, and Society.* Vol. 13: 249–271.

Conti, Paolo. 2002. "Io, Clandestino per Due Anni, Vivo Ancora nel Terrore." *Corriere della Sera.* January 20, 2002: 5.

Cooper, Marzban. 2002. "Integración Rígida o Tolerancia Humana?" *El País.* July 14, 2002: 13–14.

Cornelius, Wayne A. 1989. "The US Demand for Mexican Labor." Pp. 25–47 in *Mexican Migration to the United States: Origins, Consequences, and Policy Options,* edited by Wayne A. Cornelius and Jorge A. Bustamante. La Jolla: Center for US–Mexican Studies, University of California, San Diego.

——— 1994. "Spain: The Uneasy Transition from Labor Exporter to Labor Importer." Pp. 331–369 in *Controlling Immigration: A Global Perspective,* edited by Wayne A. Cornelius and Jorge A. Bustamante. Stanford: Stanford University Press.

Cornelius, Wayne A. and Jorge A. Bustamante. 1989. *Mexican Migration to the United States: Origins, Consequences, and Policy Options.* La Jolla: Center for US–Mexican Studies, University of California, San Diego.

Cornelius, Wayne A., Philip L. Martin, and James F. Hollifields (eds.). 2004, 2nd edn. *Controlling Immigration: A Global Perspective.* Stanford: Stanford University Press.

Corriere della Sera. 2001. "In Calabria Peschereccio Carico di Clandestini: Non Mangiavano da Giorni," July 13, 2001: 6.

——— 2002. "L'economia Italiana é Meno Competitiva," November 12, 2002: 1.

Coutin, Susan Bibler. 1994. "Enacting Law Through Social Practice: Sanctuary as a Form of Resistance." Pp. 282–303 in *Contested States: Law, Hegemony, and Resistance,* edited by Mindie Lazarus-Black and Susan Hirsch. New York: Routledge.

——— 2000. *Legalizing Moves: Salvadoran Immigrants' Struggle for US Residency.* Ann Arbor: University of Michigan Press.

Crenshaw, Kimberlé. 1990. "A Black Feminist Critique of Antidiscrimination Law and Politics." Pp. 195–218 in *The Politics of Law: A Progressive Critique,* 2nd edn, edited by David Kairys. New York: Pantheon Books.

Cusí, Anna Terrón I. 2002. "Lo que no se Ha Hecho en Sevilla." *El País.* July 3, 2002: 12.

Dáguer, Carlos. 2002. "No Tenemos el Billete de Vuelta." *El Páis.* July 15, 2002: 31.

Dahiri, Mohamed and Diamantino García Acosta. 1994. "La Inmigración en España." Pp. 115–122 in *Extranjeros en el Paraíso,* edited by El Colectivo Virico. Barcelona: Edicions La Lletra SCCL.

Danielsen, Dan and Karen Engle. 1995. *After Identity: A Reader in Law and Culture.* New York: Routledge.

Darian-Smith, Eve. 1999. *Bridging Divides: The Channel Tunnel and English Legal Identity in the New Europe*. Berkeley: University of California Press.

D'avanzo, Giuseppe. 2002. "Clandestini, Stato d'emergenza." *La Repubblica*. March 19, 2002: 1.

2002. "Perché Bossi Cavalca la Politica della Paura." *La Repubblica*. March 19, 2002: 15.

Decimo, Francesca. 1996. "Reti di Solidarietá e Strategie Economiche di Donne Immigrate a Napoli." *Studi Emigrazione*. Vol. 33: 473–494.

2003. "Gli Elementi di un Conflitto Urbano: Questione Abitativa e Immigrazione Marocchina a Bologna." Pp. 71–101 in *Stranieri in Italia: Un Immigrazione Normale*, edited by Giuseppe Sciortino and Asher Colombo. Bologna: Il Mulino.

Delgado, Manuel. 2003. "Criminalization of Immigrants?" Pp. 217–225 in *Actas de las Jornadas del Graduat en Criminologia i Política Criminal, 2000 y 2001*. Barcelona: University of Barcelona.

Delgado, Richard and Jean Stefancic. 2000. *Critical Race Theory: The Cutting Edge*. Philadelphia: Temple University Press.

D'elia, Alberto. 1999. "La Devianza dell'Immigrato Straniero nei Media: I Risultati di una Ricerca nel Salento." *Dei Delitti e Delle Pene*. September–December 1999, Vol. 6, No. 3: 77–113.

Desio, Diletta. 2001. "L'inferno Apoff." *Il Manifesto*. April 1, 2001: 5.

Diamanti, Ilvo and Fabio Bordignon. 2002. "Immigrazione e Cittadinanza in Europa." *Quaderni FNE Collana Osservatori*. Vol. 5: 12–13.

Dietz, Gunther. 2000. *El Desafío de la Interculturalidad: El Voluntariado y las ONG ante el Reto de la Inmigración. El Caso de la Ciudad de Granada*. Granada: Proyecto sur de Ediciones.

Djajic, Slobodan. 1997. "Illegal Immigration and Resource Allocation." *International Economic Review*. Vol. 38, No. 1: 97–117.

Dreier, Peter, John Mollenkopf, and Todd Swanstrom. 2001. *Place Matters: Metropolitics for the Twenty-First Century*. Lawrence, KS: University of Kansas Press.

Ebner, Adriano. 2000. *Radici Venete*. Venice: Regione del Veneto, Giunta Regionale.

Eckland-Olson, Sheldon and Steve J. Martin. 1988. "Organizational Compliance with Court-Ordered Reform." *Law and Society Review*. Vol. 22: 359–383.

Economist. 1996. "A Survey of Spain." December 14, 1996: 7.

Edelman, Murray J. 1977. *Political Language – Words that Succeed and Policies that Fail*. New York: Academic Press.

1977. *The Symbolic Uses of Politics*. Urbana: University of Illinois Press.

Eisenstadt, Todd A., and Cathryn L. Thorup. 1994. *Caring Capacity Versus Carrying Capacity*. La Jolla: Center for US–Mexican Studies, University of California, San Diego.

El Colectivo Virico. 1994. *Extranjeros en el Paraíso*. Barcelona: Virus.

El Periódico. 1997. "Boda 'Ilegal' para Denunciar los Obstaculos a los Matrimonios Interetnicos." *El Periódico*. March 29, 1997: 26.

Emerson, Robert M. and Blair Paley. 1992. "Organizational Horizons and Complaint Filing." Pp. 231–247 in *The Uses of Discretion*, edited by Keith Hawkins. Oxford: Clarendon Press.

Engel, David. 1984. "The Oven Bird's Song: Insiders, Outsiders, and Personal Injuries in an American Community." *Law and Society Review*. Vol. 18: 551–582.

Eurispes. 2001. *Rapporto Italia 2001*. Rome: Ufficio Stampa Eurispes.

Ewick, Patricia and Susan S. Silbey. 1998. *The Common Place of Law: Stories from Everyday Life*. Chicago: University of Chicago Press.

Faedda, Barbara. 2001. "Le Politiche dell'integrazione: Le Norme e le Esperienze." *Gli Stranieri*. Vol. 8, No. 2: 92–101.

      2002. "L'integrazione Attraverso il Lavoro: Il 'Caso Veneto.'" *Gli Stranieri*. Vol. 9, No. 2: 161–165.

✓ Falk, Richard. 1993. "The Making of Global Citizenship." Pp. 39–50 in *Global Visions: Beyond the New World Order*, edited by Jeremy Brecher, John Brown Childs, and Jill Cutler. Montreal: Black Rose Press.

      2000. "The Decline of Citizenship in an Era of Globalization." *Citizenship Studies*. Vol. 4: 5–17.

Fasano, Luciano and Francesco Zucchini. 2001. "L'implementazione Locale del Testo Unico sull'immigrazione." Pp. 39–50 in *Sesto Rapporto sulle Migrazioni 2000*, edited by ISMU-Cariplo. Milan: FrancoAngeli.

Fato, Manuela. 1999–2000. "Politiche Migratorie in un Paese di Vecchia Immigrazione e in uno di Nuova Immigrazione: Francia e Italia a Confronto." Masters Thesis in Sociology, University of Naples.

Fazio, Luca. 2001. "Immigrati, Sará un 2001 Record: Il Governo ne Fará Entrare 83 Mila." *La Repubblica*. March 15, 2001: 29.

      2002. "Milano, 59 Bengalesi in Tre Monolocali." *Il Manifesto*. January 5, 2002: 15.

Fedrizzi, Pier Francesco. 2001. "Clandestini Marchiati dai Boss." *La Repubblica*. July 19, 2001: 22.

Ferrer, Núria Vives i. 2001. "Las Modificaciones de la Ley de Extranjería: Historia de una Odisea Parlamentaria." Pp. 47–55 in *Informe Anual 2001 sobre el Racismo en el Estado Español*. Barcelona: Icaria Editorial.

Fishman, Robert M. 1990. *Working-Class Organization and the Return to Democracy in Spain*. Ithaca: Cornell University Press.

Fitzpatrick, Peter. 1995. "'We Know What It Is When You Do Not Ask Us': Nationalism as Racism." Pp. 3–26 in *Nationalism, Racism and the Rule of Law*, edited by Peter Fitzpatrick. Brookfield, VT: Dartmouth Publishing.

Fleishman, Jeffrey. 2002. "Low Birthrate in Italy Could Be Death Knell of Many Small Towns." *San Diego Union-Tribune*. February 10, 2002: A21 and A26.

Forbath, William. 1999. "Caste, Class, and Equal Citizenship." *Michigan Law Review*. October 1999, Vol. 98: 1–75.

Foro Civico Europeo, Comité Europeo de Defensa de los Refugiados e Inmigrantes. 2001. *El Ejido: Tierra Sin Ley*. Estella-Navarra: Gráficas Lizarra.

Forte, Francesco. 1976. *Industria, Governo, Sottogoverno*. Turin: Societá Editrice Internazionale.

Fuller, Thomas. 2002. "Low Birthrates Pose Challenge for Europe." *International Herald Tribune*. December 12, 2002: 6.

Fusani, Claudia. 2002. "Caritas e Arci Pronte a Disubbidire: 'Ospiteremo Noi gli Irregolari.'" *La Repubblica*. July 12, 2002: 3.

——— 2002. "Criminalitá, la Sfida del Governo." *La Repubblica*. May 17, 2002: 4.

Gagliardi, Andrea. 2002. "Immigrati, Bufera sulla Legge." *La Repubblica*. July 13, 2002: 21.

Gallino, Luciano. 1985. *Il Lavoro e il Suo Doppio: Seconda Occupazione e Politiche del Lavoro in Italia*. Bologna: Il Mulino.

Galluzzo, Marco. 2002. "Chi Vuole Entrare Farebbe Bene a Imparare Prima l'italiano." *Corriere della Sera*. July 12, 2002: 3.

Gans, Herbert. 1992. "Second Generation Decline: Scenarios for the Economic and Ethnic Futures of the Post-1965 American Immigrants." *Ethnic and Racial Studies*. Vol. 15: 173–192.

García, Jorge J. Maté. 1994. *Demanda, Oferta y Ajustes Salariales en el Mercado de Trabajo Español*. Valladolid: Secretariado de Publicaciones, Universidad de Valladolid.

Garrido, Diego López. 2002. "La Batalla Legal." *El País*. June 16, 2002: 16.

Gasulla, Bernat. 1997. "El Suculento Negocio de los Clandestinos." *El Periódico de la Semana*. March 17–23, 1997: 3.

Gattei, Sandro. 2002. "L'andamento del Mercato del Lavoro nelle Province Italiane tra il 1999 e il 2001." *Informazioni SVIMEZ*. Vol. 9, Nos. 1–2: 7–16.

Gavosto, Andrea, Alessandra Venturini, and Claudia Villosio. 2002. "Do Immigrants Compete with Natives?" *Labour*. Vol. 13, No. 3: 603–622.

Generalitat de Catalunya, Departament de la Presidencia, Secretaria per la Inmigració. 1995. *Entre el Sud i el Nord: Els Treballadors Immigrants Estrangers a Catalunya*. Barcelona: Generalitat de Catalunya.

Giddens, Anthony. 1990. *The Consequences of Modernity*. Cambridge: Polity Press.

Gilboy, Janet. 1992. "Penetrability of Administrative Systems: Political 'Casework' and Immigration Inspection." *Law and Society Review*. Vol. 26: 273–314.

Di Giovanni, Bianca. 2001. "Costa Caro Fare L'immigrato in Regola." *L'unitá.* July 26, 2001: 1.

Glazer, Nathan. 1993. "Is Assimilation Dead?" *Annals of the American Academy of Political and Social Sciences.* Vol. 530: 122–136.

    1998. *We Are All Multiculturalists Now.* Cambridge: Harvard University Press.

Glazer, Nathan and Daniel Patrick Moynihan. 1963. *Beyond the Melting Pot: The Negroes, Puerto Ricans, Jews, Italians, and Irish of New York City.* Cambridge: MIT Press.

Goicoechea, Eugenia Ramírez. 1996. *Inmigrantes en España: Vidas y Experiencias.* Madrid: Centro de Investigaciones Sociologicas.

Goldberg, David Theo. 1993. *Racist Culture: Philosophy and the Politics of Meaning.* Cambridge, MA: Blackwell.

Gómez, Luis. 2002. "Culpables y Víctimas de la Violencia." *El País.* June 16, 2002: 9.

    2002. "El Aumento de la Delincuencia: Culpables y Víctimas de la Violencia." *El País.* June 16, 2002: 9.

Gómez-Allende, Héctor Maravall. 1998. "Indicadores de la Inmigración y el Asilo en España." *Observatorio Permanente de la Inmigración.* May 1998, No. 1: 1.

Gómez-Reino, Margarita Cachafeiro. 2002. *Ethnicity and Nationalism in Italian Politics: Inventing the Padania: Lega Nord and the Northern Question.* Burlington, VT: Ashgate.

González, Lydia Esteve and Richard MacBride. 2000. "Fortress Europe: Fear of Immigration? Present and Future of Immigration Law and Policy in Spain." *UC Davis Journal of International Law and Policy.* Vol. 6, No. 2: 153–191.

González-Anleo, J. 1993. "El Poblado Marroquí de Manuel Garrido: Una Aproximación Sociológica." *Sociedad y Utopia: Revista de Ciencias Sociales.* Vol. 1: 171–192.

Gordon, Milton M. 1964. *Assimilation in American Life: The Role of Race, Religion, and National Origins.* New York: Oxford University Press.

Gramsci, Antonio. 1971. *Selections from the Prison Notebooks.* London: Laurence & Wishart.

De Gregorio, Concita. 2002. "Storia di Irma, Colf Peruviana, 'Ora Saró Clandestina a Vita.'" *La Repubblica.* July 13, 2002: 21.

Grion, Luisa. 2001. "I Poveri Crescono al Nord; Sono Otto Milioni in Tutta Italia." *La Repubblica.* August 1, 2001: 33.

    2002. "Italia Vicina alla Crescita Zero." *La Repubblica.* May 16, 2002: 2.

    2002. "Italia, Troppe Tasse e Caro Tariffe." *La Repubblica.* July 29, 2002: 11.

    2002. "Vicenza e Livorno Sono le 'Superstar.'" *La Repubblica.* July 29, 2002: 11.

Griseri, Paolo. 2002. "L'indotto Fiat Travolto dalla Crisi. Cancellati 24 Mila Posti." *La Repubblica*. December 30, 2002: 1.

Grisoni, Dominique and Hughes Portelli. 1977. *Le Lotte Operaie in Italia dal 1960 al 1976*. Milan: Rizzoli.

Grossman, Joel B. 1970. "The Supreme Court and Social Change." Pp. 57–73 in *Law and Social Change*, edited by Stewart Nagel. Beverly Hills: Sage Publications.

Gruppo Abele. 2001. *Annuario Sociale 2001*. Milan: Feltrinelli Editore.

Gubbini, Cinzia. 2001. "Con Tantissimo Affitto." *Il Manifesto*. January 19, 2001: 4.

Gueye, Alioune. 2000. "Il Rafforzamento della Presenza degli Immigrati nelle Aziende e la Contrattazione Sindacale." Pp. 135–143 in *Rapporto Immigrazione: Lavoro, Sindacato, Societá*, edited by Enrico Pugliese. Rome: Ediesse.

Gullo, Tano. 2001. "Se é Questo il Modo di Accoglierli." *Supplemento, La Repubblica*. July 20, 2001: 59.

Gunther, Richard, Giacomo Sani, and Goldie Shabad. 1986. *Spain after Franco: The Making of a Competitive Party System*. Berkeley: University of California Press.

Gusfield, Joseph R. 1963. *Symbolic Crusade: Status Politics and the American Temperance Movement*. Urbana: University of Illinois Press.

Hage, Ghassan. 2000. *White Nation: Fantasies of White Supremacy in a Multicultural Society*. New York: Routledge.

Haggerty, Kevin D. 2001. *Making Crime Count*. Toronto: University of Toronto Press.

Hamann, Kerstin. 1997. "The Pacted Transition to Democracy and Labour Politics in Spain." *South European Society and Politics*. Vol. 2, No. 2: 110–138.

Haney-Lopez, Ian. 1996. *White by Law: The Legal Construction of Race*. New York: New York University Press.

    2003. *Racism on Trial: The Chicano Fight for Justice*. Cambridge: Belknap Press of Harvard University Press.

Hardt, Michael and Antonio Negri. 2000. *Empire*. Cambridge: Harvard University Press.

Harris, Nigel. 1995. *The New Untouchables: Immigration and the New World Worker*. London: St. Martin's Press.

Harvey, David. 1982. *The Limits to Capital*. Oxford: Basil Blackwell.

    2001. "The Spaces of Utopia." in *Between Law and Culture: Relocating Legal Studies*, edited by David Theo Goldberg, Michael Musheno, and Lisa C. Bower. Minneapolis: University of Minnesota Press.

Haver, Flavio. 2002. "Operazione Alto Impatto: Espulsi 351 Clandestini." *Corriere della Sera*. May 17, 2002: 5.

Hoff, Joan. 1991. *Law, Gender and Justice: A Legal History of US Women.* New York: New York University Press.

Hollifield, James F. 1992. *Immigrants, Markets, and States: The Political Economy of Postwar Europe.* Cambridge: Harvard University Press.

Holzner, Claudio. 2003. "Re-Birth of Islam in Italy: Between Indifference and Intolerance." *Journal of the International Institute.* Vol. 3, No. 2.

Honig, Bonnie. 2001. *Democracy and the Foreigner.* Princeton: Princeton University Press.

Horney, Julie and Cassia Spohn. 1991. "Rape Law Reform and Instrumental Change in Six Urban Jurisdictions." *Law and Society Review.* Vol. 25: 117–153.

Huidobro, José María Ruiz de. 2001. "El Regimén Legal de la Inmigración en España: El Continuo Cambio." *Migraciones.* June 2001, Vol. 9: 69–103.

Ignatiev, Noel. 1995. *How the Irish Became White.* New York: Routledge.

Indennitate, Gloria. 2001. "Gli Sbarchi degli Immigrati in uno Spot di Trenta Secondi." *La Gazzetta del Mezzogiorno.* July 13, 2001: 24.

Instituto Nacional de Estadística. 1997. *Boletín Mensual de Estadística.* April 1997, Vol. 64.

ISMU-Cariplo. 1999. *Quarto Rapporto sulle Migrazioni.* Milan: FrancoAngeli.

2001. *Sesto Rapporto sulle Migrazioni.* Milan: FrancoAngeli.

2004. *Nono Rapporto sulle Migrazioni.* Milan: FrancoAngeli.

Istituto Nazionale di Statistica (ISTAT). 2001. "La Popolazione Straniera Residente in Italia al 1 Gennaio 2001." *Annuario Statistico Italiano.* Rome: Istituto Poligrafico dello Stato.

Izquierdo, Antonio. 1992. *La Inmigración en España: 1980–1990.* Madrid: Ministerio de Trabajo y de la Seguridad Social.

1996. *La Inmigración Inesperada.* Madrid: Editorial Trotta.

Jabardo, Mercedes. 1995. "Etnicidad y Mercado de Trabajo: Inmigración Africana en la Agricultura Catalana." *Perspectiva Social.* Vol. 36: 81–95.

Jansa, Mercedes. 2002. "Aznar Anuncia má Dura amb els Reincidents i 'Sense Papers.'" *El Periódico.* July 16, 2002: 3.

Jelloun, Tahar Ben. 1997. *Le Pareti della Solitudine.* Turin: Giulio Einaudi Editore.

Jimeno, Juan and Luís Toharia. 1994. *Unemployment and Labor Market Flexibility: Spain.* Geneva: International Labour Office.

Johnson, Kevin. 1997. "'Melting Pot' or 'Ring of Fire': Assimilation and the Mexican-American Experience." *California Law Review.* Vol. 85: 1259–1313.

Jutglar, Antonio. 1977. *La Inmigración en Cataluña.* Barcelona: Edima.

Karst, Kenneth L. 1989. *Belonging to America: Equal Citizenship and the Constitution.* New Haven: Yale University Press.

1989. "Citizenship, Race, and Marginality." *William and Mary Law Review.* Vol. 30, No. 1: 1–49.

2000. "The Bonds of American Nationhood." *Cardozo Law Review.* Vol. 21: 1141–1182.

Kazal, Russell A. 1995. "Revisiting Assimilation: The Rise, Fall, and Reappraisal of a Concept in American Ethnic History." *American History Review.* Vol. 100, No. 2: 437–471.

Kim, Claire Jean. 1999. "The Racial Triangulation of Asian Americans." *Politics and Society.* Vol. 27: 105–138.

King, Russell and Krysia Rybaczuk. 1993. "Southern Europe and the International Division of Labour: From Emigration to Immigration." Pp. 175–206 in *The New Geography of European Migrations*, edited by Russell King. London: Belhaven Press.

Kingolo, Saoka. 1994. "El Antirracismo desde la Perspectiva de los Colectivos de Inmigrantes." Pp. 155–162 in *Extranjeros en el Paraíso*, edited by el Colectivo Virico. Barcelona: Edicions La Lletra SCCL.

Kinsella, Kevin and Victoria A. Velkoff. 2001. *An Aging World.* Washington, DC: US Government Printing Office.

La Vanguardia. 1993. "El Sindic de Grueges Pide una Actitud mas Integradora hacia los Inmigrantes." *La Vanguardia.* October 8, 1993: 10.

1993. "Inmigrantes en Cataluña." March 29, 1993: 12.

1997. "Magrebíes Bajo Sospecho." June 4, 1997: 20.

Ladd, Everett Carl. 1999. *The Ladd Report.* New York: Free Press.

Lagazzi, Marco, Daniela Malfatti, E. Pallestrini, and N. Rossoni. 1996. "Immigrazione, Comportamento Criminale e Sanzione Penale." *Rassegna Italiana di Criminologia.* Vol. 1: 145–164.

Lago, Alessandro Dal. 1999. *Non-Persone: L'esclusione dei Migranti in una Società Globale.* Milan: Interzone.

Levine, James P. and Theodore L. Becker. 1970. "Toward and Beyond a Theory of Supreme Court Impact." Pp. 83–95 in *Law and Social Change*, edited by Stewart Nagel. Beverly Hills: Sage Publications.

Lipietz, Alain. 1987. *Mirages and Miracles: The Global Crisis of Fordism.* London: Verso.

Lipsky, Michael. 1980. *Street-Level Bureaucracy: Dilemmas of the Individual in Public Services.* New York: Russell Sage.

Lobo, Faustino Miguélez. 1989. "El Trabajo Sumergido en España en la Perspectiva del Acta Única Europea." *Papers: Revista de Sociologia, Universitat Autonoma de Barcelona.* Vol. 32: 115–125.

Lonardi, Giorgio. 2002. "Qui in Veneto Servono, Sanno Lavorare Bene." *La Repubblica.* July 13, 2002: 21.

Los Angeles Times. 2001. "Immigrants in Spain Protest New Law," February 5, 2001: A4.

2001. "Leftists Decry Italy's Labor Proposals," March 24, 2001: A11.

2001. "Italy: 463 Illegal Immigrants Taken Off Fishing Boat," September 30, 2001: A32.

Lowe, Lisa. 1996. *Immigrant Acts: On Asian American Cultural Politics*. Durham, NC: Duke University Press.

De Luca, Maria Novella. 2002. "Gli Immigrati Sono Molti di Piú Ma Non Sappiamo Conviverci." *La Repubblica*. March 28, 2002: 13.

De Lucas, Javier. 1994. *Europa: Convivir con la Diferencia? Racismo, Nacionalismo y Derechos de las Minorias*. Madrid: Editorial Tecnos.

1996. *Puertas que se Cierran: Europa como Fortaleza*. Barcelona: Icaria.

Lurie, Ranan R. 2002. "Siege Mentality in Fortress Europe." *Los Angeles Times*. May 12, 2002: M5.

De Lusignan, Guy. 1994. "Global Migration and European Integration." *Indiana Journal of Global Legal Studies*. Vol. 2: 179–190.

Luzi, Gianluca. 2002. " 'Piano Europeo Anticlandestini' Accordo tra Berlusconi e Aznar." *La Repubblica*. June 6, 2002: 9.

Macioti, Maria Immacolata and Enrico Pugliese. 1991. *Gli Immigrati in Italia*. Bari: Editori Laterza.

Magister, Sandro. 2002. "Lasciate che Vengano a Noi." *L'Espresso*. August 7, 2002: 58.

Magnusson, Warren. 1996. *The Search for Political Space: Globalization, Social Movements and the Urban Political Experience*. Toronto: University of Toronto Press.

Di Maio, Luigi, Maria Proto, and Maria Cristina Longarzia. 2000. *Manuale di Legislazione sugli Stranieri: Integrato dalle Norme del Regolamento di Attuazione*. Rome: Edizioni Laurus Robuffo.

Malgesini, Gabriela. 1994. "Dilemas de la Movilidad: Inmigración y Refugiados en España y la CE." Pp. 11–26 in *Extranjeros en el Paraiso*, edited by El Colectivo Virico. Barcelona: Edicions La Lletra SCCL.

Manco, Altay A. 1996. "Social Development at the Local Level and Developing Public Services." *International Sociology*. Vol. 11: 79–90.

Il Manifesto. 2001. "Case per Immigrati," January 19, 2001: 5.

2001. "Osservatorio Europeo sul Razzismo e la Xenofobia," March 21, 2001: 6.

2001. "Ma Quale Razza Padana, Quella Gente Ci Serve," August 27, 2001: 10.

Manzanos, César. 1994. "Contribución de la Política Carcelaría Estatal a la Marginación Racial." Pp. 169–188 in *Extranjeros en el Paraíso*, edited by El Colectivo Virico. Barcelona: Edicions La Lletra SCCL.

Maravall Gómez-Allende, Héctor. 1998. "Indicadores de la Inmigración y el Asilo en España." *Observatorio Permanente de la Inmigración*. May 1998, Vol. 1.

Marchena, Domingo. 1997. " 'Aquí Sólo Lloramos.' " *La Vanguardia*. June 4, 1997: 27.

Mariel. 1994. "El Reto Legal ante la Extranjería." Pp. 131–138 in *Extranjeros en el Paraíso*, edited by El Colectivo Virico. Barcelona: Edicions La Lletra SCCL.

Marshall, F. Ray. 1978. "Economic Factors Influencing the International Migration of Workers." Pp. 163–180 in *Views Across the Border*, edited by Stanley Ross. Albuquerque: University of New Mexico Press.

Marshall, T. H. 1950. *Citizenship and Social Class and Other Essays*. Cambridge: Cambridge University Press.

1964. *Class, Citizenship, and Social Development: Essays by T. H. Marshall*. Garden City, NY: Doubleday and Company.

Martinez, Antonio. 1995. "La Reagrupación Familiar." Pp. 196–208 in *Diez Años de la Ley de Extranjería: Balance y Perspectivas*, edited by Alegría Borrás. Barcelona: Itinera Libros.

Martirano, Dino. 2001. "Carceri Affollate, Rimpatriamo gli Immigrati." *Corriere della Sera*. July 25, 2001: 15.

Di Massa, Massimiliano. 2003. "Immagini d'immigrati." *Rivista Elettronica di Scienze Umane e Sociali*, Vol. 1, No. 2.

Matelli, Dante. 1997. "Melilla, Baluardo d'Europa." *L'Espresso*. January 9, 1997: 12.

Matsuda, Mari J. 1996. *Where is My Body? And Other Essays on Race, Gender, and the Law*. Boston: Beacon Press.

Maxwell, Kenneth and Steven Spiegel. 1994. *The New Spain: From Isolation to Influence*. New York: Council on Foreign Relations Press.

Mazuelos, Almudena. 1997. "Tres de Cada Cuatro Contratos Firmados en el 96 Duraron Menos de Tres Meses." *Ya*. January 24, 1997: 17.

McBritton, Monica and Mario Giovanni Garofalo. 2000. "La Legge sull'immigrazione e il Lavoro." Pp. 95–111 in *Rapporto Immigrazione: Lavoro, Sindacato, Societá*, edited by Enrico Pugliese. Rome: Ediesse.

Meillassoux, Claude. 1981. *Maidens, Meal and Money: Capitalism and the Domestic Community*. Cambridge: Cambridge University Press.

Melossi, Dario. 1999. "Multiculturalismo e Sicurezza in Emilia-Romagna: Prima Parte." *Quaderni di Cittá Sicure*. January 1999, Vol. 5, No. 15: 17–135.

2000. "Alla Ricerca di una 'Vita Tranquilla': Immigrazione, Criminalitá e *Italian Way of Life*." *Quaderni di Cittá Sicure*. Vol. 1: 17–69.

2000. "The Other in the New Europe: Migrations, Deviance, Social Control." Pp. 151–166 in *Criminal Policy in Transition*, edited by Penny Green and Andrew Rutherford. Oxford: Hart Publishing.

2003. "La 'Sovrarappresentazione' degli Stranieri nei Sistemi di Giustizia Penale Europei e Italiano." *Diritto Immigrazione e Cittadinanza*. Vol. 4: 11–27.

Menafra, Sara. 2001. "Immigrati in Fuga da Villa Magistratini." *Il Manifesto.* August 30, 2001: 10.

Mercado. 1992. "Miedo a lo Desconocido." *Mercado.* February 24, 1992: 27.

Migration News. 2000. "Southern Europe," Vol. 7, No. 9: 19.

    2001. "Southern Europe," Vol. 8, No. 3: 5.

    2001. "Southern Europe," Vol. 8, No. 5: 22.

    2002. "Southern Europe," Vol. 9, No. 3: 30.

    2002. "Southern Europe," Vol. 9, No. 4: 27.

    2002. "Southern Europe," Vol. 9, No. 6: 22.

    2002. "Southern Europe," Vol. 9, No. 9: 25–26.

    2002. "Southern Europe," Vol. 9, No. 10: 26.

De Miguel, Alberto Galerón. 2000. "Indicadores de la Inmigración y el Asilo en España." *Observatorio Permanente de la Inmigración.* January 2000, No. 10: 1.

Miller, Majorie. 2000. "In Europe, Wave of Illegal Migration Has Deadly Cost." *Los Angeles Times.* July 15, 2000: A1 and A6.

Ministerio de Asuntos Sociales, Dirección General de Migraciones. 1994. *Anuario de Migraciones.* Madrid: Ministerio de Asuntos Sociales, Secretaría General Técnica.

    1995. *Anuario de Migraciones.* Madrid: Ministerio de Asuntos Sociales, Secretaría General Técnica.

    1995. *Plán para la Integración Social de los Inmigrantes.* Madrid: Ministerio de Asuntos Sociales, Secretaría General Técnica.

Ministerio de Trabajo y Asuntos Sociales. 1997. *Boletín de Estadísticas Laborales.* Madrid: Secretaría General Técnica, Ministerio de Trabajo y Asuntos Sociales.

    2002. *Boletín de Estadísticas Laborales.* Madrid: Secretaría General Técnica, Ministerio de Trabajo y Asuntos Sociales.

Ministerio del Interior. 1996. *Normativa Básica de Extranjería.* Madrid: Secretaría General Técnica.

    2001. *Balance 2000: Extranjería e Inmigración.* Madrid: Oficina de Relaciones Informativas y Sociales.

Ministerio del Interior, Delegación del Gobierno para la Extranjería y la Inmigración. 2000. *Anuario Estadístico de Extranjería.* Madrid: Imprenta Nacionál del Boletín Oficial del Estado.

    2001. *Anuario Estadístico de Extranjería.* Madrid: Imprenta Nacionál del Boletín Oficial del Estado.

    2001. "Programa GRECO" (Programa Global de Regulación y Coordinación de la Extranjería y la Inmigración en España). Madrid: Ministerio del Interior.

Ministerio del Interior, Delegación del Gobierno para la Extranjería y la Inmigración. 2004. *Boletín Estadístico de Extranjería y Inmigración*, No, 1, March 2004.

Ministro dell'Interno. 2001. *Rapporto del Ministro dell'Interno sullo Stato della Sicurezza in Italia.* Bologna: Il Mulino.

Minuz, Fernanda. 1998. "L'esperienza dei Corsi di Formazione Linguistica per Persone Adulte Straniere dell'ISI di Bologna." *La Societá Multietnica.* December 1998, No. 3: 189–198.

Montgomery, David. 2000. "Empire, Race and Working-Class Mobilizations." Pp. 1–31 in *Racializing Class, Classifying Race: Labour and Difference in Britain, the USA and Africa*, edited by Peter Alexander and Rick Halpern. New York: St. Martin's Press.

Morandi, Alberto. 1998. "Editorial." *La Padania.* January 21, 1998.

Mottura, Giovanni. 2000. "Immigrati e Sindacato." Pp. 113–134 in *Rapporto Immigrazione: Lavoro, Sindacato, Societá*, edited by Enrico Pugliese. Rome: Ediesse.

Mughini, Luigi. 2002. *Non Passa lo Straniero: L'Italia, gli Italiani e l'Immigrazione.* Bari: Edizioni la Meridiana.

El Mundo. 2000. "Las Viviendas de Tetuán Necesitan 10,000 Millones Para Mantenerse en Pie," May 17, 2000: 2.

Navarro, Vicenc. 1997. "Un Nuevo Dogma en España." *El País.* May 5, 1997: 13–14.

Nelken, David. 1996. "Stopping the Judges." Pp. 187–204 in *Italian Politics: The Stalled Transition*, edited by Mario Caciagli and David I. Kertzer. Boulder, CO: Westview Press.

Newsweek. 2000. "Spain Has Changed: An Interview with Prime Minister José María Aznar," April 10, 2000: 24.

Nicolás, Juan Díez and María José Ramírez Lafita. 2001. *La Inmigración en España: Una Decada de Investigaciones.* Madrid: Ministerio de Trabajo y Asuntos Sociales, Secretaría General de Asuntos Sociales.

—— 2001. *La Voz de los Inmigrantes.* Madrid: Ministerio de Trabajo y Asuntos Sociales.

Noanin, Idoya. 1997. "La Crítica de la Mayoría de IU al Papel Sindical en el Pacto Laboral Hace Aflorar Contradicciones Internas." *El País.* April 20, 1997: 17.

Nogueira, Charo. 2002. "La Natalidad Crece en España por Tercer Año Consecutivo Gracias a la Inmigración." *El País.* June 27, 2002: 27.

Noguer, Miguel. 2002. "El Problema (Además) de Aprender Catalán." *El País.* June 16, 2002: 16.

OECD. 2002. *Main Economic Indicators.* May 2002, Vol. 26.

Omi, Michael and Howard Winant. 1986. *Racial Formation in the United States: From the 1960s to the 1980s.* New York: Routledge and Kegan Paul.

Ong, Aihwa. 1996. "Cultural Citizenship as Subject-Making: Immigrants Negotiate Racial and Cultural Boundaries in the United States." *Current Anthropology.* Vol. 37, No. 5: 737–762.

1999. *Flexible Citizenship: The Cultural Logics of Transnationality*. Durham, NC: Duke University Press.

2003. *Buddha Is Hiding: Refugees, Citizenship, the New America*. Berkeley: University of California Press.

Orsini-Jones, Marina and Francesca Gattullo. 2000. "Migrant Women in Italy: National Trends and Local Perspectives." Pp. 125–144 in *Gender and Migration in Southern Europe: Women on the Move*, edited by Floya Anthias and Gabriella Lazaridis. New York: Berg.

Overbeck, Henk. 1995. "Towards a New International Migration Regime: Globalization, Migration and the Internationalization of the State." Pp. 15–36 in *Migration and European Integration: The Dynamics of Inclusion and Exclusion*, edited by Robert Miles and Dietrich Thranhardt. London: Pinter Publishers.

2000. "Globalization, Sovereignty, and Transnational Regulation: Reshaping the Governance of International Migration." Pp. 48–74 in *Managing Migration: Time for a New International Regime?*, edited by Bimal Ghosh. Oxford: Oxford University Press.

El País. 2000. "Concluye el Vallado Exterior de la Frontera de Ceuta Tras Casi Siete Años de Obras," February 4, 2000: 4.

2002. "Detenidos 71 Inmigrantes y Siete Patrones de Pateras en Canarias," June 30, 2002: 30.

2002. "Una Empresa Rechaza a 250 Peticionarios de Empleo por su Raza o su Aparienzia," July 4, 2002: 1 and 4.

2002. "Aznar Propone Leyes Más Duras Contra la Delincuencia y la Inmigración Ilegal," July 16, 2002: 1.

2002. "El Empleo Ha Crecido en Cataluña el 22.1% en Cinco Años, por Debajo del 24.2% de la Media Española," July 16, 2002: 7.

2002. "La Renta 'Per Capita' en España Crece un 5.9% Hasta 16,148 Euros," July 17, 2002: 51.

2002. "La Delincuencia en España Aumentó un 5% en los Primeros Meses del Año," July 22, 2002: 1 and 18.

2002. "España Ocupa el Tercer Peor Lugar de la UE en el Índice de la ONU de Desarrollo Humano," July 24, 2002: 25.

Palidda, Salvatore. 1999. "Devianza e Vittimizzazione." Pp. 145–164 in *Quarto Rapporto sulle Migrazioni*, edited by ISMU-Cariplo. Milan: FrancoAngeli.

Papastergiadis, Nikos. 2000. *The Turbulence of Migration: Globalization, Deterritorialization and Hybridity*. Cambridge: Polity Press.

Papitto, Franco. 2002. "Immigrati, Salta l'accordo UE; Lite tra Ministri, Francia e Svezia: Niente Tolleranza Zero." *La Repubblica*. June 18, 2002: 2.

Park, Robert E. and Ernest W. Burgess. 1921. *Introduction to the Science of Sociology*. Chicago: University of Chicago Press.

Parreñas, Rhacel Salazar. 2001. *Servants of Globalization: Women, Migration, and Domestic Work*. Stanford: Stanford University Press.

Passalacqua, Guido. 2002. "Bossi, Ultimatum al Governo 'Basta Immigrati o Salta Tutto.'" *La Repubblica*. March 19, 2002: 4.

Pateman, Carole. 1988. *The Sexual Contract*. Stanford: Stanford University Press.

Patucchi, Marco. 2001. "Export Italiano in Ripresa ma il Nord-est 'Emigra.'" *La Repubblica*. July 18, 2001: 26.

Pederzoli, Patrizia and Carlo Guarnieri. 1997. "The Judicialization of Politics, Italian Style." *Journal of Modern Italian Studies*, Vol. 2, No. 3: 321–336.

El Periódico de la Semana. 1997. "Caravans of Slaves." March 17–23, 1997: 1.

Peró, Davide. 1997. "Immigrants and Politics in Left-Wing Bologna: Results from Participatory Action Research." Pp. 158–181 in *Southern Europe and the New Immigrations*, edited by Russell King and Richard Black. Brighton, England: Academic Press.

Petrini, Roberto. 2002. "Lavoro, Boom del Posto Fisso." *La Repubblica*. March 28, 2002: 6.

Piore, Michael J. 1979. *Birds of Passage: Migrant Labor and Industrial Societies*. New York: Cambridge University Press.

Piore, Michael J. and Charles Sabel. 1984. *The Second Industrial Divide*. New York: Basic Books.

Polidori, Elena. 2001. "L'Italia Frena ma Puó Ripartire con Meno Tasse e Salari Flessibili." *La Repubblica*. March 15, 2001: 3.

Polito, Antonio. 2002. "Immigrazione: La UE si Divide; Parla Aznar: Lotta Dura contro i Clandestini." *La Repubblica*. June 18, 2002: 1 and 14.

Portes, Alejandro and Min Zhou. 1993. "The New Second Generation: Segmented Assimilation and Its Variants (Interminority Affairs in the US: Pluralism at the Crossroads)." *Annals of the American Academy of Political and Social Sciences*. Vol. 530: 74–97.

Provincia di Bologna. 2001. "Immigrati a Bologna: I Numeri, Le Tendenze." *Osservatorio delle Immigrazioni*. February 2001, No. 1: 7.

Puerto, Katia Lurbe i. 2002. "Incursión Sociológico sobre la Enajenación de l@s Otr@s : Estudio sobre el Tratamiento de la Diferencia Etnica en la Salud Mental." PhD Dissertation in Department of Sociology: Universitat Autonoma de Barcelona.

Pugliese, Enrico. 1995. "New International Migrations and the 'European Fortress.'" Pp. 51–68 in *Europe at the Margins: New Mosaics of Inequality*, edited by Costis Hadjimichalis and David Sadler. New York: John Wiley and Sons.

——— 2000. "Gli Immigrati nel Mercato del Lavoro e nella Struttura dell'Occupazione." Pp. 65–87 in *Rapporto Immigrazione: Lavoro, Sindacato, Societá*, edited by Enrico Pugliese. Rome: Ediesse.

Pumares, Pablo. 1996. *La Integración de los Inmigrantes Marroquíes: Familias Marroquíes en la Comunidad de Madrid*. Barcelona: Fundación "La Caixa".

Putnam, Robert D. 2000. *Bowling Alone: The Collapse and Revival of American Community.* New York: Simon and Schuster.

Ramírez Goicoechea, Eugénia. 1996. *Inmigrantes en España: Vidas y Experiencias.* Madrid: Centro de Investigaciónes Sociológicas.

Regione Emilia-Romagna. 2000. *Economia e Lavoro in Emilia-Romagna, Rapporto Congiunturale 2000.* Bologna: Regione Emilia-Romagna.

2002. *Emilia-Romagna Lavoro.* Bologna: Regione Emilia-Romagna.

Regione Emilia-Romagna, Giunta Regionale. 2001. *Con Questa Faccia da Straniero: Rapporto sull'immigrazione in Emilia-Romagna.* Bologna: Regione Emilia-Romagna.

Reich, Robert. 1991. *The Work of Nations.* New York: Knopf.

Renfrew, Barry. 2002. "Europe Giving the Boot to Left-Leaning Governments." *San Diego Union-Tribune.* June 17, 2002: A3.

La Repubblica. 1999. "Fazio: 'Saranno gli Immigrati a Salvare le Pensioni Italiane,'" July 31, 1999: 23.

2001. "Crimini, Alto Rischio nelle Grandi Cittá," March 16, 2001: 25.

2001. "Non Affitto agli Immigrati," May 30, 2001: 10.

2002. "L'italia si é Fermata: Tredici Milioni in Sciopero, Centinaia di Migliaia nelle Piazze," April 17, 2002: 1.

2002. "Ciampi: Meno Immigrati," May 17, 2002: 1.

2002. "Disoccupati: Il Sud Peggio della Bulgaria," August 6, 2002: 25.

Revista Española de Derecho Internacional. 1996. "El Nuevo Reglamento de la Ley de Extranjería de 2 de Febrero de 1996." *Revista Española de Derecho Internacional.* Vol. 48: 466–471.

Rhode, Deborah L. 1989. *Justice and Gender.* Cambridge: Harvard University Press.

Ribas-Mateos, Natalia. 2000. "Female Birds of Passage: Leaving and Settling in Spain." Pp. 173–197 in *Gender and Migration in Southern Europe: Women on the Move,* edited by Floya Anthias and Gabriella Lazaridis. New York: Berg.

Richards, Andrew J. 1999. "Spain: From Isolation to Integration." Pp. 161–196 in *Europe Today: National Politics, European Integration, and European Security,* edited by Ronald Tiersky. Lanham: Rowman and Littlefield.

Richburg, Keith B. 2002. "Widely Scorned, Illegal Workers Do Europe's Heavy Lifting." *Washington Post.* August 3, 2002: A16.

Rizza, Roberto. 2000. "Trasformazioni del Lavoro, Nuove Forme di Precarizzazione Lavorativa e Politiche di Welfare: Alcune Riflessioni Preliminari." *Sociología del Lavoro.* Vols. 78–79: 13–27.

Rodríguez, Jorge A. 2002. " 'La Solución es que el Gobierno no Nos Envíe ni un Inmigrante Más.' " *El País.* July 5, 2002: 24.

Román, Ediberto. 2000–2001. "Members and Outsiders: An Examination of the Models of United States Citizenship as Well as Questions Concerning

European Union Citizenship." *University of Miami International and Comparative Law Review*. Vol. 9: 81–113.

Roncone, Fabrizio. 2002. "Immigrati, Decine di Migliaia contro le Espulsioni." *Corriere della Sera*. January 20, 2002: 5.

Roquero, Esperanza. 1996. "Asalariados Africanos Trabajando Bajo Plástico." *Sociología del Trabajo*. Vol. 28: 3–23.

Rosaldo, Renato. 1988. "Ideology, Place, and People without Culture." *Cultural Anthropology*. Vol. 3, No. 1: 77–87.

1994. "Cultural Citizenship in San Jose, California." *PoLAR*. Vol. 17: 57–63.

Rosato, Sergio. 2001. "Preface." P. 9 in *Il Mercato del Lavoro nel Veneto*, edited by Bruno Anastasia, Anna de Angelini, Maurizio Gambuzza, and Maurizio Rasera. Milan: FrancoAngeli.

Rotella, Sebastian. 2003. "Spain Arrests 16 in Terror Crackdown." *Los Angeles Times*. January 25, 2003: A3.

Rouse, Roger. 1991. "Mexican Migration and the Social Space of Postmodernism." *Diaspora*. Spring 1991, Vol. 1, No. 1: 8–23.

Ruiz, José Luis Solana. 2002. "Análisis y Reflexiones en Torno a una Década (1990–1999) de Intervención y Trabajo Social con la Población Inmigrante." Pp. 257–311 in *Las Migraciones a Debate: De las Teorias a las Prácticas Sociales*, edited by Francisco Checa. Barcelona: Icaria Editorial.

Ruiz-Huerta, Jesús and Rosa Martínez. 1994. "La Pobreza en España: Que Nos Muestran las EPF?" *Documentación Social*. Vol. 96: 15–109.

Rumbaut, Rubén G. 1997. "Assimilation and Its Discontents: Between Rhetoric and Reality." *International Migration Review*. Vol. 31, No. 4: 923–960.

Rumiz, Paolo. 2003. "Viaggio sul 'Treno degli Africani.'" *La Repubblica*. January 19, 2003: 21.

Sagarra, Eduard and Pedro Aresté. 1995. "Evolución en la Administración desde 1985 en el Tratamiento de la Extranjería." Pp. 163–174 in *Diez Años de la Ley de Extranjería: Balance y Perspectivas*, edited by Alegría Borrás. Barcelona: Itinera Libros.

Said, Edward W. 1979. *Orientalism*. New York: Vintage Books.

Sanchez, Lisa E. 2001. "Enclosure Acts and Exclusionary Practices." Pp. 122–140 in *Between Law and Culture: Relocating Legal Studies*, edited by David Theo Goldberg, Michael Musheno, and Lisa C. Bower. Minneapolis: University of Minnesota Press.

Sansa, Ferruccio. 2002. "E Per Salvare le Prostitute Corsi da Sarte e Cameriere." *La Repubblica*. July 29, 2002: 3.

Santamaría, Enrique. 1993. "(Re)presentación de una Presencia. La 'Inmigración' en y a Través de la Prensa Diaria." *Archipielago: Cuadernos de Critica de la Cultura*. Vol. 12: 65–72.

2002. *La Incógnita del Extraño. Una Aproximación a la Significación Sociológica de la 'Inmigración no Comunitaria'*. Barcelona: Anthropos.

Santos, Lidia. 1993. "Elementos Jurídicos de la Integración de los Extran-jeros." Pp. 91–125 in *Inmigración e Integración en Europa*, edited by Georges Tapinos. Barcelona: Itinera Libros.

Sapelli, Giulio. 1997. "The Transformation of the Italian Party System." *Journal of Modern Italian Studies*. Vol. 2, No. 2: 167–187.

Sarat, Austin and Thomas R. Kearns. 1993. *Law in Everyday Life*. Ann Arbor: University of Michigan Press.

Sassen, Saskia. 1982. "Recomposition and Peripheralization at the Core." *Contemporary Marxism*. Summer 1982, Vol. 5: 88–100.

 1996. *Losing Control? Sovereignty in an Age of Globalization*. New York: Columbia University Press.

 2001. *The Global City*. Princeton: Princeton University Press.

Sayad, Abdelmalek. 1996. "La Doppia Pena del Migrante: Riflessioni sul 'Pensiero di Stato.'" *Aut Aut*. Vol. 275: 8–16.

Sayer, Andrew and Richard Walker. 1992. *The New Social Economy: Reworking the Division of Labor*. Cambridge: Blackwell.

Scanlan, John A. 1994. "A View from the United States – Social, Economic, and Legal Change, the Persistence of the State, and Immigration Policy in the Coming Century." *Indiana Journal of Global Legal Studies*. Vol. 2: 79–141.

Schuck, Peter H. 1998. *Citizens, Strangers, and In-Betweens: Essays on Immigration and Citizenship*. Boulder, CO: Westview Press.

Sciotto, Antonio. 2001. "Dopo il Lavoro, una Casa." *Il Manifesto*. July 19, 2001: 12.

Segura Sánchez J. 1993. "Spain: Shaping Factors." Pp. 400–423 in *The European Challenges, Post-1992: Shaping Factors, Shaping Actors*, edited by Alexis Jacquemin and David Wright. Brookfield, VT: Edward Elgar Publishing.

Selva, Andrea. 2003. "'Vagoni Separati per gli Immigrati.'" *La Repubblica*. January 18, 2003: 27.

Sengenberger, Werner and Frank Pyke. 1992. *Industrial Districts and Local Economic Regeneration*. Geneva: International Institute of Labour Studies.

Sennett, Richard. 1999. "Growth and Failure: The New Political Economy and Its Culture." In *Spaces of Culture: City-Nation-World*, edited by Mike Featherstone and Scott Lash. London: Sage.

Sennett, Richard and Jonathan Cobb. 1993. *The Hidden Injuries of Class*. New York: Norton.

Serrano, Carlos García, Miguel Ángel Malo, and Luís Toharia. 2000. *La Pobreza en España*. Madrid: Ministerio de Trabajo y Asuntos Sociales.

Silbey, Susan. 1997. "'Let Them Eat Cake': Globalization, Postmodern Colonialism, and the Possibilities of Justice." *Law and Society Review*. Vol. 31: 207–235.

Simmel, Georg. 1950. *The Sociology of Georg Simmel*. New York: Free Press.

Simon, Jonathan. 1993. *Poor Discipline: Parole and the Social Control of the Underclass, 1890–1990*. Chicago: University of Chicago Press.

Skocpol, Theda and Morris Fiorina (eds.). 1999. *Civic Engagement in American Democracy*. Washington, DC: Brookings Institution Press.

Smith, Jeffrey. 2000. "Europe Bids Immigrants Unwelcome." *Washington Post*. July 23, 2000: A1 and A18.

Solé, Carlota. 1982. *Los Inmigrantes en la Sociedad y en la Cultura Catalanas*. Barcelona: Ediciones Península.

——— 1995. *Discriminación Racial en el Mercado de Trabajo*. Madrid: Consejo Economico y Social.

Solé, Carlota, Rosa Alcalde, Josep Pont, Kátia Lurbe, and Sónia Parella. 2002. "El Concepto de Integración desde la Sociología de las Migraciones." *Migraciones*. Vol. 12: 9–41.

SOS Racismo. 1995. *Informe Anual sobre el Racismo en el Estado Español*. Barcelona: SOS Racismo.

——— 1996. *Informe Anual sobre el Racismo en el Estado Español*. Barcelona: SOS Racismo.

——— 2000. *Informe Anual sobre el Racismo en el Estado Español*. Barcelona: SOS Racismo.

——— 2001. *El Ejido: Racismo y Explotación Laboral*. Barcelona: Icaria.

——— 2001. *Informe Anual 2001 sobre el Racismo en el Estado Español*. Barcelona: Icaria Editorial.

——— 2002. *Informe Anual 2002 sobre el Racismo en el Estado Español*. Barcelona: Icaria Editorial.

Soverini, Angela. 2002. "Il Profilo dell'Economia Regionale." Pp. 9–13 in *Emilia-Romagna Lavoro*. Bologna: Agenzia Emilia-Romagna.

Soysal, Yasemin Nuhoglu. 1994. *Limits of Citizenship: Migrants and Postnational Membership in Europe*. Chicago: University of Chicago Press.

Stanley, Alessandra. 2000. "Immigration is Emerging as Early Issue in Italy's Vote." *New York Times*. August 8, 2000: A7.

Starr, Paul. 2000. "The Public Vanishes." *New Republic*. August 14, 2000: 35–37.

Stella, Gian Antonio. 2001. "Altivole, Un Abitante su Sette é Immigrato." *Corriere della Sera*. March 19, 2001: 17.

Stolcke, Verena. 1993. "El 'Problema' de la Inmigración en Europa: El Fundamentalismo Cultural Como Nueva Retórica de Exclusión." *Mientras Tanto*. Vol. 55: 73–90.

——— 1994. "Europa: Nuevas Fronteras, Nuevas Retóricas de Exclusión." Pp. 235–266 in *Extranjeros en el Paraíso*, edited by El Colectivo Virico. Barcelona: Edicions La Lletra SCCL.

Gli Stranieri. 2002. "Leggi, Decreti e Circolari," Vol. 9, No. 2: 142–143.

Suarez-Orozco, Marcelo M. 1987. "Becoming Somebody: Central American Immigrants in US Inner-City Schools." *Anthropology and Education Quarterly*. Vol. 18, No. 4: 287–299.

Sudnow, David. 1965. "Normal Crimes: Sociological Features of the Penal Code in the Public Defender Office." *Social Problems*. Vol. 12: 255–276.

Tagliabue, John. 2002. "Italy Issues Decree to Destroy Ships Used in Refugee Transport." *San Diego Union-Tribune*. March 29, 2002: A18.

Tartaglione, Clemente. 2001. "Riallineamento e Sommerso nel Mezzogiorno." In *Presentazione dell'Osservatorio per l'Emersione nel Mezzogiorno*. Rome: IRES CGIL.

Thomas, William Isaac and Florian Znaniecki. 1927. *The Polish Peasant in Europe and America*. New York: Knopf.

Thranhardt, Dietrich and Robert Miles. 1995. "Introduction." Pp. 1–12 in *Migration and European Integration: The Dynamics of Inclusion and Exclusion*, edited by Dietrich Thranhardt and Robert Miles. London: Pinter Publishers.

Tobarra, Sebastián. 2002. "Una Fuente de Riqueza." *El País*. June 16, 2002: 10.

Tonkin, Elizabeth, Maryon McDonald, and Malcolm Chapman. 1989. *History and Ethnicity*. New York: Routledge.

Touraine, Alain. 1995. "Minorias, Pluriculturalismo e Integración." *El País*. January 12, 1995: 12.

Trigilia, Carlo. 1997. "The Political Economy of a Regionalized Capitalism." *South European Society and Politics*. Vol. 2, No. 3: 52–79.

Turner, Bryan S. 1993. *Citizenship and Social Theory*. London: Sage Publications. 2000. "Citizenship Studies." *Review Essay: Citizenship and Political Globalization*. Vol. 4: 81–86.

Unguendoli, Chiara. 2000. "Biffi Insiste: Fermiamo gli Islamici." *Corriere della Sera*. October 1, 2000: 5.

United Nations. 2000. *The World's Women, 2000: Trends and Statistics*. New York: United Nations Secretariat.

United Nations Population Division. 2000. *Replacement Migration: Is It a Solution to Declining and Ageing Populations?* New York: United Nations Secretariat.

Valdes, Francisco, Jerome McCristal Culp, and Angela P. Harris. 2002. *Crossroads, Directions, and a New Critical Race Theory*. Philadelphia: Temple University Press.

Valls, Andreu Domingo, Jaume Clapés Estrada, and Maria Prats Ferret. 1995. *Condicions de Vida de la Població d'origen Africà i Llatinoamericà a la Regió Metropolitana de Barcelona: Una Aproximació Qualitativa*. Barcelona: Diputació de Barcelona.

Valls, Carles. 2001. "Es Busca Pis per Immigrant." *La Veu del Carrer*. March–April 2001: 5.

2001. "La Revolta dels 'Sense Papers.'" *La Vue del Carrer*. January–February 2001: 3.

Venturini, Alessandra and Claudia Villosio. 2002. "Are Immigrants Competing with Natives in the Italian Labour Market? The Employment Effect." *Institute for the Study of Labor*. April 2002, Vol. 467: 1–27.

Visa, Lluís. 2002. "Más de 3000 Inmigrantes Vagan Sin Trabajo en Lleida por la Disminución de la Cosecha de Fruta." *El País*. July 8, 2002: 25.

2002. "Miles de Temporeros Vagan por Lleida sin Trabajo tras las Últimas Tormentas de Granizo." *El País*. July 22, 2002: 1.

2002. "Temporeros sin Trabajo." *El País*. July 24, 2002: 1.

de Vito, Gianluigi. 2002. "Non Piace la Bossi-Fini." *La Gazzetta del Mezzogiorno*. July 13, 2002: 4.

2002. "Lavoro Dunque Non Sono." *La Gazzetta del Mezzogiorno*. February 13, 2002: 15.

Volpp, Leti. 2001. "'Obnoxious to their Very Nature': Asian Americans and Constitutional Citizenship." *Citizenship Studies*. Vol. 5, No. 1: 57–71.

Wacquant, Loic. 2000. *Parola d'Ordine: Tolleranza Zero*. Milan: Feltrinelli.

Wal, Jessika Ter. 2000. "Comparing Argumentation and Counter-Argumentation in Italian Parliamentary Debate on Immigration." Pp. 129–154 in *The Semiotics of Racism*, edited by Martin Reisigl and Ruth Wodak. Vienna: Passagen Verlag.

2000. "The Discourse of the Extreme Right and Its Ideological Implications: The Case of the Alleanza Nazionale on Immigration." *Patterns of Prejudice*. Vol. 34, No. 4: 37–51.

Walzer, Michael. 1983. *Spheres of Justice: A Defense of Pluralism and Equality*. New York: Basic Books.

Warner, W. Lloyd and Leo Srole. 1945. *The Social Systems of American Ethnic Groups*. New Haven: Yale University Press.

Waters, Mary C. 2001. *Black Identities: West Indian Immigrant Dreams and American Realities*. Cambridge: Harvard University Press.

Watts, Julie R. 2000. *An Unconventional Brotherhood: Union Support for Liberalized Immigration in Europe*. La Jolla, CA: Center for Comparative Immigration Studies, University of California, San Diego.

Wilkins, Roger. 2001. *Jefferson's Pillow: The Founding Fathers and the Dilemma of Black Patriotism*. Boston: Beacon Press.

Wills, Garry. 2000. "Putnam's America." *American Prospect*. Vol. II. July 17, 2000.

Woolard, Kathryn A. 1986. "The 'Crisis in the Concept of Identity' in Contemporary Catalonia, 1976–1982." Pp. 57–71 in *Conflict in Catalonia: Images of an Urban Society*, edited by Gary McDonogh. Gainesville, FL: University of Florida Press.

Yamaguchi, Masao. 1977. "Kinship, Theatricality, and Marginal Reality in Japan." P. 154 in *Text and Context: The Social Anthropology of Tradition*, edited by Ravindra K. Jain. Philadelphia: Institute for the Study of Human Issues.

Young, Alison. 1996. *Imagining Crime: Textual Outlaws and Criminal Conversations*. London: Sage Publications.

Young, Iris Marion. 1995. "Polity and Group Difference: A Critique of the Ideal of Universal Citizenship." Pp. 175–207 in *Theorizing Citizenship*, edited by Ronald Beiner. Albany: State University of New York Press.

Young, Jock. 1999. *The Exclusive Society: Social Exclusion, Crime and Difference in Late Modernity*. London: Sage Publications.

———. 2003. "Merton with Energy, Katz with Structure: The Sociology of Vindictiveness and the Criminology of Transgression." *Theoretical Criminology*. Vol. 7, No. 3: 389–413.

Yuval-Davis, Nira. 1997. *Gender and Nation*. Thousand Oaks, CA: Sage Publications.

Zaguirre, Manuel. 1997. "Un Acuerdo Histórico." *El País*. May 9, 1997:64.

Zanfrini, Laura. 1996. "Il Lavoro degli 'Altri': Gli Immigrati nel Sistema Produttivo Bergamasco." *Quaderni ISMU*. Vol. 1.

Zanon, Raffaele. 2001. "Veneto Approva Piano Triennale Immigrazione." *Veneto Globale*. June 2001, Vol. 4, No. 6: 1.

Zapata-Barrero, Ricard. 2002. *L'hora dels Immigrants: Esferes de Justícia i Polítiques d'acomodació*. Barcelona: Laia Tresserra.

Zarzalejos, José Antonio. 2002. "Ma l'Europa non Tornerá Indietro: Sará Lotta Dura Contro i Clandestini." *La Repubblica*. June 18, 2002: 3.

Zaurín, Luís. 2002. "La Inmigración Marca el Futuro de Santa Coloma." *La Veu del Carrer*. January–February 2002: 7.

Zincone, Giovanna. 2000. "Immigrati: Quali Politiche per l'integrazione?" *Il Mulino*, January–February 2000: 80–91.

———. 2000. "A Model of 'Reasonable Integration': Summary of the First Report on the Integration of Immigrants in Italy." *International Migration Review*. Vol. 34, No. 3: 956–968.

———. 2000. *Primo Rapporto sull'integrazione degli Immigrati in Italia*. Bologna: Il Mulino.

———. 2001. *Secondo Rapporto sull'integrazione degli Immigrati in Italia*. Bologna: Il Mulino.

Zolberg, Aristide. 1987. "Wanted But Not Welcome: Alien Labor in Western Development." Pp. 261–297 in *Population in an Interacting World*, edited by William Alonso. Cambridge: Harvard University Press.

———. 1994. "Changing Sovereignty Games and Internation Migration." *Indiana Journal of Global Studies*. Vol. 2: 153–170.

———. 1997. "Modes of Incorporation: Toward a Comparative Framework." Pp. 139–154 in *Citizenship and Exclusion*, edited by Veit Bader. London: Macmillan Press.

Zuccolini, Roberto. 2001. "Sí Solo agli Immigrati con un Lavoro." *La Repubblica*. July 13, 2001: 6.

———. 2002. "Immigrati, Espulsioni Piú Facili." *Corriere della Sera*. July 27, 2002: 1.

———. 2002. "La Loggia: La Lega ha Ragione, Rigore Necessario." *Corriere della Sera*. March 20, 2002: 8.

Statutes, regulations, and legal cases

Italy

National statutes

Legge 30 dicembre 1986, No. 943. "Norme in materia di collocamento e di trattamento dei lavoratori extacomunitari immigrati e contro le immigrazioni clandestine" (Foreign Workers and the Control of Illegal Immigration). *Gazzetta Ufficiale*, No. 8, January 12, 1987.

Legge 28 febbraio 1990, No. 39. "Norme urgenti in materia di asilo politico, di ingresso e soggiorno dei cittadini extracomunitari e di regolarizzazione dei cittadini extracomunitari ed apolidi giá presenti nel territorio dello Stato" (Martelli Law). *Gazzetta Ufficiale*, No. 49, February 28, 1990.

Legge 6 marzo 1998, No. 40. "Disciplina dell'immigrazione e norme sulla condizione dello straniero" (Turco-Napolitano Law). *Gazzetta Ufficiale*, No. 59, March 12, 1998.

Decreto Legislativo 25 luglio 1998, No. 286. "Testo unico delle disposizioni concernenti la disciplina dell'immigrazione e norme sulla condizione dello straniero" (Executive Regulations for Turco-Napolitano Law). *Gazzetta Ufficiale*, No. 191, August 18, 1998.

Decreto del Ministro per la Solidarietá Sociale, 6 dicembre 1999. "Linee guida per la predisposizione dei programmi regionali e del modello uniforme" (Guide for the Preparation of Regional Programs). *Gazzetta Ufficiale*, No. 47, February 26, 2000.

Decreto del Presidente del Consiglio dei Ministri, 18 dicembre 1999. "Istituzione in ciascuna Provincia di un Consiglio territoriale per l'immigrazione" (Establishment in Every Province of Territorial Councils for Immigration). *Gazzetta Ufficiale*, No. 13, January 18, 2000.

Legge 1 marzo 2002, No. 39. "Disposizioni per l'adempimento di obblighi derivanti dall'appartenenza dell'Italia alle Comunitá Europee" (Principle of Non-Discrimination Based on Race and Ethnic Origin). *Gazzetta Ufficiale*, No. 91, April 18, 2002.

Legge 30 luglio 2002, No. 189. "Modifica alla normativa in materia di immigrazione e di asilo" (Bossi-Fini Law). *Gazzetta Ufficiale*, No. 199, August 26, 2002.

Regional statutes

Legge Regionale Emilia-Romagna, 12 gennaio 1985, No. 2. "Riordino e programmazione delle funzioni di assistenza sociale" (Reorganization of Social Assistance Services). *Bollettino Ufficiale della Regione Emilia-Romagna*, No. 8, January 16, 1985.

Legge Regionale Piemonte, 8 novembre 1989, No. 64. "Interventi regionali a favore degli immigrati extracomunitari in Piemonte" (Regional Law in Support of non-EU Immigrants in Piedmont). *Bollettino Ufficiale della Regione Piemonte*, No. 46, November 15, 1989.

Legge Regionale Veneto, 30 gennaio 1990, No. 8. "Interventi nel settore dell'immigrazione" (Regional Law in the Sector of Immigration). *Bollettino Ufficiale della Regione Veneto*, No. 8, 1990.

Legge Regionale Emilia-Romagna, 21 febbraio 1990, No. 14. "Iniziative regionale in favore dell'emigrazione e immigrazione" (Regional Law in Support of Emigration and Immigration). *Bollettino Ufficiale della Regione Emilia-Romagna*, No. 27, March 26, 1990.

Legge Regionale Toscana, 22 marzo 1990, No. 22. "Interventi a sostegno dei diritti extracomunitari in Toscana" (Regional Law in Support of the Rights of Non-EU Immigrants in Tuscany). *Bollettino Ufficiale della Regione Toscana*, No. 20, March 31, 1990.

Legge Regionale Veneto, 30 agosto 1993, No. 42. "Modifiche della legge regionale di contabilitá 9 dicembre 1977, No. 72 e sue successive integrazioni e modificazioni" (Reform of the Regional Law of December 9, 1977, No. 72). *Bollettino Ufficiale della Regione Veneto*, No. 73, 1993.

Legge Regionale Lombardia, 5 dicembre 2000, No. 7/2526. "Istituzione dell'osservatorio regionale per l'integrazione e la multietnicitá" (Establishment of the Regional Observatory for Integration and Multiethnicity). *Bollettino Ufficiale della Regione Lombardia*, No. 52, December 27, 2000.

Spain

Ley Orgánica (LOE) 1985. "Ley Orgánica sobre Derechos y Libertades de los Extranjeros en España" (Organic Law on the Rights and Liberties of Foreigners in Spain), Congreso de los Diputados, *Boletín de las Cortes Generales*, No. 132, May 8, 1985.

Ley Orgánica (LOE) 7/1985. "Ley Orgánica sobre Derechos y Libertades de los Extranjeros en España" (Organic Law on the Rights and Liberties of Foreigners in Spain), July 1, 1985, Congreso de los Diputados, *Boletín Oficial del Estado*, No. 158, July 3, 1985.

Ley General de Sanidad. (General Health Law), April 25, 1986. *Boletín Oficial del Estado*, No. 102, April 29, 1986.

Real Decreto, No. 1088. "Por que se Extiende la Cobertura de la Asistencia sanitaria de la Seguridad Social a las Personas sin Recursos Suficientes" (Law to Extend Health Coverage to those without Sufficient Resources), September 8, 1989. *Boletín Oficial del Estado*, No. 219, September 9, 1989.

Ley Orgánica 4/2000. "Ley Orgánica sobre Derechos y Libertades de los Extranjeros en España y su Integración Social" (Organic Law on the Rights and Liberties of Foreigners in Spain and their Social Integration), *Boletín Oficial del Estado*, No. 10, January 12, 2000.

Ley Orgánica 8/2000. "Derechos y Libertades de los Extranjeros en España y su Integración Social, Texto Integrado de las Leyes Orgánicas 4/2000 y 8/2000" (Organic Law on the Rights and Liberties of Foreigners in Spain and their Social Integration, Integration of Law 4/2000 and Law 8/2000), *Boletín Oficial del Estado*, No. 307, December 23, 2000.

Plan Interdepartamental de Inmigración 2001–2004: Aprobado en la Sesión del Gobierno de la generalidad del Día 18 de julio de 2001. Barcelona: Generalitat de Catalunya, 2002.

Tribunal Constitucional, Sentencia No. 115, July 7, 1987.

Cortes Generales, *Diario de Sesiones del Congreso de los Diputados*, No. 100, April 9, 1991: 4889.

Cortes Generales, *Diario de Sesiones del Congreso de los Diputados*, No. 580, December 9, 1992: 17465.

INDEX